William Francis

C000144013

William Francis Bartlett

Biography of a Union General in the Civil War

RICHARD A. SAUERS *and*
MARTIN H. SABLE

McFarland & Company, Inc., Publishers
Jefferson, North Carolina, and London

LIBRARY OF CONGRESS CATALOGUING-IN-PUBLICATION DATA

Sauers, Richard Allen.
  William Francis Bartlett : biography of a Union general in
the Civil War / Richard A. Sauers and Martin H. Sable.
      p.   cm.
  Includes bibliographical references and index.

  ISBN 978-0-7864-4146-4
  softcover : 50# alkaline paper ∞

  1. Bartlett, William Francis, 1840–1876.   2. Generals —
United States — Biography.   3. United States — History —
Civil War, 1861–1865 — Biography.   4. United States —
History — Civil War, 1861–1865 — Campaigns.   5. Soldiers —
Massachusetts — Biography.   6. United States. Army —
Biography.   I. Sable, Martin Howard.   II. Title.
E467.1.B29S28   2009
973.7092 — dc22   2009002555
[B]

British Library cataloguing data are available

©2009 Richard A. Sauers and Martin H. Sable. All rights
reserved

*No part of this book may be reproduced or transmitted in any form
or by any means, electronic or mechanical, including photocopying
or recording, or by any information storage and retrieval system,
without permission in writing from the publisher.*

On the cover: William Francis Bartlett Portrait, courtesy
Berkshire Athenaeum, Pittsfield, MA; American flag background
©2008 Shutterstock.

Manufactured in the United States of America

McFarland & Company, Inc., Publishers
  Box 611, Jefferson, North Carolina 28640
  www.mcfarlandpub.com

TABLE OF CONTENTS

ACKNOWLEDGMENTS

A number of people provided assistance over the years of research and writing of this book. Some of them I've never met since Martin corresponded with them before I became involved with this project. I am especially indebted to Donna Kasuba, Pittsfield, MA, for going above and beyond my request for research help by tracking down many of the illustrations in this book and for locating details that helped answer some questions I had about the general's family. I am also appreciative of Blake Magner and his superb cartographic skills for executing the maps based on rough information I gave to him. Others who helped in various ways include Dr. Art Bergeron, U.S. Army Military History Institute, Carlisle, PA; Vincent T. Brooks, Library of Virginia, Richmond, VA; Charles Dew, Williams College, Williamstown, MA; Dan Essigmann, Massachusetts National Guard Military Archives and Museum, Worcester, MA; Patrick Flynn, Berkshire Historical Society, Pittsfield, MA; Ann H. Gutting, Winthrop Public Library, Winthrop, MA; Ann-Marie Harris, Senior Technician, Berkshire Athenaeum, Pittsfield, MA; Leanna Hayden, Director of Collections, Berkshire Athenaeum; Dr. Earl Hess, Lincoln Memorial University, Harrogate, TN; Harley P. Holden, Harvard University Archives, Cambridge, MA; G. David Hubbard, Winthrop, MA; Shannon Humphreys, Richmond Public Library, VA; Roger D. Hunt, Gettysburg, PA; Edward Hutchinson, Massachusetts Historical Society, Boston, MA; Interlibrary Loan Department, University of Wisconsin-Milwaukee; Robert E. L. Krick, Richmond National Battlefield Park, VA; Susan Greendyke Lachevre, Commonwealth of Massachusetts, Art Commission, Boston, MA; Elizabeth M. Lockyer, Librarian, Berkshire Athenaeum, Pittsfield, MA; Jeannie Maschino, Librarian/Archivist, *The Berkshire Eagle*, Pittsfield, MA; Andrew Mick, Publisher, *The Berkshire Eagle*; Megan Milford, Massachusetts Historical Society, Boston, MA; Richard F. Miller, Concord, MA; Leslie Morris,

Houghton Library, Harvard University, Cambridge, MA; Stephen Z. Nonack, Boston Athenaeum; Norma Purdy, Volunteer, Berkshire Historical Society, Pittsfield, MA; Ruth Quattlebaum, Archivist, Phillips Academy, Andover, MA; Kathleen M. Reilly, Berkshire Athenaeum, Pittsfield, MA; Henry F. Scannell, Boston Public Library; Aleta L. Sousa, Phillips Academy, Andover, MA; Brian A. Sullivan, Harvard University Archives, Cambridge, MA; Daniel J. Sullivan, Winthrop, MA; Jennifer Tolpa, Massachusetts Historical Society, Cambridge, MA; Special Collections Department, Davidson Library, University of California, Santa Barbara; and David Ward, Hotchkiss School, Lakeville, CT.

I thank the following institutions for permission to use quotations: Historical Society of Pennsylvania; Houghton Library, Harvard University; Davidson Library, Special Collections, University of California, Santa Barbara; University Press of Mississippi; and Wesleyan University Press.

All credits for illustrations in this book can be found at the end of individual captions.

R.A.S.

PREFACE

Before I began this book I was aware of Major General William Francis Bartlett only vaguely. As a student primarily of the eastern theater of operations during the Civil War, I knew about Bartlett's role in the fiasco of the Crater. To me, he was merely one of over five hundred Union generals, and a not very important one at that.

In early 2002, I received an e-mail from Kay Jorgensen, the managing editor for *Civil War News*, informing me of a gentleman in Milwaukee who was looking for an author to write a Civil War book for him. Martin H. Sable was a retired professor from the University of Wisconsin–Milwaukee. He had been born in Haverhill, Massachusetts, Frank Bartlett's hometown. Naturally, he considered General Bartlett a local hero and determined to write a book about him so that more people would realize his role in nineteenth century America. He had spent years collecting material about the general and his family, but needed someone to write the book. After speaking with him via telephone, I agreed to examine his material and possibly write a biography of the general.

At the time, I lived in northern Wisconsin, several hours from Milwaukee. Martin trusted me enough to part with two boxes of material, which arrived by special delivery. After sifting through the scores of folders, I realized that he had done a prodigious amount of research and there was indeed enough material for a biography.

In early 2003, I began serious work on the book after returning to Pennsylvania. Although Martin had done a lot of work on Bartlett, there were gaps in the research, which I began to research and fill. Martin aided me by helping locate additional sources of information as he was able. He also read early drafts of chapters and offered his viewpoint on numerous occasions.

Through the years of work, I learned a great deal about Frank Bartlett and came to respect this man. Wounded three times during the Civil War, Frank could have quit at any time and returned home, but his sense of loyalty to the Union cause kept him in the field until he was finally captured at the Crater. Worn out in body, Frank went on to a postwar career in the iron industry but was only marginally successful. The stress attendant to his work in the iron industry, made worse by the Panic of 1873, when combined with his frail postwar health, eventually killed Frank Bartlett at age thirty-six.

Because Bartlett was wounded so often, he never had the chance to remain in active military service for enough time to earn more recognition than he actually did. He finally received some national recognition late in life when his speeches about North-South reconciliation were circulated in newspapers across the nation. However, Frank's name quickly disappeared after his early death in 1876. Though his name appears in standard battle histories in which he was engaged, and in the regimental histories of the units he commanded, Frank's name is not widely circulated even today. A perusal of books on postwar reconciliation clearly shows that few historians remember the general's early efforts at national unity.

Francis Palfrey, one of Frank's brother officers in the 20th Massachusetts, had access to Bartlett's letters and journals, from which he quoted copiously for his 1878 *Memoir of William Francis Bartlett*. Thereafter, however, Frank's papers simply disappeared. No historian has ever found them. After Mary Agnes died in 1909, did her husband's papers go to one of the surviving children? If so, perhaps Frank's papers lie in a trunk in an attic, waiting for the time in which they will be rediscovered and throw additional light on this true American hero.

Martin Sable and I are proud of our effort to rescue Frank Bartlett's name and bring his deeds to the notice of the current generation of history buffs. We are sure you will enjoy the story of an American who encountered numerous obstacles and setbacks during his short life, but never gave up hope.

Richard A. Sauers
Sunbury, Pennsylvania
Spring 2009

INTRODUCTION

During the four bloody years of the American Civil War, more than five hundred Union officers wore general's stars on their shoulders to signify their rank. Many of them are well known yet today, more than one hundred forty years after the war. Names such as Ulysses S. Grant, George G. Meade, George B. McClellan, and William T. Sherman are all justly famous.

On the other hand, a large number of generals in blue remain obscure. Some, like Andrew Jackson Smith, were above average officers who emerged from the war with good combat records but left no known memoirs or manuscripts which historians could use to reconstruct their careers. Others left in disgrace and were abysmal failures as military men. James H. Ledlie is a prime example of this class of generals.

The subject of this book, William Francis Bartlett, was a civilian without prior military experience when Fort Sumter was fired upon in April 1861. Born in 1840, young Frank Bartlett seemingly had no plans for his career. He was an indifferent student at both Phillips Academy and Harvard University. As it did for many others of his generation, the conflict gave Frank Bartlett an opportunity and he made the most of it. His wartime experience clearly indicated that the civilian turned soldier quickly adapted to military life and emerged as a fine leader of men.

However, Bartlett was cursed with bad luck throughout his military service. During his first engagement as a captain in the 20th Massachusetts, Frank managed to escape the debacle at Ball's Bluff. He was hit in the knee at Yorktown and lost a leg. Undaunted, Frank chose to remain in the service and was promoted to colonel of the 49th Massachusetts, which he whipped into shape by the time the Port Hudson Campaign began. On May 27, 1863, Frank led his regiment during the first attack on Port Hudson and was again wounded, this time in the arm. After recuperating, Frank went into the field in May 1864 as colonel of the 57th Massachusetts Veteran Volunteers, only to be lightly wounded in the Wilderness. Promoted to brigadier general, Bartlett returned to duty in time to be captured in the Crater. After a sojourn in two Rebel prisons, he was exchanged and promoted to major general.

Frank's postwar career was a struggle to provide for his growing family. He married in 1865 and fathered six children. Thanks to his father-in-law, Bartlett became associated with the iron industry and managed plants in Massachusetts and Virginia. Disgusted with Grant's presidency and Congressional reconstruction, Frank began to speak about national reconciliation a decade or more before it became popular. Although his speeches earned him some national recognition, Frank's death at age thirty-six meant a rapid eclipse of his name. An 1878 memoir penned by a brother officer earned plaudits from reviewers, but since that time, the Bartlett name remains largely unknown in Civil War history. But Bartlett deserves to be remembered because he typifies the American volunteer officer who rose to the challenge offered by the war and did his part to preserve the union. His is the story of a humble American hero.

1

"HE WAS NOT A CLOSE STUDENT"

Prelude to War

The subject of this biography, William Francis Bartlett, was born in Haverhill, Massachusetts, on January 6, 1840. According to family records, the earliest form of the family name was Berthelot, which included a nephew of Charlemagne. In 1066, Brian Barttelot, a Norman knight, and his esquire, Adam Barttelot, accompanied William the Conqueror from Normandy to England. In return for their help in defeating the Saxons by supplying ships and men, the Barttelots were awarded large estates in Sussex County, around the village of Stopham. Eventually, so goes the story, the family name was anglicized to Bartlett.[1]

The first ancestors of the future general came to Massachusetts in the 1630s. John Bartlett arrived in Newbury in 1634; his younger brother Richard arrived the next year. Richard's son, also named Richard, had been born in England in 1621 and died in Newbury in 1698. This Richard Bartlett was at various times a shoemaker, cordwainer, and yeoman. Richard's son Samuel (1646–1732) also lived in Newbury and worked as a cordwainer. His son Thomas (1681–1744) was Frank Bartlett's great-great-grandfather. Thomas was a tanner by trade and had several sons. His grandson Israel (1748–1838) had a son who later achieved much fame; Enoch Bartlett (1779–1860) was the namesake of the "Bartlett Pear." Enoch purchased an estate in Roxbury in 1821. The previous owner had imported several varieties of fruit trees, among which were two pear trees that bore a hitherto unknown type of pear. Enoch exhibited these pears, which were named after him.[2]

Thomas Bartlett's son Enoch (1715–1789) was the general's great-grandfather. He was born in Newbury like so many of his ancestors, but after marrying in 1749 he moved to Haverill, where his son Bailey was born in January 1750. Bailey, Frank's grandfather, had a distinguished civil career in

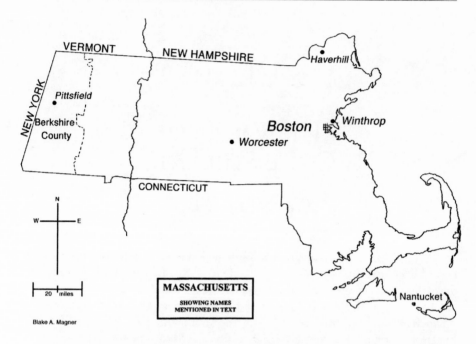

VERMONT   NEW HAMPSHIRE   Haverhill

NEW YORK   Pittsfield

Berkshire   County

Boston   Winthrop

Worcester

CONNECTICUT

N

W——E

20 miles

MASSACHUSETTS
SHOWING NAMES
MENTIONED IN TEXT

Nantucket

Blake A. Magner

Massachusetts. Bailey at first followed in his father's footsteps as a dry goods store owner, but became interested in politics. One of his close friends was John Adams, and it is reported that Bailey was present in Philadelphia when the Declaration of Independence was first proclaimed to the crowd on July 14, 1776. Bailey was later a state representative (1781–1784) and senator (1789), and was a member of the state delegation to the Constitutional Convention. In 1789, Governor John Hancock appointed him sheriff of Essex County, a post he held until his death in 1830. Bailey was also a representative in the federal House from 1797 to 1801.[3]

Bailey Bartlett sired fifteen children, one of whom, Charles L. Bartlett, was Frank's illustrious father. Charles was born in Haverhill on August 15, 1802, the tenth of fifteen children. After being educated at Bradford Academy, young Charles began employment as a clerk in a Boston counting house. Charles then moved to Savannah, Georgia, to work in a commercial house there, after which he gained employment as a commission merchant at Port au Prince, Trinidad, where he also functioned as the American consul. When his uncle retired as cashier of the Merrimack Bank in Haverhill, Charles returned to his birthplace and succeeded his uncle in that position. Shortly after moving back home, he married Harriet Plummer in 1836. This was the family situation when Frank was born in January 1840. He was the couple's third child and only son. Daughters Anna (1837) and Eliza (1838) were followed by William F. (1840), Florence (1842), and Edith (1844).[4]

In 1847, Charles moved his growing family to Winthrop, a growing suburb of Boston located on the northeast side of Boston harbor. Three years earlier, he had accepted the position of shipping agent and commission merchant in the firm of Seecomb, Taylor & Company, which was engaged primarily in trade from the Cape of Good Hope. His office was only ten miles away in central Boston. Charles built a new house for his growing family on a hill overlooking the harbor. His wife's parents — Hiram and Eliza Plummer — moved with them.[5]

Two years after moving to Winthrop, Charles changed jobs for the last time. His brother Edwin, in a partnership with some other investors, had founded in 1847 the Pacific Mail Steamship Company in an attempt to cash in on the increasing westward movement of settlers to the Pacific northwest. When the United States and England concluded a treaty that established a firm boundary line between America and Canada, the American government authorized the Secretary of the Navy to contract for mail service between New York and the mouth of the Columbia River in the Oregon Territory. The winning bidder assigned the contract to Edwin and five other partners, who obtained a New York state charter in 1848. Starting with an investment of $400,000, the company began operations when its first ship departed New York in October 1848. The company grew steadily and soon was reaping profits of more than $1,000,000 per annum. Charles joined his brother and became a very successful agent for the company.[6]

There are very few surviving accounts of Frank Bartlett's childhood. Long-time Winthrop historian G. David Hubbard told of the time when nine-year-old Frank was late for school one winter's day. He rode his sled to school until he spied a huge snowdrift outside the schoolhouse. He pulled his sled up to the top and slid down the other side, hitting the school door and opening it. When the sled stopped, Frank looked up to see his teacher, Nahum Smith, standing there above him. Young Frank stood up, removed his cap, and then apologized.[7]

In 1853, the Italian patriot Giuseppe Garibaldi came into Frank's life. Garibaldi had come to New York in 1850 and remained here for nine months before heading off to Peru. While in South America, he captained an Italian trading ship that went to China and back. He then took command of a ship filled with copper and wool from Chile and Peru to Boston. According to one of Charles Bartlett's obituaries, Garibaldi's vessel was consigned to Bartlett, who welcomed the Italian hero with open arms and insisted he spend time in the Bartlett home in Winthrop. The thirteen-year-old Frank took an instant liking to Garibaldi, and the two friends could be seen strolling around town, exploring the bays and inlets and talking about a wide range of topics, including Garibaldi's military experiences in Italy and South America. Before he departed America, Garibaldi gave Frank a walking stick.[8]

Charles Bartlett moved his family to this house in Winthrop in 1847. William Francis Bartlett lived here from 1847 until his marriage in 1865. The house remained in the Bartlett family until 1887, then became a seaside hotel before it was demolished. Courtesy Winthrop Public Library.

On October 13, 1853, Frank Bartlett enrolled at Phillips Academy, located in Andover, Massachusetts, twenty-one miles north of Boston. This elite boarding school had been founded in 1778 and many of its students went on to Harvard or other Ivy League schools. Frank only stayed at Phillips for one year. His course of study is listed as scientific, which means that he took mathematics and related courses rather than a standard classical approach to education. Given his later demerits at Harvard, Frank's indifference to education may have started by this time.[9]

Following Frank's discharge from Phillips, there is a dearth of information about his activities in the next several years. It is quite probable that his parents tried to get their son ready for the next stage of higher education — college. For the scions of the more important families in the Boston area, college meant Harvard University, the venerable institution founded in 1636 by the Massachusetts Bay Colony legislature. Although not directly affiliated with any church, Harvard was strongly Congregational, thanks in large part to its Puritan colonial heritage. Harvard was America's oldest college and trained its students to be both gentlemen and scholars. In 1849, a faculty member described the typical Harvard graduate as

one of a great family, who have gone forth from her instruction, and borne manfully the honorable burdens of life. He is bound to them and to her by a thousand ties, which nothing in after-years can break. He and they may be rivals in business, struggling hand in hand in the competition for wealth; but, when they meet ... they are indeed on common ground, with common tastes, feelings, and hopes.[10]

Harvard's gentleman scholars were groomed to have three major attributes — wealth, cultivation, and education. To accomplish the final product, students were educated to appreciate "cleanliness, grooming, and fashion; a facility with conversation, alcohol, and ladies; an acceptance of the virtues of nature as well as of books; a commingling of sophisticated excess with responsible self-control and worldly grace with physical vigor."[11]

Frank Bartlett was thrust into this program when he entered Harvard in the fall of 1859. His biographer Francis W. Palfrey described Bartlett's college years briefly. "He was not a close student, and perhaps a little young for his years. He was rather fond of billiards, suppers, college clubs, and the society of young ladies, and very fond of skating, boating, novels, and the theatre." As a result of his lack of attention to his studies, Frank's class rankings on two occasions were ninety-second in a class of 106 and eighty-fifth in a class of 110.[12]

Frank's lack of interest in serious studying is clearly shown in the existing records of Harvard University. He was privately admonished for improper conduct in the Greek recitation room, for absence from recitations, and for his part in a noisy disturbance of a meeting of the Institute of 1770. Frank

General Bartlett was honored at Phillips Academy when this oil portrait by Jane Bartlett was given to the school by the general's family. Courtesy of Phillips Academy Andover.

received public admonishment for absence from recitation and was required to study while on vacation. On May 22, 1860, Cornelius C. Felton, Harvard's president, wrote a letter to Frank's father, informing the elder Bartlett that his son had been publicly admonished for "offering an exercise in Greek written by another person," or, in other words, Frank copied someone else's Greek assignment. Frank was also fined $2 for cutting benches in the Mathematical room.[13]

For the most part, owing to the lack of records, we do not know what Frank Bartlett thought of the slavery issue in the late 1850s as North and South drifted apart. He seems to have made several friends of Southern students while at Harvard. On January 2, 1861, Bartlett wrote an essay in which he defended the rights of the South under the Constitution. Eight days later, Frank recorded in his journal that "all these troubles have arisen from the interference of the North." Still, Frank decided to join the New England Guards and begin drilling with his classmates, which he did on January 4. His drill instructor was Sergeant Thomas G. Stevenson, who would go on to command the 24th Massachusetts before being promoted to brigadier general. Stevenson was shot dead by a sharpshooter during the Battle of Spotsylvania in May 1864.[14]

John A. Andrew was inaugurated as governor of Massachusetts on January 5, 1861. The new governor was a fierce anti-slavery man and had defended John Brown's raid back in 1859. He was a noted lawyer who specialized in divorce and criminal law. Andrew was not well liked by the Boston elite, but when Andrew became governor, he began to cultivate their support that would be needed in the months ahead. But it would take a lot to galvanize public support of abolitionists. On January 24, abolitionist Wendell Phillips had to be protected from a hostile mob when he arrived in the city to attend an anti-slavery meeting. It's more than likely that Frank Bartlett was among those who looked down on these abolitionists for disturbing the unity of the country by attacking slavery.[15]

Frank surely followed the deteriorating relations between North and South. By the time Abraham Lincoln was inaugurated as the nation's sixteenth president on March 4, 1861, the states that had seceded from the Union had formed the Confederate States of America. On the morning of April 12, Confederate batteries positioned in the harbor of Charleston, South Carolina, opened fire on Fort Sumter, igniting four years of civil war. On the fifteenth, President Lincoln issued a call for 75,000 three-month militia to suppress the Southern rebellion. The next day, Governor Andrew called up the Massachusetts militia. Harvard students who had joined militia units were excused from class. "The college is full of the spirit of war & indignant at the treatment of the country's flag," wrote university librarian John Sibley.[16]

Sometime early on April 17, a pensive Frank Bartlett recorded in his journal that going to war "would be fighting rather against my principles, since I have stuck up for the South all along. We shall see." But, later that day, Frank enlisted as a private in the 4th Battalion, Massachusetts Volunteer Militia, the new name for the New England Guards. A week later, as the unit organized, the officers and men met and agreed to accept a proposal from the state to garrison a fort in Boston harbor. The following morning, April 25, 120 young men clad in dark blue caps and trousers assembled in line outside Boylston Hall and then marched to Liverpool Wharf at the foot of Pearl Street. Here, students from a local girls' school presented the unit with a flag, while a private citizen donated fatigue coats to all the soldiers.[17]

Following the ceremonies at the wharf, the battalion boarded a ferryboat for the two-mile ride to Fort Independence on Castle Island. This masonry fort was armed with twenty-four cannon to keep enemy ships from entering the harbor. Here, for the next thirty days, Major Stevenson's companies garrisoned the fort and drilled incessantly. The battalion's former commander, George H. Gordon, who was appointed to command the 2nd Massachusetts Volunteer Infantry, had recognized that the battalion contained men from the best classes in the city. He suggested to Governor Andrew that these men should be used "to organize and drill the bone and muscle of those upon whom we must rely for our armies." Thus, he believed, the 4th Battalion would produce "a small body of well-instructed gentlemen" who would lead the "undisciplined mobs of raw militia" into battle. These gentlemen required promotion rather than waste their talents as privates, concluded Gordon.[18]

Frank Bartlett enjoyed his month away from Harvard. He remained in the fort the entire month except for a two-day furlough. "What have I gained during the last month?" he wrote after returning to school. "I have learned more military than I could have learned in a year in the armory or from books.... I value the knowledge acquired in the last month more highly than all the Greek and Latin I have learned in the last year.... I look back on the past month as one of the pleasantest and most useful that I remember." Frank's experience mirrored that of his comrades in the 4th Battalion. Whether they consciously knew it or not, the month of military service had given these privileged men a new experience. Harvard student Henry Abbott perhaps summed it up best when he wrote his parents that the army was a cure for school, with its over-controlled schedules and boring recitations. Abbott was like Frank, as both acquired a sense of usefulness that they had not yet learned in school. Abbott wrote that he had gotten "disgusted with being nothing and doing nothing, & resolved that if I couldn't do much, to do what so many other young men were doing."[19]

2

"CAPTAIN BARTLETT IS ONE OF THE NOBLEST FELLOWS"

The Harvard Regiment

Not long after the mustering out of the 4th Battalion, Francis W. Palfrey was offered the lieutenant colonelcy of the new 20th Massachusetts Volunteer Infantry, a unit that was to be formed for a service of three years. William R. Lee, a West Point graduate with military service in the Seminole wars in Florida, was appointed by Governor Andrew to command this new unit. Lee, an older gentleman who had left the army to practice civil engineering, asked Palfrey to recommend younger men for the positions of captain and lieutenant in the ten companies that would form the regiment. Lee himself, in addition to nominating Palfrey to be his second in command, had also nominated Paul J. Revere to be major, as well as two other men to be adjutant and regimental quartermaster.[1]

> Friday, June 28. Palfrey came up to me on the Common, and said he had received the Lieutenant-colonel's commission of the Twentieth Regiment; that he had several commissions at his disposal, and asked me if I wanted one. I replied in the affirmative. I take it as a compliment, his coming and asking me, when there are so many begging him for them.[2]

For Frank Bartlett, Palfrey's confidence in his martial abilities was a surprise. Yet at the same time, young Bartlett sensed an opportunity to make a name for himself in this great civil war. Thousands of men from the Bay State were flocking to the colors, many drawn by an extreme sense of patriotism and a desire to restore the Union, others by peer pressure, many by the excitement and a chance to make more money in the army than in their professions.

12

Frank Bartlett's induction into the growing volunteer army also resulted in the first photographs we have of the twenty-one-year-old man from Haverhill. Colonel Palfrey described his young friend as "tall, straight, and slender, with a certain air of reserve and dignity of carriage which corresponded with his yet undeveloped character." And indeed the images of the new captain clearly show his tall, thin figure. Records indicate that Frank had brown hair and blue eyes. The photos also show that his eyes were sharp and focused, perhaps piercing, indicating an intentness of purpose. Palfrey described Frank's voice as "deep, full-toned, and powerful." Furthermore, Frank would prove to be "a born leader of the best men, and he had large endowments for controlling the worst."[3]

On July 2, Palfrey confirmed to Frank that he had been appointed a captain, with authority to lead a company. Word quickly spread of Bartlett's appointment, and the very next day several applicants approached him with the desire to serve in his company. Bartlett eventually selected two Harvard classmates as his lieutenants. George N. Macy became Bartlett's first lieutenant, and Henry L. Abbott his second lieutenant. On July 5, the new captain set out on a recruiting expedition to locate suitable men for his company. The nucleus of his command, which would eventually become Company I of the 20th, was composed of men from the island of Nantucket, together with contingents of recruits from elsewhere in the state.[4]

In the meantime, Colonel Lee decided that the regiment would form at a camp near Readville Station on the Boston and Providence Railroad, eight miles from Boston. The colonel and a detachment of men laid out the camp on July 8. "It was an ideal place for a camp,—a gentle slope with sandy soil which quickly dried after a rain, covered with a thick carpet of grass, bordered on two sides by beautiful old elms, and with the 'Blue Hills' of Milton but a mile away. Close by was a pond of clear, cool water .... A short distance beyond the pond was the Neponset River, while the railroad station was only a pistol-shot from camp." The first men arrived on July 10 and pitched their tents at "Camp Massasoit," as it was named. As the regimental historian noted, recruiting proceeded at a slow pace, which meant that a number of officers were forced to go on recruiting service. The initial wave of patriotic enthusiasm had already run its course, and as a result, the strength of the 20th grew slowly.[5]

The formation of a typical Union regiment was a slow process at this time. Most of the officers were unfamiliar with military service unless they had served in the state militia. Even so, once in camp, the officers as well as the men had to learn the basic ideas of soldiering. Officers were instructed by their peers who had seen prior service, at times even by privates who had been in the army before the war. Once they learned the basic drill maneuvers, the officers then drilled their companies incessantly until every man in blue could go through the evolutions without hesitation. Men learned the basic of drill at first in squads, then in companies, and as the individual companies improved, the colonel would assemble the entire regiment for drill. Men learned how to march in step, perform left and right wheels, deploy into column and line of battle, how to hold and move their weapons, performed bayonet drill, and occasionally got the chance to fire live rounds at target practice. They also had to learn the basics of army hygiene, where to dig their latrines so they would not interfere with the fresh water supply, how to cook their rations, and other essential duties of the soldier. The men in camp also had to learn the basics of guard duty, that universally hated duty in which men were placed on guard according to regulations, no matter where the camp was located or what the weather conditions were.

Major Revere reported for duty on July 12 and proved to be a big help to Colonel Lee and Lieutenant Colonel Palfrey. Battalion drill commenced almost immediately after Revere's arrival, every afternoon, so that the men would improve rapidly in efficiency. Still, many of the new recruits had to learn army discipline the hard way when they tried sneaking out of camp to visit a local tavern. Each and every man was also subjected to a medical examination by the regiment's surgeons. Captain Bartlett's recruits gathered during his recent expedition were included in this July 16–18 inspection. On July 18, Captain Thomas J. C. Amory mustered the regiment into the service of the United States for a period of three years. Amory was evidently not pleased by what he saw, remarking that "the men already enlisted as so deficient in stamina and capability that not more than one third of them were equal to the average of his experience as mustering officer for Massachusetts." Alarmed, Colonel Lee ordered the surgeons to conduct another inspection and discharge those unable to stand the rigors of army life.[6]

When the regiment was formed, Colonel Lee, in consultation with his two chief subordinates — Palfrey and Revere — decided that the seniority ranking of the ten company captains would not be established until the three officers had several weeks to watch the progress of the regiment as it drilled. On August 19, the colonel received orders to be ready to move to Washington at a moment's notice. The Battle of Manassas had taken place on July 21. The Confederate army under the command of General Joseph E. Johnston had sustained the attack of General Irvin McDowell's Union army, and managed to repel the Yankee attacks. In the ensuing retreat, many of McDowell's green regiments broke and fled, turning the retreat into a panic-stricken rout. McDowell was relieved from command soon after and replaced by Major General George B. McClellan, who began to rebuild the army defending Washington.[7]

Upon receiving orders to be ready to march, Lee, Palfrey, and Revere decided that Captain Bartlett, commanding Company I, would be the senior captain, followed in turn by the other nine captains in the regiment. Each commission was then dated to July 10, with Bartlett's first in order of commission. Lieutenant Macy ranked third among first lieutenants, with Abbott at the head of the regiment's second lieutenants. Still, the regiment was not yet ready to take the field. A full-strength Union infantry regiment consisted of field and staff officers and ten infantry companies. Each company, at full strength, would field one captain, one first lieutenant, one second lieutenant, one first sergeant, four sergeants, eight corporals, and 85 privates (two of which were detailed as musicians, and one as a wagoner), making a total of 101 for the company. There were to be fifteen field and staff officers, with a regiment fielding 1,025 officers and men at full strength. However, the 20th Massachusetts morning report for August

Henry L. Abbott was Bartlett's first Lieutenant in Company I, 20th Massachusetts. He developed into a very capable officer. As major commanding the 20th, Abbott was killed in the Wilderness. Courtesy United States Army Military History Institute, Massachusetts MOLLUS Collection.

21 showed only 538 officers and men present in camp. Recruiting was indeed going slowly. When three Massachusetts regiments left the state for Washington on August 27, the recruiting officer for the state was ordered to send all recruits to Colonel Lee until the 20th should be filled. During the ensuing week, more than 250 men arrived in camp, but when the regiment left the state in early September, its ranks were still not at full strength.[8]

While waiting for definite orders to break camp, the regiment continued to attract a few new recruits. On August 30, a group of ladies came to camp to present a regimental color to the 20th. Governor Andrew was also in attendance and made the actual presentation to the assembled regiment, accompanied by the usual flowery patriotic speech. The regiment also received new British-made Enfield rifle-muskets, purchased in England by a state agent.[9]

The long-awaited orders reached camp on September 2. Two days later, the 20th Massachusetts struck camp and prepared to leave for Washington. Eighty men were detached to take the regimental wagon train (baggage wagons and ambulances) and horses to Boston and place them on the train. The regiment left Camp Massasoit at four o'clock on the afternoon of September 4. An hour later, the men were all aboard and the train steamed south to Groton, Connecticut, where the regiment boarded a steamer for New York City. Once the unit debarked at New York, Governor Andrew and a deputation of Massachusetts citizens had a splendid dinner awaiting the men at Park Barracks. Then, after a march up Broadway to a boat wharf, the regiment again embarked on a steamer and reached Philadelphia at 6:30 A.M. on September 6. The 20th debarked and was marched to the Cooper Shop Volunteer Refreshment Saloon to receive an "excellent breakfast." The volunteers working at the Cooper Shop served 861 breakfasts to the Harvard Regiment that morning. After a three-hour stay in Philadelphia, the regiment was taken by train through Baltimore to Washington, reaching the national capital on the morning of September 7.[10]

That afternoon, the regiment marched down Pennsylvania Avenue, passing in review before General Winfield Scott, before marching out to Georgetown Heights to Camp Kalorama. Two days later, just when the men had gotten their camp fairly in order, the 20th received instructions to move to a new camp about three miles away, which was accomplished on September 10. However, no sooner had the regiment arrived at this new camp on Meridian Hill than orders were received to move across the river onto Virginia soil the next day. On September 12, the tents were struck and baggage packed and the regiment started down the hill for Virginia. Just then, another order came for the 20th to reverse its march and instead head for Poolesville, Maryland, and report to Brigadier General Frederick W. Lander.[11]

The 20th Massachusetts marched about nine miles that afternoon. "It was hot and dusty," recalled Bartlett, and they marched "over an uneven road." At seven o'clock, the regiment fell out to bivouac for the night "in wet grass about a foot high, a pleasant reflection for a landsman," wrote Lieutenant Macy.[12]

The next morning — September 13 — Captain Bartlett's Company I stepped out at the head of the 20th's long column of march.

> I led the column at a smart step until the Colonel rode up and said
> that the men were complaining of having to march too fast, and asked

> for an easier gait. We slackened up. We marched on through a hilly
> country for some miles, when we struck off the main road to the left
> for Rockville. It now began to look more like my idea of an army on
> the march, now fording a shallow stream and now climbing a long,
> steep, and rocky hill. Being at the head of the column, I could look
> back as we reached the top, and see the bayonets glisten down the nar-
> row road until the rear was lost in a cloud of dust.

After halting outside of Rockville at noon for lunch, the regiment formed ranks, passed through Rockville in step to the beat of the regimental drum corps, then kept on going. By sunset, the regiment halted to camp on a steep hillside at a place called Muddy Branch, "well named" said Lieutenant Macy, who described the place as having "mud, rocks, stumps, streams, bad water & no supper." However, Macy's servant had somehow procured a turkey, which was roasted as a meal for the company. Colonel Lee got a whiff of roasting turkey and asked if he could buy it, but was turned down. However, to show their appreciation of the colonel, he did receive a drumstick.[13]

As the regiment prepared to march on September 14, General Lander sent an order to Colonel Lee to be wary, as he had received reports of Rebel cavalry having crossed the Potomac River. Thus, Colonel Lee created both an advance and a rear guard to protect his regiment. Captain Bartlett, with a portion of Company I, again led the march, his men with loaded and capped rifles. The 20th moved fifteen miles this day and encamped near Poolesville, close to the camp of the 15th Massachusetts, which had arrived a few days before.[14]

The next afternoon, the 20th moved about two and a half miles to a better location for a permanent camp. Here, the regiment unpacked its baggage and laid out Camp Benton in a large wheatfield surrounded by a stream of clear water, situated on a plateau overlooking the Potomac River valley and about two miles from Edwards Ferry. Here the regiment would remain for more than six months. Colonel Lee's regiment became part of General Lander's First Brigade of the Corps of Observation, under the command of Brigadier General Charles P. Stone. This corps — in effect a division — was tasked with keeping an eye on the Confederate forces across the river in the vicinity of Leesburg, Virginia. Stone's 11,000 men were spread out in camps and sent out daily picket details to patrol the river to watch especially Edwards and White's ferries and the fords in between. On the opposite bank of the river, the Yankee pickets could see their counterparts. On occasion they exchanged gunfire, but on the whole, the men in blue and gray had an understanding not to fire on each other unless provoked.[15]

The regimental historian long afterward described the daily life that now took place in the regiment:

> From this time began our regular work, company drill every morning,
> battalion drill and dress parade every afternoon, with occasional

reviews and brigade drills, and regular Sunday morning inspection. Every other night two companies were detailed for outpost duty at the Potomac River in the neighborhood of Edwards Ferry, with other troops of the brigade and two guns from Vaughn's [Rhode Island] Battery. The reserve was placed in a thick piece of woods some two hundred yards back from the river, where they soon built a group of very pretty rustic houses, with pickets on the tow-path between the Chesapeake & Ohio Canal and the river. This duty was made as pleasant as possible under the circumstances, and it was relieved from monotony by an occasional conversation with the rebel pickets a quarter of a mile away across the river, as well as by an occasional shot and by constant alarming rumors of raids by large forces of the enemy, which sometimes aroused the entire brigade. Very few men were killed or wounded, but it served to teach us that there was no certain time for rest in the front line, and it was an excellent training for the officers and men. Skirmishing drill was now begun and a school was opened for non-commissioned officers in tactics, bayonet exercise, and discipline.[16]

Lieutenant Macy was sent to Washington soon after the regiment set up camp to obtain hospital supplies as well as additional supplies and extra horses. When he returned to camp, the lieutenant found that Captain Bartlett's company was down along the river on picket duty. Excited by the prospect of seeing the enemy, Macy hastened to join his company. "I found our boys in a thick piece of wood on a high hill immediately before the enemy's pickets," he wrote. The young lieutenant was a bit disappointed, however. "The pickets are in plain sight on the other side but they have the same instructions as ours not to fire unless fired upon or an advance made upon them. Our pickets are forbidden to speak to the enemy but the Minnesota pickets who were posted next to ours did talk frequently." Macy wrote that he would sneak down to the river and hide behind a tree to eavesdrop on the conversation, learning only that their opponents were Rebel cavalry. A Rebel officer came down to the river to water his horse after ascertaining that he would not be fired upon. Complained Macy, "This does not seem like warfare." The enemy were in plain sight on the other side of the Potomac, constructing an earthen fort for their artillery, but were not fired upon — that is, until one day when an officer of the Rhode Island battery was fired upon twice by the enemy. In response, the Rhode Islanders fired two well-aimed shells at the fort under construction and sent the enemy flying head over heels. Bartlett's three-company picket detail was relieved on Sunday morning, September 22, and returned to camp in a pouring rain.[17]

That evening, as the men of Company I lay quietly in their tents resting, the drums beat assembly and word was received that the enemy had crossed a force several miles upriver. Bartlett was placed in charge of three companies and sent out to check this report. The column moved down the hill two miles to the towpath of the canal, then went four miles north along the path. "I marched them at single file," reported the captain, "open order. I marched ahead with a few sharpshooters. We bivouacked on the path, where we halted. It was very wet before morning. We returned to camp by daylight, without having a skirmish." "A bloodless affair," quipped Lieutenant Macy.[18]

Yet another report of enemy activity swept through the regimental camp on Tuesday evening, September 24. This time Captain Bartlett set out with half the regiment—five companies—to investigate. When they reached Edwards Ferry, Bartlett halted three companies and sent Captain Henry M. Tremlett four miles upriver with the other two. Bartlett formed his soldiers into a hollow square, stacked arms, posted guards, and instructed the men to rest. The captain himself slept in a deserted house nearby, with guards ordered to awaken him if they heard any suspicious noise. At four o'clock in the morning of September 25, satisfied that there was nothing going on, Bartlett formed his detachment and was back in camp in time for reveille. "Another bloodless victory," penned Lieutenant Macy.[19]

Having witnessed Bartlett's actions now for several weeks, Lieutenant Macy took the time to write his views on his company. "Capt. Bartlett is one of the noblest fellows I ever saw. He will make his mark anywhere, and would today be made major in a moment if a vacancy occurred. I should dislike to part from him even for promotion." Continued Macy, "Lieut. A[bbott] is also all I could wish and I assure you this is very happy to be so pleasantly situated especially when out nights. I love them both as brothers. Our company and its officers have by far the best reputation of any in the camp although it may not become me to say so."[20]

By the end of the first week in October, in spite of recurring rumors of enemy river crossings, "our sudden alarms have begun to be 'played out,'" wrote Lieutenant Macy. The men were getting tired of being roused from camp and sent to the river, only to discover no enemy. Another such alarm sent Company I and another company racing toward Edwards Ferry on the evening of October 8. Two more companies followed. "We went to the ferry and remained until 4 A.M. when we were relieved by two companies and returned to camp," penned a disgusted Macy. The lieutenant found out that the alarm started when Union pickets occupied a large island about three miles long in the river. When discovered by the enemy, a force advanced to dispute possession of the island and the Yankees fell back to the Maryland shore. When the enemy fell back, the men in blue returned to occupy this island. The four companies of the 20th Massachusetts moved up as reinforcements.[21]

Macy remarked that his men left their overcoats and blankets in camp and were tired and cold by the time they returned, even though the lieutenant himself bragged that he experienced "no inconvenience" in spite of such a "rough" night. Macy also wrote, "Our men seem indifferent whether we whip or are whipped if they can only catch a chance at the Rebels who line the shore opposite." He had no way of knowing that this chance was very close for himself, Captain Bartlett, and the rest of the 20th Massachusetts.[22]

3

"ONE OF THE MOST COMPLETE SLAUGHTER PENS EVER DEVISED"

The Battle of Ball's Bluff

"We had [a] terrible fight yesterday. Went in with 22 officers and returned with but 9. Bartlett, Abbott & myself safe. Regiment literally cut to pieces. My knee is a little hurt that's all." With these words, Lieutenant Macy summarized the costly defeat at Ball's Bluff, Virginia, on October 21, 1861. Captain Bartlett's Company I was in the thick of this horrible battle, which turned into a rout for the defeated Yankees as they fled from the enemy in hope of escaping the bad situation in which they had been positioned.[1]

The fighting at Ball's Bluff was not supposed to happen, but a series of events ultimately led to this costly Union defeat. This chain of events began on the evening of October 16, when Confederate Colonel Nathaniel G. Evans, in command of a brigade charged with the defense of the Leesburg, Virginia, area, decided to fall back to a more defensible position some seven or eight miles south of town. Evans was apparently worried over the large number of blue-clad troops across the Potomac, but his unauthorized move was quickly countermanded by his superior, General P. G. T. Beauregard. The general advised Evans that the Leesburg defenses, which consisted primarily of an earthwork fort appropriately named Fort Evans, were strong enough to defend, but gave Evans the option to spread his men out as far as Goose Creek.[2]

However, Evans' troop movements were seen by Union observers and reported to Major General George B. McClellan, in command of all the Union troops. Wondering what the enemy was up to, McClellan decided to find out. He sent orders to Brigadier General George A. McCall to move his Pennsylvania Reserves division from its camp near Langley, Virginia, and reconnoiter the territory between there and the village of Dranesville, about halfway between Langley and Leesburg. McClellan told McCall that his chief duty was to map the terrain before returning to camp. McCall's Pennsylvanians moved out on the morning of October 19 and occupied Dranesville without opposition. He then sent out scouting parties to map the area. McClellan authorized McCall to remain in the area until his mapping project was done, then march back to camp on Monday, October 21.[3]

On October 20, McClellan dispatched an aide with the following message to General Stone: "General McClellan desires to inform you that General McCall occupied Drainesville [sic] yesterday, and is still there. Will send out heavy reconnaissances to-day in all directions from that point. The general desires that you keep a good lookout upon Leesburg, to see if this movement has the effect to drive them away. Perhaps a slight demonstration on your part would have the effect to move them." Stone immediately took steps to comply with McClellan's directive. His troops had several crossing points available to them over the Potomac River. On the south end of his division's front was Edwards Ferry, located at the point where Goose Creek flows into the Potomac. Three miles upriver was Harrison's Island, a low, flat island about two miles long and 300–400 yards in width. Stone's troops already picketed this island, which could provide a jumping off point for a foray across the river. Two miles upriver from Harrison's Island was Conrad's Ferry. Stone's men picketed the entire river between the two ferries.[4]

General Bartlett's military gear including his sword, shown here draped over a photo, was once displayed in the Berkshire Museum. The sword is engraved "Col. William F. Bartlett from the citizens of Winthrop, Mass. as a token of their appreciation of his gallant and patriotic military service." Reprinted with permission from *The Berkshire Eagle*.

On October 20, Stone sent part of General Gorman's brigade to Edwards Ferry to draw the enemy's attention to that point. Later in the day, a few companies of the 1st Minnesota crossed into Virginia but did not remain long, recrossing before dark. Stone also moved half the 15th Massachusetts to Harrison's Island, then sent most of the 20th Massachusetts, part of the 42nd New York, and a section of artillery, to the Maryland shore opposite the island. The Yankee actions compelled Colonel Evans to move part of his brigade toward Edwards Ferry. Evans also knew of McCall's presence at Dranesville, and worried that this strong division would continue to advance, cross Goose Creek, and head for Leesburg.[5]

And then, to ascertain if his movements had distracted the enemy and opened Leesburg for occupation, General Stone ordered Colonel Charles Devens, commanding the 15th Massachusetts, to send a patrol from Harrison's Island across the river and scout toward Leesburg, searching for any signs of the enemy. Devens in turn detailed Captain Chase Philbrick to head the reconnaissance. Accompanied by about twenty of his men, Philbrick used two small skiffs to ferry his men the from Harrison's Island to the Virginia shore. Once across, Philbrick was confronted by Ball's Bluff, a sheer rock cliff about 110 feet high, thickly wooded, and scalable only by a small path slightly down river from his crossing site. There was a piece of flat land along the river that was less than fifty yards wide to the base of the bluff, allowing the Yankees to move quietly along it to the path. The Rebels did not regularly picket the bluff, apparently believing that it would be foolish for their adversaries to mount an offensive there.[6]

Captain Philbrick and his men crossed at dusk and wound their way up the path to the summit of the bluff. Here they found a "cart path" that led inland through the woods. Cautiously taking this route, Philbrick and his men moved perhaps three quarters of a mile to the crest of a slight ridge on the opposite side of the woods. Lieutenant Church Howe, the regimental quartermaster of the 15th, later chronicled the scene: "We saw what we supposed to be an encampment. [There was] a row of maple trees; and there was a light on the opposite hill which shone through the trees and gave it the appearance of the camp. We were very well satisfied it was a camp." Philbrick's men could discern the town of Leesburg, less than two miles distant. There had been a full moon two nights earlier and there was moonlight yet remaining to bathe the night with enough light for the Yankees to survey the landscape. Yet the camp seemed deserted. There were no pickets visible, nor did any campfires burn in the night. Philbrick believed that his men were as yet undetected by the enemy.[7]

Philbrick decided not to press his luck and fell back, sending Lieutenant Howe to report to General Stone what the patrol had discovered. Upon hearing the news of a small Rebel camp, Stone decided to take advantage of the situation by sending over a larger force to launch a surprise attack and scatter the occupants of the camp. Sometime around midnight, Lieutenant Howe relayed General Stone's instructions to Colonel Devens:

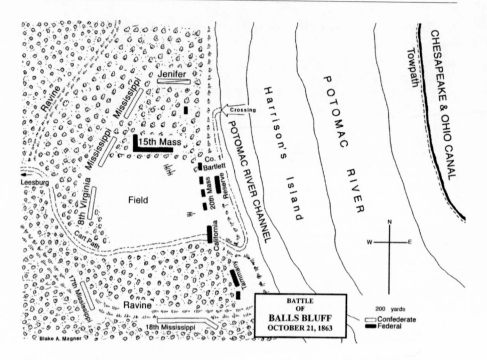

Colonel Devens will land opposite Harrison's Island with five companies of his regiment, and proceed to surprise the camp of the enemy
discovered by Captain Philbrick in the direction of Leesburg. The
landing and march will be effected with silence and rapidity.

Colonel Lee, Twentieth Massachusetts Volunteers, will immediately
after Colonel Devens' departure occupy Harrison's Island with four
companies of his regiment, and will cause the four-oared boat to be
taken across the island to the point of departure of Colonel Devens.

One company will be thrown across to occupy the heights on the
Virginia shore after Colonel Devens' departure to cover his return....

Colonel Devens will attack the camp of the enemy at daybreak, and,
having routed them, will pursue them as far as he deems prudent, and
will destroy the camp, if practicable, before returning....

Having accomplished this duty, Colonel Devens will return to his
present position, unless he shall see one on the Virginia side, near the
river, which he can undoubtedly hold until re-enforced, and one
which can be successfully held against largely superior numbers. In
such case he will hold on and report.[8]

Colonel Devens' five companies were ferried across the river by the two
skiffs and the boat dragged across the island by Colonel Lee's command. This
latter boat was actually a metallic lifeboat capable of holding approximately
fifteen men. All three craft could handle 30–35 men on one trip, and thus,
the ferrying process of Devens' companies and two companies of the 20th

occupied most of the rest of the early, pre-dawn morning. Lee, though authorized to send one company across, selected two — Bartlett's Company I and Captain Caspar Crowninshield's Company D — for the mission of covering the rear of Devens' troops. Together, the seven companies totaled just over 400 officers and men. Lee's men also supported two 12-pounder mountain howitzers from the 2nd New York State Militia, which moved the two small cannon into position on Harrison's Island to cover the Yankees atop the bluff.[9]

Once on the bluff, the Bay Staters discovered that the cart path led through a cleared field of sorts that was several acres in size and shaped somewhat like the African continent. The remainder of the area within view was wooded. According to Lieutenant Abbott: "When we get on the top, we are drawn up in the only open space there is, about wide enough for the front of two regiments, & about a short rifle shot in length, surrounded on every side by large, unexplored woods. It was in fact one of the most complete slaughter pens ever devised. Here we were kept, while the 15th marched off to surprise the rebel camp."[10]

Colonel Devens started his battalion along the cart path sometime around six on the morning of October 21. Sunrise was actually at 6:26, so Devens had his men moving to take advantage of the waning night. They advanced into the open on the other side of the woods and moved toward the row of trees, beyond which the Rebel camp had been located by Captain Philbrick's patrol. Devens recorded what happened next: "We came out upon the open field, which rises gradually. At the head of the rise there was a single row of trees — I think of fruit trees — of some description.... the light coming through between part of the branches of the trees gave very much the appearance of a row of tents." Devens was nonplussed — there seemed to be no camp. An embarrassed Philbrick at first insisted that the row of trees was not the same he had seen that night. So the colonel placed his men under cover and crept forward to investigate. He and a few men moved several hundred yards forward to the top of a small rise in the distance, where they could see Leesburg in the distance. They spied four white military tents close by the town, and clearly saw the Jackson farmhouse just to their north.[11]

Colonel Devens, after finding that there was no enemy camp, could simply have marched his men back to Ball's Bluff, descended the path, and embarked across the river to Harrison's Island, followed by the rearguard of the two 20th Massachusetts companies. If he had done so, there would have been no battle and no costly defeat. But General Stone's orders to the colonel left him the discretion to remain on Virginia soil. Devens did so, later arguing that his orders gave him this flexibility. The colonel thought at that moment that his troops had not been detected by the enemy. Instead of withdrawing, Devens decided to keep his troops near the Jackson farmstead and sent Lieutenant Howe to report the situation to General Stone.[12]

However, events were not what they seemed to Colonel Devens. Once his troops had marched out of sight, Colonel Lee, waiting with Crownin-shield's and Bartlett's companies, decided to send out patrols to scour the woods to the left and right of their position to ascertain whether any Confederates might be concealed nearby. Bartlett dispatched Sergeant William R. Riddle and three men from Company I out through the woods to their right, or roughly north, somewhat inland from the bluff's steep slope. Captain Crowninshield in person, followed by a private, walked north along the bluff's edge, were seen by Yankees on Harrison's Island, and fired at before the captain waved his arms and halted the few shots fired at him.[13]

Sergeant Riddle's men encountered a Confederate patrol from the 17th Mississippi, stationed north of Leesburg. During the ensuing exchange of gunfire, Riddle was wounded in the right elbow before his men fell back. Wrote Bartlett: "It was now about sunrise, when we heard three or four shots in rapid succession on our right. In a few minutes my First Sergeant (Riddle) was brought in, shot through the elbow. He was fainting from loss of blood. We tied a handkerchief around his arm and sent him down to the river."[14]

Colonel Devens seems not to have heard this brief skirmish; perhaps the woods muffled the shots. But the Confederates sent a runner back to warn the Mississippi commander, who in turn dispatched a mounted courier to Colonel Evans. So, while Devens remained in place and sent Lieutenant Howe across the river and down to Edwards Ferry to report to Stone, Evans was being warned about the presence of Yankees on Virginia soil.[15]

General Stone, meanwhile, had decided to draw the attention of the enemy to Edwards Ferry to allow Devens' raid to occur unmolested. On the morning of the twenty-first, Stone directed General Gorman to send two companies of the 1st Minnesota across the river, followed by a detachment of the 3rd New York Cavalry, which landed, then headed inland to scout. After covering three miles, the horsemen encountered Rebel infantry, exchanged gunfire, then headed back to the ferry. By that time, Stone had sent several regiments across the river and thus forced Colonel Evans to respond to this threat by moving much of his brigade toward the crossing site.[16]

After Lieutenant Howe departed the scene to report to General Stone, Colonel Devens spied enemy infantry approaching his position from the right. This was a lone company of Mississippi troops heading south toward Leesburg to avoid being cut off by the Yankee force. The sighting took place around eight o'clock, followed by some skirmishing as Devens pushed forward a company to investigate. This Mississippi unit (Company K, 17th Mississippi) was later reinforced by a mixed force of three cavalry companies, gathered together by a lieutenant colonel who heard of the Yankee advance from the courier sent to Colonel Evans. The colonel also detached four companies of infantry from his Mississippi units and sent them toward Ball's Bluff. [17]

Both Colonel Lee ("a heavy volley") and Captain Bartlett ("a splendid volley") heard the firing when Devens' men encountered the lone Mississippi company. Men wounded in the brief gunfight began coming back down the road to be evacuated across the river. Bartlett was worried. "The firing ceased and we were in suspense, thinking that they might have been surrounded and waiting to see the enemy come down that road and sweep our one hundred men into the river." The captain surmised that the 15th would coming running back past the two companies of the 20th, who would be expected to engage the pursuers until the 15th could recross the river. "I never expected to see Camp Benton again," Frank mused. [18]

Shortly thereafter, Colonel Devens led his battalion back to the clearing in front of Colonel Lee's position, remained there for perhaps half an hour while his scouts searched the woods, then led his troops back to their original position near the Jackson farmhouse. The two colonels had conversed, but Lee was mystified by Devens' retrograde movement. When the 15th headed back toward the enemy, Lee sent word to Major Revere to bring over the five companies of the 20th stationed on Harrison's Island, along with the two howitzers. "Colonel Devens has fallen back on my position; we are determined to fight," was the brief message from Lee to Revere. [19]

While all of this was going on, Lieutenant Howe reported to General Stone that the Confederate camp was not there. The general told Howe to take his order to Lieutenant Colonel George Ward of the 15th Massachusetts to cross the remaining half of his regiment, but also to cross at Smart's Mill, upriver from Ball's Bluff where the terrain was flatter and commanded by Union artillery across the river. This way, Ward would cover Colonel Devens, who was instructed to reconnoiter farther inland toward Leesburg without getting into a fight. Stone did not yet know about the morning skirmish. [20]

Howe returned to find Devens and learn about the fighting. The lieutenant immediately set off for Stone, talked to Ward on Harrison's Island, and suggested that he go directly across the river instead of upstream to the mill. While Howe went back to Edwards Ferry, Ward crossed and reinforced Devens, who now had his entire regiment in line at the Jackson farm. The 15th sent out skirmishers, who were attacked and driven back to the main line by the arrival of the Confederate cavalry, who attacked both mounted and dismounted. But Devens remained in position and still outnumbered the enemy. After this Confederate attack, there was a lull in the fighting, shortly after noon. [21]

While all this was going on, Colonel Lee remained stationary with the 20th Massachusetts. The seven companies of the regiment were drawn up in line, facing inland, with Company I on the right. Wrote Bartlett, "[Y]ou can imagine what a long morning it was, waiting either for reinforcements or the order to withdraw, with nothing to eat since dinner the day before. My company being deployed as skirmishers, I had given the order 'Lie down,' and I myself reclined on my elbow and dozed for half an hour. I woke up and found that nearly all my skirmishers lying down had taken the opportunity to go to sleep...."[22]

As Lieutenant Howe was making his way back from his last report to General Stone, he encountered Colonel Edward D. Baker riding south in search of Stone. Baker commanded one of the division's brigades, four regiments at the time numbered the 1st, 2nd, 3rd, and 5th California; most of the soldiers were recruited in Pennsylvania, though, and would be renumbered the 69th, 71st, 72nd, and 106th Pennsylvania before year's end. Baker, born in England in 1811, had migrated to Pennsylvania with his family in 1815, then went to Illinois, where he studied law and got to know Abraham Lincoln very well. Baker actually defeated Lincoln in a Congressional election before serving in the Mexican War. After this conflict, Baker resumed his political office, moved to California in 1851, then was invited to Oregon where he was appointed a United States senator in 1860. Baker, a Republican, was credited with helping spread Unionist sentiment along the west coast and thus saved these states for the Union. He was elected colonel of the 1st California (71st Pennsylvania) in 1861 and was also under consideration for a general's commission.[23]

Earlier in the day, Stone had ordered Baker to have his troops ready for a movement at a moment's notice. Observing the buildup of troops at Harrison's Island, Baker decided to report to Stone for more information. The general advised him of the situation and detailed Baker to go to the island and take charge, giving him discretionary authority to assess the situation and either evacuate the troops on the Virginia side or reinforce them as the situation warranted. Under no circumstances, said Stone, was Baker to advance his troops unless the enemy numbers were clearly inferior to his own. When Baker encountered Lieutenant Howe, he learned of the skirmish before Stone did. Even after reporting to Stone, Howe was told that Colonel Baker was in charge of the area and would act according to the developing situation.[24]

But Baker shirked his responsibilities and remained on the island, issuing instructions for crossing and making sure that the troops kept moving. Worried about the lack of boats, the colonel had a flatboat lifted out of the Chesapeake and Ohio Canal and dragged over to Harrison's Island to facilitate the crossing. He sent no orders to the troops on Ball's Bluff. And so, when the 8th Virginia arrived in front of the 15th Massachusetts shortly after 12:30 P.M., Devens' regiment again engaged the enemy with no support. But even with the 8th Virginia's support, the Rebels could not force Devens back. Finally, around 2:00 P.M., Devens withdrew his isolated regiment back toward Ball's Bluff. The Rebels did not pursue.[25]

By the time Devens withdrew, Colonel Baker had finally crossed to Ball's Bluff and assumed command of the troops. Union soldiers were still crossing the river when Baker arrived. When the Union troops finished crossing, Baker had a line of battle established parallel to the river. The left flank was covered by Company D, 20th Massachusetts, followed in line by six companies of the 1st California, some companies of the newly-arrived 42nd New York, both of which units were formed along the east side of the clearing. Five companies of the 20th Massachusetts were formed in line behind the New Yorkers. Colonel Devens formed his unit on the northern side of the clearing, with his right and rear protected by two of his companies, one (H) from the 20th Massachusetts, and one from the 42nd New York. Two companies of the California Regiment also formed on the north side of the clearing, perpendicular to Colonel Lee's men. Baker's three fieldpieces — the two howitzers and a James rifle — were placed along the east edge of the clearing.[26]

The action began to heat up shortly after three o'clock, when Colonel Baker, after talking with Colonel Milton Cogswell of the 42nd New York, decided to send a reconnaissance out to his left to see if there were any Rebels in that direction. General Stone had earlier informed Baker that perhaps as many as 4,000 Confederates were in the Leesburg area. The feint at Edwards Ferry was designed to draw most of them in that direction while the original raid took place toward the Leesburg camp that Captain Philbrick had located. Now the situation had changed and Baker decided to find out what troops he was facing.[27]

Accordingly, two companies of the 1st California advanced southwest into the woods on the south side of the clearing. This force ran headlong into the 8th Virginia, was which also advancing into the area, and a fierce combat erupted. The two Yankee companies lost two-thirds of their men and fell back as the enemy opened fire all along the line. The Yankees returned fire and caused the 8th Virginia to begin to fall back; some of the Southerners even panicked and began to head farther to the rear out of range of the fighting. As the Virginians fell back, the newly-arrived 18th Mississippi formed and advanced diagonally into the same area. As the Mississippians emerged from the woods, they exposed their left flank to the 15th Massachusetts, which, combined with the Yankee frontal fire, decimated the enemy, mortally wounding their colonel and forcing the regiment to retreat.[28]

After the repulse of the Mississippi regiment, the fighting seems to have become general all along the line. Captain Bartlett recounted his experience in his first time under hostile fire:

> Well the first volley came and the balls flew like hail.... The whizzing of balls was a new sensation. I had read so much about being under fire and flying bullets that I was curious to experience it. I had a fair chance. An old German soldier told me that he had been in a good

many battles, but that he never saw such a concentrated fire before. They fired beautifully, too, their balls all coming low, within from one to four feet of the ground. The men now began to drop around me; most of them were lying down in the first of it, being ordered to keep in reserve. Those that were lying down, if they lifted their foot or head it was struck. One poor fellow near me was struck in the hip while lying flat, and rose to go to the rear, when another struck him on the head, and knocked him over. I felt that if I was going to be hit, I should be, whether I stood up or lay down, so I stood up and walked around among the men, stepping over them and talking to them in a joking way, to take away their thoughts from the bullets, and keep them more self possessed. I was surprised at first at my own coolness. I never felt better, although I expected of course that I should feel the lead every second, and I was wondering where it would take me.[29]

Lieutenant Abbott's recollections matched his captain's. "It seemed as if every square inch of air within six feet of the ground was traversed by bullets as they whistled by us," wrote Abbott the next day. The lieutenant also wrote that the men had taken off their winter great coats and hung them on trees behind the line of battle. The coats were lined with red, making them conspicuous targets for the enemy, one reason for the great rate of fire over the heads of the Bay Staters. "Though we were lying down," continued Abbott, "our men were shot on every side of us. And yet Capt. Bartlett, though standing up nearly all the time, wasn't so much as scratched."[30]

The fighting intensified throughout the late afternoon. During the early course of this last phase of the battle, the companies of the 42nd New York, originally deployed in front of the Harvard Regiment, were disorganized by the heavy fire and fell back through the ranks of the Bay Staters. Wrote Bartlett: "The field now began to look like my preconceived notion of a battle field. The ground was smoking and covered with blood, while the noise was perfectly deafening. Men were lying under foot, and here and there a horse struggling in death. Coats and guns strewn over the ground in all directions."[31]

The 18th Mississippi, once it reorganized following its unsuccessful charge, deployed on the Union left flank and began working its way toward the river. Evans had sent word for the 17th Mississippi to march to the battlefield, and once this regiment arrived, it deployed between the 18th Mississippi and 8th Virginia. The firing was heavy. The three Union artillery pieces were silenced during this intense phase of the battle, the cannoneers shot down, horses slain, and ammunition in short supply. Colonel Baker, attired in his full dress uniform, was conspicuous, walking up and down the front line on the Union left, encouraging his men as best he could. Sometime between 4:30 and 5:00, Baker was hit, fell down, got up and was again felled by several bullets almost at once, killing him. Captain Crowninshield of the 20th recorded that Baker was within six feet of him when he was shot.[32]

Baker's death demoralized the already-shaken Yankee battle line. Men instinctively began to fall back from the heavy fusillade of bullets. A number of men rallied, however, and surged forward to rescue the colonel's body. Colonel Lee was quickly informed of the colonel's death and assumed command temporarily. He and Colonel Devens were talking when Colonel Cogswell came up and, as the senior officer present, took command. Cogswell was well aware of the difficult situation faced by the Union forces atop Ball's Bluff. Earlier, he had advised Baker to collect all the troops and move them south and strike the enemy left flank, break through, and head downriver to Edwards Ferry to join Gorman's forces there. This tactic might have worked earlier in the day, but ws now well nigh impossible because the main strength of the enemy was facing the Union left.[33]

But Cogswell was determined to try. He ordered Colonel Devens to withdraw his regiment from the woods and lead it around behind the 20th to the Union left. Once the 15th vacated their position, the Rebels advanced and fired into the Union right flank with great effect. Cogswell then ordered an advance by his right at the same time that one of Evans' staff officers rode out of the woods to the companies of the 42nd New York, which he mistakenly thought were Confederates since the Tammanies were wearing their old gray militia uniforms, and ordered them to attack. Cogswell also seemed to have thought that Lee's five companies of the 20th Massachusetts would join this attack. Events surrounding this portion of the battle are very confusing, however, and the contradictory reports of officers involved makes it difficult to determine exactly what happened.[34]

Colonel Lee had appointed Major Revere of the 20th to the command of a covering force to protect the rear of the Union infantry as it tried to move south and break out. The two howitzers had been abandoned by the survivors of the gun crews and stood in the open clearing, a prize for the advancing Confederates. Revere counterattacked just as the 8th Virginia came out of the woods to seize the guns. Revere's men were repelled and the Virginians overran the two guns.[35]

At about the same time as Revere attacked, Captain Bartlett also decided to charge the enemy. The captain had apparently located Colonel Lee, sitting behind a tree, tired and dispirited. The colonel told Frank that the battle was lost and everyone must surrender to avoid being "murdered" by the heavy enemy fire. But Frank thought otherwise. "I thought it over in my mind, and reasoned that we might as well be shot advancing on the enemy, as to be slaughtered like sheep at the foot of the bank."[36]

Continued Bartlett: "I called for Company I for one last rally." His men sprang forward, followed by men from other companies. The band of Yankees bravely charged uphill from near the top of the bluff to the crest of a small ridge. "As we reached the top, I found Little (Abbott) by my side. We came upon two fresh companies of the enemy which had just come out of the woods; they had their flag with them. Both sides were so surprised at seeing each other ... that *each side forgot to fire.* And we stood looking at each other (not a gun being fired) for twenty seconds, and then they let fly their volley at the same time we did. If bullets rained before, they came in sheets now. It is surprising that any one could escape being hit. We were driven back again. I had to order sharply one or two of my brave fellows before they would go back. Everything was lost now."[37]

Lieutenant Abbott also described this last valiant charge:

> But we were determined to have one more shot. So Frank ordered a charge & we rushed along, followed by all our men without an exception, & by Lieut. Hallowell with about 20 men, making about 60 in all. So we charged across the field about half way, when we saw the enemy in full sight. They had just come out of the woods & had halted at our advance. There they were in their dirty gray clothes, their banner waving, cavalry on the flank. For a moment there was a pause. And then, simultaneously, we fired & there came a murderous discharge from the full rebel force. Of course we retreated, but not a man went faster than a walk.[38]

The two Company I officers described the last charge made by the 20th Massachusetts and the intensity of the rifle fire against them. The 8th Virginia at this time was short on ammunition when it again moved onto the battlefield and headed toward the two abandoned howitzers. Accompanying the Virginians were at least one or two companies of Mississippians, one of which, at least, had a full supply of ammunition. It was probably at this time that the 8th Virginia's color bearer, Sergeant Clinton Hatcher, was killed, perhaps by Company I's parting volley before they fell back.[39]

While Bartlett charged the enemy, Colonel Cogswell was directing the breakout attempt on the Union left. The companies of troops had begun moving off but as they began their attack, both the 17th and 18th Mississippi, with perhaps 1,000 men yet in the ranks in both regiments, began their own attack, sweeping across the cleared field under a heavy fire from the Yankees on the opposite side. The Mississippi advance effectively halted Cogswell's plan, and the colonel realized that the only alternative was to retreat before it was too late. An orderly retreat was almost impossible, with the near approach of the enemy and the cliff behind the Yankees. In the rush to fall back, the Union line simply dissolved into a mass of soldiers trying their utmost to get down to the river and get across to Harrison's Island. Scores of men were captured by the oncoming Confederates, who then lined the top of the bluff and opened a murderous fire on the men in blue below.[40]

When Captain Bartlett rallied his survivors after falling back from their charge, they found Colonel Lee, sitting under a tree, exhausted. Lieutenant Abbott recorded that the colonel swore he could not go another step and that he would rather surrender. Wrote Bartlett: "The Adjutant took his left arm and I his right, and we got him down the bank unhurt." Once down at the cliff's base, Bartlett saw "a horrible scene. Men crowded together, the wounded and the dying. The water was full of human beings, struggling with each other and the water, the surface of which looked like a pond when it rains, from the withering volleys that the enemy were pouring down from the top of the bank. Those who were not drowned ran the chance of being shot."[41]

The captain then went about collecting the men of his company, and when he returned to the riverbank, could not find Colonel Lee. Someone informed Frank that the adjutant had gotten Colonel Lee into a boat and rowed across the river, so the captain told all those within earshot that they were free to swim across the river to safety. Frank thought it his duty to remain behind with those who were unable to swim, but since most of Company I hailed from Nantucket Island, the majority of the men were swimmers. Lieutenant Abbott stayed with Frank, while Macy decided to swim the river. The lieutenant, like many of the men, stripped off his uniform to swim easier. Macy lost his swordbelt en route and had to jettison his sword before successfully getting across. "Many were drowned right side of me," he penned. "I ran naked two miles after getting over." Captain Crowninshield also made it across, wearing at least his flannel underwear, found a haystack on the island, and crawled underneath it to sleep, completely worn out by his ordeal.[42]

Once all those who could swim had left the riverbank, Bartlett gathered a number of men of the 20th around him and headed upriver, determined to avoid the volleys from the bluff and find someone to surrender his men without further casualties. Captain Henry M. Tremlett and Lieutenant Charles A. Whittier, both of Company A, followed Frank and Lieutenant Abbott, with about twenty others from the regiment. Approximately sixty men from the 15th Massachusetts, 42nd New York, and 1st California also followed the captain. The group eventually reached Smart's Mill, where an elderly slave informed the captain that there was an old boat nearby that they could use. Bartlett went to investigate and found a small skiff capable of holding five men half sunk in the mill race. His men dragged it out, repaired it, and Bartlett decided to try to save his men, expecting full well that they would be discovered any moment. But it was now dark and this probably more than anything was the major reason why the Rebels failed to see his band of soldiers. When the boat was lowered into the Potomac, the men instinctively made a rush for it. "I had to use a little persuasion by stepping in front of it, drew my pistol (for the first time this afternoon), and swore to God that I would shoot the first man who moved without my order." Frank selected five men from his own company to go first, along with a man to pole the boat back. Lieutenant Whittier went over in the second load to take command on the opposite shore. Bartlett, Tremlett, and Abbott went over last. All eighty men reached the northern end of Harrison's Island without incident.[43]

Captain Bartlett and the survivors of his company reached the Maryland shore opposite Harrison's Island sometime around midnight. "Then we had still that long walk down the tow-path and up to our camp from the river, where we arrived at three a. m. I got to bed pretty well tired out at half past three." For the 20th Massachusetts, the Battle of Ball's Bluff was a terrible defeat. Colonel Lee, Major Revere, and Adjutant Charles L. Peirson were all captured, much to Frank's amazement. The story that he was told — these three had gotten safely across the river — was false. Colonel Lee had actually gone upriver long before Bartlett assembled his party, had been shown the half-sunk boat at Smart's Mill, but was captured by a roving Confederate patrol around eight o'clock that evening. The regiment's seven companies that were present on the battlefield totaled 340 officers and men. Casualties were tallied as 15 killed, 44 wounded, and 135 captured or missing, a total of 194. Captain Bartlett had 48 men in his company, which suffered a loss of one man killed, eleven wounded, and nine missing, a total of twenty-one, or almost half. The entire Union loss was calculated at 49 killed, 158 wounded, and 714 captured or missing, for a total of 921 out of about 1,600 engaged.[44]

Frank's Company I performed well, though, in its first engagement. Lieutenant Abbott admired the way his men stood their ground. They "couldn't possibly have behaved better," he wrote. "They never fired once without an order. They never advanced without an order, as all the rest did. They never retreated without an order, as some of the others did. In short, they never once lost their presence of mind, & behaved as well as if on the parade ground." Abbott himself was pleasantly surprised that he was physically brave during the fighting. Lieutenant Abbott was equally happy with his company commander, whose newspaper report was perhaps the only accurate account of the battle that the lieutenant read. Frank "...deserves all [the praise] he gets," recounted Abbott. Later in the year, Abbott wrote that Bartlett was "a person of more natural military aptitude & genius than anybody I have ever met.... Not only military aptitude, but the power of governing men with vigor & firmness, so that they not only look up to him in every moment of doubt but also love him."[45]

Frank himself, a few days after the battle, recorded in his journal that the newspapers "compliment me too highly, who did nothing more than my duty. My coolness was in me. I ought not to have the credit of it, but be grateful to God, who in his mercy has spared me, for granting me the courage and self-possession."[46]

4

"OUR REGIMENT MET WITH THE GREATEST LOSS"

The Road to Yorktown

The debacle at Ball's Bluff was costly to the 20th Massachusetts. Over half the men taken into action were casualties. Colonel Lee, Major Revere, the adjutant, surgeon, and many others were prisoners of the Confederacy. Lieutenant Colonel Palfrey was the senior officer remaining in the regiment. But when Frank Bartlett and the other survivors of the battle all drifted back to camp, Palfrey was absent, having marched the remainder of the regiment toward Edwards Ferry to support the operations there. So Frank, as senior captain present, assumed temporary command of the regiment. "[T]o let the men see that everything was not broken up, and to cheer them with the music," wrote Frank, he issued orders for the usual evening dress parade on October 23. During the formal occasion of the parade, Bartlett issued a congratulatory order to the survivors, praising their "admirable conduct" in the battle. "Your courage and bravery under a galling fire for hours was only equaled by your coolness and steadiness throughout."[1]

Once the three companies under Palfrey's command returned to camp, the lieutenant colonel felt that the regiment needed a temporary reorganization until the prisoners were exchanged. On October 24, he issued an order that detailed Bartlett for duty as acting lieutenant colonel, Captain Crowninshield as acting major, and, among other such details, Lieutenant Macy assumed the role of captain of Company I. Since Company G had lost heavily, the survivors were temporarily assigned to Company A; Company E's survivors were merged temporarily with Company I; and Company D was merged with Company H. A recruiting party was soon dispatched to Boston to seek new members for the regiment. The 20th had left the state understrength, and the loss at Ball's Bluff seriously depleted the ranks.[2]

Years after the war, when Colonel Palfrey edited Frank's letters and journal accounts for publication, he praised the young captain for taking on the role of second in command and fulfilling his duties far beyond expectations. Palfrey wrote that he personally was deluged with mail from families of men in the regiment, seeking answers to the fates of their loved ones. Civilians from the Bay State descended on the camp, demanding the colonel's attention. After the day's work was over, Palfrey would visit the hospitals to check on his wounded men. Lieutenant Macy was pressed into service writing letters to the families of those killed in battle to help ease the burden on the regimental staff.[3]

With Palfrey busy, Acting Lieutenant Colonel Frank Bartlett tended to the business of keeping the regiment in shape. Palfrey praised Frank's work in the months after Ball's Bluff. "He took a great interest in tactics, and rapidly made himself a proficient in the school of the battalion, and drilled the regiment constantly and well. His height, fine carriage, good horsemanship, and powerful voice, caused him to appear in such positions to the greatest advantage. It was characteristic of him, that at this time he learned to play the bugle sufficiently well to sound the infantry calls." By early December, Palfrey invited Bartlett to join his tent, and their friendship grew.[4]

Under Frank's tutelage, the regiment rapidly improved in drill. October gave way to November, bringing howling winds and cold. The regiment remained at Camp Benton through the fall and winter, picketing the Potomac, drilling, and growing restless. A federal paymaster arrived in camp on November 12 and paid the regiment through November 1, the first pay since leaving Massachusetts. The men sent over $8,000 to their families. "[W]e live like princes," penned Lieutenant Macy. Since the fight at Ball's Bluff, loyal Bay Staters had showered their largess upon the survivors, sending all sorts of delicacies to the men to show their appreciation of their bravery in the face of the enemy. "Wine and all luxuries sent us in quantities for us personally as well as for our sick." For Thanksgiving, the regiment feasted on a dinner of turkey and plum pudding. Company I's 35 men were given five bottles of whiskey by the officers, "& I am happy that there wasn't the slightest trouble," wrote Lieutenant Abbott.[5]

Unfortunately for history, Palfrey, when editing Bartlett's writings, jumped over this period in the regiment's history. Today, over 140 years later, Frank's reflections on the state of affairs in the regiment would be invaluable for historians attempting to reconstruct what was happening behind the scenes. Colonel Bruce's regimental history, like most others of this genre, glosses over any problems in the interest of telling a good story about a band of patriotic soldiers. But, in the 20th Massachusetts, there was dissension and controversy.[6]

In late November, Governor John Andrew of Massachusetts received an anonymous letter complaining about certain officers in the 20th Massachusetts. The writer stated that General Stone had sent an order to his division officers describing two escaped slaves and directing their return to their masters should they be apprehended. Stone's order eventually reached Lieutenant Macy, who, on a Sunday morning, arrested two black peddlers as they sold their wares in camp. The letter writer informed Governor Andrew that the general's order was illegal because it did not pertain to any military matter. What was worse, continued the writer, was the fact that the lieutenant "glories in the act ... as though he had performed some noble and praiseworthy deed. And in this view of the case, I am sorry to say, he does not appear to be alone. With but two or three exceptions those of our officers boast of their pro-slavery opinions and purposes."[7]

Francis W. Palfrey was lieutenant colonel of the 20th Massachusetts during the time Frank Bartlett was with the regiment. Palfrey recognized Bartlett's aptitude for military life and discipline and allowed his senior captain to drill the regiment after Ball's Bluff. Courtesy United States Army Military History Institute, Massachusetts MOLLUS Collection.

The governor had, just two days previous to receiving this letter, approved of Macy's promotion to captain, part of a number of promotions in the regiment, which included Abbott's elevation to first lieutenant. Andrew immediately fired off an angry letter to Colonel Palfrey, stating that if he had known of Macy's political stance, he would not have promoted the officer. Palfrey replied to the governor and suggested that Andrew was trying to interfere with military discipline. Angered further by Palfrey's letter, Andrew complained to General McClellan, who politely informed the governor that the 20th Massachusetts had been mustered into federal service and was thus removed from state control. Not content to be treated so, Andrew informed the general in chief that the 20th had been raised, manned, and equipped at state expense. Moreover, the governor did not appreciate the general's procrastination in moving against the rebels in Virginia.[8]

The feud between Palfrey and Andrew was just the tip of the iceberg. At this stage of the war, most Union soldiers were in the army to preserve the

Union, not to destroy slavery. Abolitionists were yet a growing, but very vocal, minority across the North. Massachusetts was one of the leading abolition states, but that did not mean that every officer in her regiments was in favor of abolishing slavery. Many officers in the 20th obeyed orders and followed the Constitution, even if it meant delivering escaped slaves to their owners. It is interesting to note that Lieutenant Macy never mentioned the incident of arresting the two slaves in any of his letters to his friend Lincoln. To the lieutenant, the incident was just another routine military matter. Considering that Frank Bartlett had a number of Southern friends previous to the war, he more than likely sided with the "strict constructionists" and allowed his officers to uphold the Constitution as it was then written.[9]

About this same time, Captain Crowninshield of Company D, who was the acting major of the regiment, managed to secure a transfer to the 1st Massachusetts Cavalry. Lieutenant Macy was sorry to see him go. "...[A] finer and more honorable fellow never lived," he wrote. Crowninshield was a cavalry hobbyist, said Macy, and though he possessed "no great military genius," his action at Ball's Bluff, where his company held the left flank for quite some time, showed his bravery under fire. However, once he left the regiment, the captain badmouthed his former comrades; his comments seem to have appeared in a Boston newspaper that angered the officers in the regiment. Lieutenant Abbott was terribly upset and penned his opinions in a letter to his industrialist father. As far as Abbott was concerned, Crowninshield's jealousy of Frank Bartlett's military aptitude was the real reason for his transfer to the cavalry. Abbott commented that Crowninshield hated to play second fiddle to Bartlett. The officer was "perfectly selfish & indifferent to everybody else, though ordinarily too shrewd & wellbred to show it.[10]

Company I, during Bartlett's tenure as acting lieutenant colonel, served as a model company for the regiment. With Bartlett acting as a field officer, and Macy transferred to Company B, Abbott was promoted to first lieutenant and a new second lieutenant-Arthur Curtis-arrived from Massachusetts to begin his military career with the 20th. As late as December 16, Lieutenant Abbott surmised that not a single man from Company I had been sent to the guardhouse for any military infraction. Wrote Abbott, " ... they are such a good set of boys that I never have a word of complaint from them of any kind, not even looks ...." In one example, Colonel Lee had ordered that the men in the regiment did not have to attend Sunday religious services. In other companies, the audiences became smaller over time, but not in Company I. When three men took the day off, Abbott detailed them to carry water to camp during the service and for a couple of hours afterward. That punishment ended any further holdouts.[11]

On the last day of the year, Abbott again praised Company I and its effect on the entire regiment. "Since Palfrey & Bartlett have had charge of the regt. you see a complete change all through. Instead of blacked boots & washed hair being confined to one company you see all companies alike in that respect. Instead of the majority of the men being merely a pack of Broad St. & Northstreet roughs who are just working along as little as possible for their pay, ... you see them actually vying with each other who shall be the best soldier, most tidy with his equipments & most active in his duty. And all this done with very little punishment...." Indeed, Abbot's genteel upbringing shows through in many of his letters. Harvard-educated and well-bred, Abbott, Macy, Bartlett, and other officers sometimes came off as haughty New Englanders. Two of the regiment's companies — B

Here, Frank strikes a jaunty military pose common during the war — hand stuck in his coat, hat cocked at an angle, courtesy Berkshire Athenaeum, Pittsfield, MA.

and C — were composed of German immigrants living in Boston. Occasionally, New England contempt for ill-educated and poor foreigners came through in their writings. In spite of such prejudices, Frank Bartlett and his brother officers, throughout the fall and winter of 1861–1862, slowly turned the 20th Massachusetts into a superior Yankee regiment.[12]

The winter months were generally uneventful for the 20th Massachusetts. The normal routine of picket duty occupied much of the regiment's time, as well as Frank's relentless drilling of the officers and men. In spite of such boring daily routine, picket duty remained a hard task because of the long hours involved and the ever-present possibility that there would be firing in case of attack. "I have just come off the hardest week's duty I ever had in my life," penned Lieutenant Abbott on February 5, 1862. With 97 men and two lieutenants, Abbott was in charge of patrolling eight miles of the Potomac River, his men deployed on the towpath between the river and the canal. Every night, complained Abbott, he had to make the entire rounds of every picket station, sixteen miles in all, "through the most horrible mud that the mind of man can conceive of." On one occasion, he was in a small boat that tipped over, drenching the hapless lieutenant. And since the rounds were made after midnight, in the perpetual winter darkness, Abbott kept slipping and tripping in the muddy, rutted path. To make matters even worse, one night after returning to camp, heavy winds started a fire in camp and his tent burned, leaving him with singed hair and a burned neck as he worked to save some of his belongings.[13]

Behind the scenes, trouble was brewing. Ever since the debacle at Ball's Bluff, politicians, newspaper reporters, soldiers, and civilians, wondered who was to blame for the defeat. Lieutenant Abbott had scathing words to write about General Stone, blaming him for allowing his subordinates to decide the issue rather than coming to see firsthand the events at Ball's Bluff. Others blamed McClellan as well, for not informing Stone of McCall's retrograde movement. Colonel Baker also came in for criticism by those who fought in the battle for refusing to listen to other colonels as to the disposition of the troops.[14]

In December 1861, Congress created the Joint Congressional Committee on the Conduct of the War, a body tasked with the broad investigation of the Union war effort, "past, present, and future." Led by Republican senators Benjamin F. Wade (Ohio) and Zachariah Chandler (Michigan), the committee was dominated by Radical Republicans who mistrusted West Pointers and wanted a quick victory over the Confederacy. Stone's conduct of the Ball's Bluff affair was an early prime topic of committee meetings. Using their power of subpoena, the committee members began hearing testimony from participants in January 1862. Although Stone ably defended himself against insinuations that he had allowed Confederate sympathizers to cross the Potomac, engaged in correspondence with Rebel officers, and effectively mismanaged the battle, the committee agenda triumphed and Stone was arrested on February 8, then imprisoned at Fort Lafayette, New York harbor. Transferred later to another fort, Stone remained in prison for 189 days without any charges being brought against him. Finally, after a personal appeal to the president, he was released in July, but his military career was a shambles.[15]

Stone's arrest elicited sympathy from the 20th, though. Abbott thought that the general had "offended the abolitionists." "[T]o doubt his loyalty is simply ridiculous. I wouldn't send a private to the guard house on such absurd charges as have been trumped up to enable Charles Sumner to have a gentleman dragged away in the night from a dying wife & shut up in a prison. Every decent man here feels shocked beyond expression." Stone's arrest meant more changes in his command. Earlier, General Lander's slight wounding at Edwards Ferry forced him away from active duty at the time and he never returned to the division. Now, with Stone gone, his replacement was Brigadier General John Sedgwick, a Connecticut-born professional soldier who assumed command on February 19. The three brigadiers now were Willis A. Gorman (First Brigade), Napoleon J. T. Dana (Second), and William W. Burns (Third). On March 13, Sedgwick's division became the Second Division, Second Army Corps, with Burns' brigade becoming the Second Brigade (Baker's old command), and Dana's the Third. The 20th Massachusetts, together with the 19th Massachusetts, 7th Michigan, and 42nd New York, constituted Dana's command.[16]

On February 26, the 20th Massachusetts broke camp and moved a short distance to the old camp of the 15th Massachusetts, close to Poolesville, Maryland. The men christened their new abode "Camp Lee," in honor of their colonel, who, together with other Ball's Bluff prisoners, had been released and sent north. Lee was in Boston at this time, having signed a parole. He would not be able to resume duty until officially exchanged. On March 11, the regiment again broke camp and marched to the mouth of the Monocacy River, where the men were placed on canal boats and sent upriver to Harper's Ferry. On the twelfth, the regiment marched eight miles to Charlestown, Virginia, and went into camp. The next day, the regiment, with Sedgwick's division, moved farther south to Berryville.[17]

The movement was part of a larger general advance by Federal troops in Virginia. On March 8, the Confederate army began to evacuate its positions around Manassas and withdraw to Fredericksburg; Leesburg was evacuated the same day and was occupied by Union soldiers the same day. General McClellan quickly moved elements of the Army of the Potomac toward Manassas, but the Yankees found only empty camps and smouldering supplies that had not been carted away. McClellan, who was planning an attack on Richmond, the Confederate capital, decided to move the army via ship to Fort Monroe, then advance up the peninsula to Richmond rather than move overland. As the column under General Banks moved up the Shenandoah Valley, the fewer Southern troops under Stonewall Jackson's command evacuated Winchester. While Banks consolidated his hold on the lower Valley, McClellan's army began to board ships at Alexandria on March 17.[18]

Meanwhile, the 20th Massachusetts marched back to the Harper's Ferry area, bivouacking in abandoned houses in Bolivar, a small village up on the ridge overlooking the larger town down on the Potomac. Here, the men of Sedgwick's division learned that they had been assigned to the new Second

Army Corps, led by Brigadier General Edwin V. Sumner, a white-haired, 65-year-old West Pointer. The regiment remained on Bolivar Heights until March 24, drilling and preparing for a new campaign. While here, another episode in the regiment's history erupted, as Lieutenant John W. LeBarnes of Company B sent a protest letter to Governor Andrew, then tendered his resignation the same day. Earlier, Lieutenant Colonel Palfrey had issued an order to his regiment to expel from camp all fugitive slaves who had come in the camp and had been hired as personal servants by officers. LeBarnes refused to comply with Palfrey's order and was arrested, but resigned and went home. To Lieutenant Abbott, LeBarnes was "a long haired abolitionist & spy of Gov. Andrew's." In leaving, LeBarnes denounced the aristocratic clique of Harvard officers — Bartlett and Abbott among them — who followed Palfrey's orders and actually inspired such orders.[19]

In spite of such problems, the regiment was more than ready to move. Many officers and men were afraid that the war would end before they got a chance to share in the victory. They read with glee the recent Northern victories at Roanoke Island, Forts Henry and Donelson, and elsewhere. Lieutenant Abbott was particularly outraged that they were not able to capture Leesburg, especially after "watching it for six long & dreary months in a muddy Maryland cornfield." Sedgwick's division was delayed, however, for on March 23, Stonewall Jackson, acting on erroneous information, attacked a Union division at Kernstown, south of Winchester. Jackson's attacks were repulsed and he withdrew southward before Union reinforcements managed to reach the battlefield. The next day, the 20th packed up camp, marched down through Harper's Ferry, crossed the Potomac on the railroad bridge, and halted at Sandy Hook, Maryland, where the men were packed on rail cars and sent to Washington. On the 27th, the Harvard Regiment boarded the steamer *Catskill*, disembarking on the final day of March at Fort Monroe.[20]

General McClellan had figured that a waterborne movement to Fort Monroe would surprise the Rebels and allow his army to move quickly up the peninsula toward Richmond before enough troops could be moved to oppose the 110,000 Yankees landing at the fort. But the general was slow and methodical most of the time, and as his troops began heading up the peninsula, they ran into opposition from Major General John B. Magruder's Confederate force that watched the Yankee base at Fort Monroe. Magruder initially had far less than 10,000 troops to oppose the Yankee juggernaut, but Magruder skillfully deployed his men in the wooded terrain and managed to convince McClellan that there were a lot more Rebels than actually opposed him. Magruder had erected earthwork fortifications at Yorktown that stretched across the peninsula. His men had dammed up some of the creeks to create boggy lowlands that made direct assault very difficult. And on top of this,

Union maps of the peninsula were wrong. The maps showed the smaller Warwick River as running parallel to the James and York rivers that framed the peninsula, when in reality the Warwick flowed across the peninsula. And so, the Yankee advance reached the Rebel lines on April 5 and halted. Then rain set in that lasted more than twenty-eight hours, turning the roads to mud. General Joseph E. Johnston's troops began arriving at Yorktown on April 7 to reinforce Magruder. As a result of delay and weather, McClellan's rapid advance ground to a halt and the general decided to undertake siege operations by bringing up heavy guns and preparing to batter his way through the enemy earthworks.[21]

This was the situation that confronted the 20th Massachusetts. Sumner's two divisions — Israel Richardson's and John Sedgwick's — occupied the center of the Union position. As they approached the Rebel lines, the men were heartened because they had advanced past abandoned enemy earthworks that appeared strongly built. Lieutenant Henry Ropes, a new lieutenant assigned to the regiment in early 1862, recalled catching a glimpse of General McClellan as he rode through his advancing troops. "He looks as if nothing can daunt him, and nothing discourage him," penned Ropes. As the columns advanced on April 5, Ropes could hear distant cannon fire, then the rattle of musketry, a signal that the enemy's current position had been located. Frank was yet in overall command of the 20th Massachusetts as the army came to a halt before the Yorktown entrenchments. Lieutenant Colonel Palfrey developed a lame foot and spent a lot of the time laying in his tent. Colonel Lee and Major Revere were close by, at Fort Monroe, awaiting formal word of their exchange.[22]

A day after the army halted before the enemy positions, McClellan sent out engineers to survey the Rebel lines to see if a weak spot could be located. April 7 was a day of incessant rain, but orders were orders, and General Dana set out with the 19th and 20th Massachusetts and a company of independent sharpshooters from the Bay State.[23] Frank described his part in this brief affair, and how the regiment moved forward through the woods and mud, to within sight of the Rebel works, fronted by a dammed stream which covered the ground with water:

> The engineer who went with the General reconnoitered it, covered by
> our skirmishers. We exchanged perhaps a hundred shots with them,
> without doing any damage to any one, and, the engineer having
> accomplished his object, we left, and kept to the left; about two miles.
> We came to another battery on the same stream. Here they opened on
> us with shell from a thirty-two pounder. Three men of the Nineteenth
> were wounded. One died that night. We got under cover of some
> woods and covered the engineer while he reconnoitered. It looked
> pretty squally when they opened on us with shell, as we had no
> artillery with us. We withdrew about dark, having effected the object

of the reconnoissance. We had to march home in the dark, through
the woods, in mud up to our knees. It had rained hard all day.[24]

Lieutenant Ropes wrote that the men advanced with loaded muskets at the
half cock. While the engineer surveyed the enemy line after the two regiments
halted at first, Bartlett sent out pickets to watch for the enemy. Some of the
Bay Staters were excited to actually see the enemy, and became careless as they
crossed an open space, prompting an exchange of gunfire. After moving to
the left, past the burning ruins of a "fine house," the 20th halted and the men
threw off their gum blankets and overcoats, left behind under guard as they
moved forward. The 19th became engaged with the enemy, who opened fire
from an artillery piece. Dana ordered Bartlett to send forward skirmishers,
and the acting colonel sent out companies A, F, and I. Frank even told Lieutenant Ropes that the regiment might assault the enemy works, but after the
engineer completed the survey, the wet, tired men were withdrawn.[25]

Once back in camp, the men were exposed to the all-night rain because
the brigade baggage trains had not yet brought up their shelter tents. Only
Lieutenant Colonel Palfrey had a tent, which Frank Bartlett shared that night.
The acting colonel recorded that most of the men stayed up all night, standing around fires to keep warm. "I managed to get two dozen bottles of whiskey
from the sutler, which he had brought for officers, and distributed it so that
each man got a small drink of hot whiskey and water. I stayed out till eleven
o'clock in the rain doing it. I then came in, took off my stockings and pants,
which were wet through, rubbed my feet dry, and slept soundly enough."[26]

Once the enemy lines were surveyed, McClellan moved his troops up
and began erecting siege batteries to smash the Rebel defenses, especially in
the Yorktown area itself. The numerous regiments took turns doing picket
duty, drilling in camp, and waiting for action. The 20th Massachusetts went
out on picket every third day. Lieutenant Abbott called picket duty "bar-
barous & unchristian warfare.... The result is that a man or two is picked off
every day, without getting anything to compensate for the loss of life, slight
as it is." Annoyed with the constant popping of muskets, Abbott decided to
order his men not to place caps on the nipples of their rifles, and avoid firing.
If the enemy made any action to advance, they were to fall back on the picket
reserve, where the lieutenant himself was posted. Thus, firing on the 20th's
front subsided and allowed the Harvard man to get some rest. He knew by
this time the propensity of the men to fire at anything that moved, then continue firing at all sorts of imaged enemies after night set in. Frank himself,
in a letter home, described how the false alarms and reports of enemy advances
forced the general to call out the brigade and have the men ready to fight at
a moment's notice. The constant rain did not improve matters, and made the
sick list grow daily.[27]

When the tents finally came up, the 20th set up a permanent camp, complete with drilling and evening dress parades to keep the men sharp. General McClellan issued an order for all music to cease so that the enemy could not locate the Yankee camps and open on them with artillery. The men were anxious to take part in the giant impending battle that all thought would close with a Union victory and end the war. Though Lieutenant Colonel Palfrey was the commander of the regiment, Frank Bartlett, as the senior captain, still ran the day-to-day affairs. Yet there was still an undercurrent of dissatisfaction among some of the officers. Lieutenant Ropes, who once thought, as did many others in the regiment, that the 20th Massachusetts was well drilled and stood above other Yankee regiments, soon commented that the 20th was not all that different from the other units he observed on a daily basis. Ropes criticized Palfrey as not being a "real, active, wide awake man, nor a man of self reliance and force. Of course he is personally brave, but does not keep up the officers and the regiment to the mark." The lieutenant wrote that Palfrey "lies abed so late, and many of the company officers do so too ...." Although not a direct criticism of Bartlett, Ropes' observations indicated that not everyone was happy with the state of affairs in the 20th.[28]

April 24, 1862, was another day on picket for the 20th Massachusetts. As usual, Frank Bartlett had charge of the picket line. Earlier, almost as if he had a premonition of danger, Bartlett had told Lieutenant Ropes that he hated picket work, "and felt sure he should sometime be shot while on picket. He said he would much rather meet the enemy in open fight." Ropes had pointed out an exposed position that gave a good view of a newly-constructed Confederate rifle pit. While Captain Bartlett and Lieutenant Abbott were examining the Rebels from behind a tree, the enemy noticed them and fired a shot at them without hitting either officer.[29]

Frank Bartlett would not be so lucky on April 24, though. Lieutenant Herbert C. Mason of Company H was in charge of the regimental picket line that day. The lieutenant recounted how he was lounging under a tree reading when Bartlett came up from the rear, field glasses in hand. When asked, Frank replied that he was going to visit the pickets. Herbert warned Frank to be careful; although there was not much firing that day, most casualties recently were on the regiment's picket line.[30]

Around 11:15 that morning, Frank was kneeling behind a tree, using his field glasses to examine the enemy earthworks. Lieutenant Abbott described what happened:

> He was kneeling, looking through his glass, when the ball (an Enfield rifle) struck his [left] knee, passed along, shattering the bone to pieces & stopped just on the surface of the calf. When I came up to him, they had just ripped up his trousers, & Frank sat up & took the ball out of the wound & then picked 2 or 3 pieces of bone out. when he

saw the bone, he said his leg was a goner. The ball, as he picked it out, was so covered with bone & flesh that I thought it a huge gobbet of flesh.[31]

Lieutenant Mason's letter of April 26 provided more details about Frank's wounding. He recalled that a corporal came in from the picket line and yelled that someone had been shot, possibly the captain.

I sprang to my feet and call'd two or three of my men to follow me and bring him in. I had just gained the wood when two of my men came out of it bearing poor Bartlett on their shoulders. He was as pale as death, his mouth shut tight, but not a groan escaped him. I thought at first he was killed and asked him where he was struck and was much relieved when he told me in the leg. I had him carried to my blanquet & laid out, with my knife I ripped his pants up and had his boot taken off. The ball a conical rifle ball had entered his knee and came out low down in the calf of his leg where we found it. I took it; it was all torn & jammed and covered with small triangular pieces of bone. I gave him some water and sent for Dr. Hayward. He was in terrible pain but stood it splendidly.... Frank told me he had dropt his glass when he fell and he wanted it.... In the meantime I took off my sword and crept down the opening in the woods from tree to tree to find his glass on the left side of the very same tree behind which I came near being shot and of which I wrote you about.[32]

Lieutenant Colonel Palfrey continued the story:

When I got to him his color had not left him, and he was suffering only at intervals, when spasms of pain seized him for a moment, and quickly passed and left him comparatively comfortable again.... He was carried to a house near by, and then the surgeons gave him chloroform and examined his wound. Drs. Hayward and Crehore of the Twentieth, Dr. Haven of the Fifteenth, and Dr. Clark, a surgeon from Worcester, were unanimous in the opinion that amputation was not only proper, but necessary. I urged upon them to be sure, before proceeding, that there was no chance of recovery, and that it would not do to delay for consultation with other surgeons.

They assured me positively that there was no room for doubt, and that the operation must be performed immediately; that the ball had totally destroyed the knee joint, and shivered and destroyed the bone of the leg for six inches below; furthermore that delay would materially diminish the chances of recovery. The leg was taken off by Dr. Hayward, in the lower third of the portion above the knee.[33]

"It was a pretty mournful sight to see him lying there with only one leg," penned Abbott two days later, "both as the dearest fellow in the regiment, & as the man that the regiment has got to depend on in battle." Abbott wrote to his mother that Frank was the bona fide commander of the regiment, the man to whom everyone looked for guidance. "Poor fellow, to be cut off for good from a military career when he had so much talent for it." The lieutenant wrote that he was afraid, that without Frank to lead them, the men would not do as well in their next battle. Lieutenant Ropes echoed Abbott's sentiments. "[Y]esterday our regiment met with the greatest loss it could possibly sustain," he wrote on April 25. "This of course ends the military career of one of the most promising young men in the army.... He was the right hand man of the regiment, and I do not see who can fill his place." Lieutenant Colonel Palfrey described Frank to his father as "the most brilliant soldier I have known in the Volunteer Army, and I anticipated for him the highest distinction."[34]

Lieutenant Colonel Palfrey apparently remained at Frank's bedside until he awoke after the operation. "He suffered a good deal after he returned to consciousness, but not to the point of faintness," penned the colonel. Frank was not surprised about the entire operation because once he saw the bone was smashed, he had expected to lose his leg. The maimed captain was soon transferred to a four-horse ambulance and sent to Ship Point, on the York River, for transportation to Washington, attended by Dr. Clark and Palfrey's own servant. A detachment from Company I also went along; in case the roads proved bumpy, they would take turns carrying Frank on a litter to decrease his suffering. Frank was placed on board the transport *Commodore* for the trip up the Potomac to Washington.[35]

5

"WE ARE LEARNING SUBORDINATION WITHOUT COMPLAINING"

The 49th Massachusetts Volunteer Infantry

Once Frank Bartlett's leg was amputated, he was conveyed to Fort Monroe and placed on a northbound steamer. His family was notified, and the young captain was landed at Baltimore, where his mother met her crippled son and took him to a relative's house to recuperate a bit before going on to Boston. On the eighth of May, his mother penned a short note to Colonel Palfrey, informing him that her patient "had been improving in general health and strength, and looking more like himself that I supposed he would in so short a time. The main cause of his troubles gives him almost constant twinges of pain, and he suffers much, although he tries to make very light of it." When the captain wrote a letter to his colonel, he admitted that the writing was interspersed "between spasms of dreadful pain." In another letter, Frank wondered whether his amputated limb had been given a Christian burial, "for my foot torments me as if it were ill at rest." He also told Palfrey that his thoughts constantly were of the war, "with a vain regret at being snatched away just at the moment when we were about to see something of glorious and victorious *war*."[1]

Once Frank got stronger, his family moved him to Winthrop, where he continued to recuperate. On June 20, Bartlett participated in Harvard's annual Class Day as part of the graduating class of 1862. A *Boston Daily Advertiser* reporter was on hand to record the day's events. "The class was forcibly reminded, however, of the demands of patriotism, by the presence of their former classmate, Capt. W. F. Bartlett of the 20th Regiment, walking on his crutches, and pale and thin from the effects of his wound. He stood by the church door and was warmly greeted by his former classmates."[2]

Frank's letters of this period reflect his constant worry about the fate of his beloved 20th Massachusetts, which took part in the Battle of Fair Oaks (May 31–June 1), then in the Seven Days' Battles as McClellan's Army of the Potomac retreated from its position near Richmond to Harrison's Landing on the James River (June 25–July 1). Friends at home touted the crippled Bartlett as a war hero and began circulating his name as possible colonel of one of the new regiments to be raised. "I have been very grateful for the offers, of course," mused Frank in a letter to Palfrey, "but have invariably discountenanced them. You know that I had rather be a captain in the Twentieth than colonel of any regiment that may be raised."[3]

And indeed, there was a hue and cry across the North after McClellan's defeat before Richmond. Shortly before this campaign, the War Department, anticipating that the war would soon be over once McClellan captured Richmond, had ill-advisedly suspended recruiting efforts. Then, with the shock of the defeat in Virginia, recruiting began in a frenzy. On August 4, President Lincoln issued a call for 300,000 soldiers, the bulk of them to be drafted from existing militia if numbers were not forthcoming. To entice recruits, the War Department authorized troops to be recruited for nine months rather than the standard three years. Massachusetts supplied a dozen nine-month regiments for the war effort.

One of the new regiments was recruited entirely in Berkshire County, Massachusetts. Numbered the 49th Massachusetts Volunteer Infantry, it was brought together at Camp Briggs, located just outside Pittsfield, beginning in September 1862, the first company arriving just after the departure of the new 37th Massachusetts, a three-year regiment organized in late August. Shortly after the new companies began arriving at Camp Briggs, Captain Bartlett appeared on the scene, after reluctantly accepting the governor's offer to assume command of the camp and train this regiment of fresh fish. On September 6, the captain was offered the command of the camp, with orders to whip the new recruits into shape. "With some reluctance," Frank accepted the state's offer and arrived at Camp Briggs on the 20th of September.[4]

Private Henry T. Johns, who would become the quartermaster of the 49th, noted Captain Bartlett's arrival: "His appearance denotes much of intelligent energy, and his gentlemanly manner, his soldierly bearing (for he looks the soldier even on crutches), and our sympathy with him in his great loss, have made him at once a universal favorite." The recruits did not yet have their uniforms, and were living in A tents, with six men per crowded tent. They were just beginning to realize what soldiering was all about. Johns wrote that it was strange to have butter but once or twice a week, and to have to arise with the morning drum beat. Standing guard was also a pain, as most soldiers would recall, but to Johns, it gave him the chance to be alone and appreciate the quietude of night duty.[5]

The new recruits had a regulated day of work while at Camp Briggs. The men were awakened about sunrise, formed in line, then roll call was taken. Then came an hour of drilling, followed by breakfast. Once the meal was consumed, the men were detailed to police the camp and clean up any messes. At eight o'clock came the guard mounting, when men were detailed for guard duty and sent off to their posts. While this was going on, the policing continued and cooks were detailed to start preparing the next meal. At ten o'clock came another hour or more of drill for those not off on some detail. Then came the noon meal, followed by an afternoon drill session. The formal day was closed with a dress parade, when the entire regiment was formed on the drill field and went through a formal ceremony according to army regulations. Once this "spectacle" was over (remember the men as of yet had not received uniforms or weapons), they were dismissed to supper, which was followed by free time until the drums signaled evening roll call, which in turn was soon followed by "taps," after which all lights were extinguished except for those officers who wished to remain awake. The next day this routine started all over again. The routine varied a bit on Sundays when a regimental inspection took the place of more drilling.[6]

As the companies arrived in camp and reported, the regiment came together. The 49th was a typical Union regiment, with ten companies, lettered A, B, C, D, E, F, G, H, I, and K. Each company recruited elected its own officers — captain, first lieutenant, second lieutenant. These men in turn appointed the first sergeant, four other sergeants, and eight corporals, from among the enlisted men. In general, the man who recruited a company was usually elected the captain, with his choices as lieutenants generally followed by the rest of his men when voting. Then Governor Andrew had to approve these elections and issue commissions to the elected officers. When the regiment was ready to be formed, the company officers voted for the three field officers — colonel, lieutenant colonel, and major. Once these men were voted on, the governor again would generally rubber stamp the choices and commission these officers. Then, if the field officers were elected from among the captains, those elevated to field command would be replaced by new elections from each company. The field officers would appoint individuals to other key positions, such as adjutant, quartermaster, and sergeant major. They would also agree on the choice of a sutler and regimental chaplain. This was a democratic process in the Union and Confederate armies throughout the Civil War. Often though, the men elected to officer rank had no prior military experience. Only time and combat would weed out the incompetent ones, who would be replaced by veterans from the ranks as the war went on.

As Captain Bartlett became better known to the regiment of raw recruits,

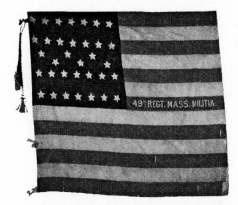

Top left: National color issued to the 49th Massachusetts at some point prior to its departure from the state in the fall of 1862. Courtesy Commonwealth of Massachusetts, Art Commission. *Right:* Massachusetts issued this state color to the 49th Massachusetts in the fall of 1862, before the regiment left for New York. Courtesy Commonwealth of Massachusetts, Art Commission.

some began to think that he would make the best choice as colonel. Private Johns realized, as no doubt did some of his comrades, that Colonel Lee of the 20th Massachusetts would not have appointed Bartlett as senior colonel of his regiment unless he knew that the youngster was worthy of the position. "That alone would warrant his election to the colonelcy," penned Johns, who continued, "As few men, *he looks* the soldier. Though quiet, there is an air of command about him that would make obedience to his orders almost involuntary."[7] The men were amazed by the way Bartlett took the lead in drilling them. Johns, in early October, penned perhaps the most eloquent tribute to Bartlett that could be written, when describing the captain's determination to overcome the loss of his leg:

> It is a treat to see that man go through the manual of arms. He puts such a finish, such a *vim* to every motion. For two hours at a time, he will stand on that remaining leg, till half of us believe he never had any need of the one buried at Yorktown, but it was only a superfluous member or mere ornament. Sometimes we try to see how long *we* can stand on one leg; a few short minutes, and we require the use of both, or find ourselves reeling about like decapitated hens. If the colonel (I will call him such) needs rest, he takes it as part of the exercise, so we cannot tell which is manual of arms and which rest. The cords of that right leg must stand out like great whip lashes. There is a *will* about all this. It is the quiet, intense determination, this fixedness of will, that makes us desire Colonel Bartlett, with but one leg, for our commander, over any other man with the full complement of limbs. Somehow or other, we cannot tell why, we believe that he will not be the mere buffet of circumstances, but will ride over, and lead us over

all difficulties. Every man salutes him, and he *always* salutes in return. In saluting, the back of the right hand is brought up to the visor of the cap, then the arm is fully extended, and brought down to the side. You can see it is no easy thing to be done *walking* on two crutches, but the Colonel does it, not halting to do it, but while walking on and in the most approved military manner. This may seem to you a small matter, but to us it indicates the *born* soldier, the man who *will* do the duties he has assumed. The other day, while riding in his carriage, he put the regiment through battalion drill. What a noble voice he has, a deep bass, yet as clear and distinct as any tenor. It is full of command. He doesn't have to put in any expletives to insure attention and prompt obedience. They are all in the mere voice. Over, or rather under all noise, with apparently no effort, that voice carries his orders to the remotest soldier. Take him all and in all, I have yet to meet one who so fully embodies any conceptions of a commander as Colonel Bartlett.[8]

By the time Johns wrote these observations, the 49th was beginning to look like a military unit. Uniforms finally arrived and the men drew their first quotas of them. Instead of sky blue trousers, the 49th was issued dark blue ones, with the regulation dark blue sack coats and forage caps. The dress Hardee hat, two pairs of flannel shirts, drawers, and stockings, a single pair of army shoes, a great black overcoat (instead of the usual sky blue), and a rubber blanket completed the regiment's first issue of regulation uniforms. The men were further heartened because Camp Briggs was close to home for many of them. Their friends and families were able to watch the progress of the recruits, deliver all sorts of goodies to them, and in general provide a smooth transition from civilian to soldier.[9]

The camp's location also provided an unexpected benefit for Colonel Bartlett. Frank somehow met the Robert Pomeroy family while in camp with his new regiment. The Pomeroy family was counted among Pittsfield's elites, having made its money in the textile business. Robert Pomeroy was one of the owners of his late father's firm, Lemuel Pomeroy & Sons, which owned several mills in Berkshire County. Robert's eldest daughter, Mary Agnes, had been born in 1841. She was educated at local schools and was attending a New York City school when war erupted in 1861. She returned to Pittsfield and helped her aunt in local Pittsfield hospitals, taking an active interest in the local soldiers and their welfare. When Frank went to Pittsfield to train the 49th Massachusetts, he took along letters to the family by comrades in the 20th. Oliver Wendell Holmes, for example, had spent summers in Pittsfield and knew the Pomeroys quite well. Frank and Mary Agnes evidently took a liking to each other and began a correspondence that intensified as the war went on.[10]

On November 7, the 49th was ordered to move to Camp Wool, located near Worcester. The regiment boarded twenty passenger cars for the trip, and

Colonel William F. Bartlett, his wounded left arm in a sling, is seated on the left of this photography, taken at Dewey's Gallery in Pittsfield, after the return of the 49th Massachusetts in August 1862. Also seated is Lieutenant Colonel Samuel B. Sumner. Standing, left to right, are Major Charles T. Plunkett, First Lieutenant Benjamin Mifflin, and Surgeon Frederick Winsor. Courtesy United States Army Military History Institute.

was seen off by an immense crowd of well-wishers. Frank Bartlett's adjutant tallied the regimental strength at 963 officers and men. En route to Worcester, the train halted for a brief twenty minute stop at Springfield, then arrived at Camp Wool in the midst of a driving storm. The men were delighted to find that their new quarters were new wooden barracks buildings instead of tents. They also found that the 51st Massachusetts was already in camp, occupying an old pistol factory, with Colonel George H. Ward in command of the camp. Once ensconced in their new buildings, the men began drilling yet again in preparation for the upcoming campaign.[11]

Three days after arriving at Camp Wool, the company officers gathered to elect the field and staff officers. Frank Bartlett was unanimously elected colonel. For his second in command, Samuel B. Sumner of Great Barrington was elected lieutenant colonel, and Charles T. Plunkett of Pittsfield as major. Sumner, age 31, was the oldest of the three. He was a graduate of Williams College, a lawyer by profession, and formerly the youngest Massachusetts state senator. Sumner also had a reputation as a fine poet and orator, and had prior military experience in the state militia. Plunkett, age 23 and six and a half feet tall, was living in Connecticut when war broke out in 1861. Though a young member of the state legislature and a successful cotton manufacturer, he suspended his career, returned to Pittsfield, and raised Company C of the 49th. When elected colonel, Frank told his other officers that he would prefer to appoint his own adjutant, and selected Benjamin C. Mifflin, a "personal friend and college associate" of the colonel. Fresh from Harvard, Mifflin was only 22 years old, had scant militia experience, but was ready and willing to follow his friend Bartlett.[12]

The regiment continued to improve in drill during its stay at Camp Wool. Weapons and accoutrements arrived and were distributed on November 25, finally allowing the regiment to actually handle instruments of death and destruction. The regiment's arms were new British-made .577 caliber Enfield rifle-muskets. Weighing almost ten pounds, though, the new arms also showed the recruits that "it is no light task to keep a gun in perfect order." The 49th also received new sky blue wool overcoats, replacing the worn black ones the regiment had left Camp Briggs with. Thanksgiving day saw a bountiful meal provided to the regiment, a combination of a thoughtful colonel, good sutlers, and packages from friends in Berkshire County. Rumors also began circulating through camp that the regiment would be a part of an expedition being prepared by Major General Nathaniel P. Banks, a Massachusetts-born political general who had just been ordered to supersede Major General Benjamin Butler in Louisiana.[13]

While the regiment was at Camp Wool, Colonel Bartlett went to Boston and returned with a wooden leg and a "fiery little" black horse. Penned Johns, "His appearance before the troops on horseback, seemingly a whole man, drew forth hearty spontaneous cheers, not ungrateful to any man who knows that the confidence of his men is a sure guarantee of success." Shortly thereafter, on the morning of November 28, the regiment packed up its gear, boarded a train, and went by rail to Norwich, Connecticut, where the men were packed on board the steamer *Commodore* for the voyage to New York

City, arriving on the morning of the 28th. After a brief halt in the City Hall Park, a drizzle of rain began and the colonel received orders to march his regiment to the Franklin Street barracks, located in an old, dilapidated six-story building.[14] A correspondent for the *Home Journal* was present when Frank and the 49th marched the regiment up a crowded Broadway.

> The Colonel ... was mounted on a Vermont horse with shaggy brown mane and fetlocks, an animal that looked as sensible in the face as he was lithe of limb-a most capital friend for a soldier to take with him to the wars. The equipments, as well as the limbs of the rider, were apparently all complete, each long boot with its spur riding gracefully in its stirrup. Pistols and sword were in their places. At the horseman's back, however — poised like a long spear at the back of the lancer — swung the strange implement which told the story, a long crutch with velvet handle, betraying the wooden leg for which it stood ready to do service.... He rode up and down the lines, in fact, with the confidence and ease of a fine horseman.... We were pleased with the physiognomy of the wounded Colonel. His head was well set upon an unusually slight frame, and his features were of the most intellectual cast, pale and thin. He had the sandy hair and blue eye of New England, and under the slouched hat of a cavalry officer, he was the picturesque type of the intellectual energy which the sculptor would strive to express in modeling "the Yankee." [15]

Here was Frank Bartlett in one of his finest public performances! Observers in the crowd that witnessed the steady march of the 49th Massachusetts up Broadway all noticed the military bearing of the regiment's colonel, wounded with the loss of a limb yet still willing to remain in the army and take an active role rather than passively staying behind to manage a camp. Bartlett had obtained a wooden leg to make him a bit more mobile during the coming months, but the presence of his crutch signaled to all that his grim determination to continue a career at which he excelled and in which he was happy showed a character of great strength. The martial appearance of his untested regiment demonstrated Frank's previous training and how determined he was to ensure that the 49th would somehow at least be disciplined enough to make a good showing when the firing started, similar to the 20th Massachusetts' stand at Ball's Bluff, where the core of the regiment, in spite of bad leadership at the top and equally bad terrain, remained on the field and put up a good fight.

The men were not pleased with the Franklin Street barracks, a behemoth of a structure that could house more than fifteen hundred soldiers. The building fronted on a narrow, muddy street, and when the soldiers crowded against the windows to see out, they were afforded only a "dim and distant view of the thoroughfare." "Here we are in the Western Babylon," penned a disgusted Henry Johns on December 4. The regiment had not been paid in months, and thus most soldiers had little or no money to spend on the city's temptations. "In squads, under the charge of officers, we wander round the city, attend churches, and visit places of amusements. A great treat this to many who were never before in this heart of the western world." But, continued John, "Empty pockets enable us to be proof against all the snares of Sodom."[16]

The stay of the 49th at the Franklin Street barracks was very brief, for on December 4 the regiment formed in march order, waited impatiently for two hours while standing in the street, then moved back down Broadway to a dock on the East River, crossed, and marched out Long Island to Camp Banks, where the units assigned to Banks were concentrating. Here were more than thirty new units, boarding ships and heading south as shipping was available. Brigadier General George L. Andrews, Banks' chief of staff, was in charge of the camp, but when duty called him into New York or Boston for a day or more, he left Colonel Bartlett in command. Frank wrote that there were perhaps eight thousand soldiers in camp at the time. Occasionally while on such duty, there came questions that needed answers but could not wait until General Andrews returned. "In cases of doubt, which have required my authority and decision," wrote Bartlett, "I have kept an old maxim of mine before me. Do that, which according to your impartial judgment, tends most to promote the good of the service."[17]

Colonel Bartlett did not fail to ensure that his regiment made steady progress while in camp on Long Island. "I drill the non-coms in the manual an hour every morning, standing on one leg. In the afternoon, I drill the whole line in the manual an hour and a half. I visit the guard every night after twelve, to see that the officer of the guard and day are doing their duty." Private Johns, a keen and literate observer, recognized the continuing progress his comrades were making toward becoming good soldiers. "Daily he draws the reins of discipline tighter," wrote Johns, "but with such judgment, that we are learning subordination without complaining ... singular, what command he has over men. He is a *born* commander. Quiet, reserved, yet there is not a man or officer in the regiment who does not feel that obedience to him is half involuntary. While no one more than himself is a stickler for military etiquette and for a proper respect paid to superior rank, yet no one is less assuming or dictatorial. Emphatically, he treats a private as well as an officer."[18] And here Johns recognized the colonel's capacity for leadership. Although born into a superior societal rank, Frank was not overbearing or dictatorial in his work with the 49th. The colonel was even known, after wrongly blaming a private for some misdeed, to call him into his tent and apologize for falsely accusing him. In general, Frank used the required Sunday readings of the Articles of War to accent to his men what the rules stated. A deeply religious man, he even read the Episcopal service to his men on an occasional Sunday, prior to the appointment of the regimental chaplain. The colonel was worried, as Johns also noticed, in the increased use of profanity by his men. This was one of the usual criticisms of soldiers by their more religious comrades, who blamed army life for such profanity, which would not be tolerated at home. Frank instituted a system of fines in an attempt to curtail profanity, officers and men alike subject to a fine if heard cursing. All in all, Colonel Bartlett endeavored to instill a sense of discipline and pride in the 49th to make them as good as the 20th was before its first engagement with the enemy.[19]

The 49th remained on Long Island for seven weeks, occasionally sending detachments into New York City to act as provost guards and arrest deserters. Corporal John Gamwell wrote that scores of men left camp for the comfort of the city. They left because army food was in scant supply, the weather was cold, and the camp lacked enough wood to keep the campfires burning. Gamwell himself was part of a detachment sent to New York and described his work:

> Dec. 9. One at night. Have been patrolling the City from morn till now. Have visited *very many* dens of infamy, both high and low, but have just commenced. Their name is legion & every one has its victims. Many books have been written of the mysteries & miseries of N. Y., but the half has not, nor can ever be told. To know it one must see it, & to see it singlehanded would be at the imminent danger of his life. Loaded muskets with glittering bayonets wielded by strong and fearless soldiers is the only safe pass to those dens of crime.[20]

At first lodged in tents in the cold weather, the 49th moved into some wooden stables associated with the Union Course (a horse racing track) later in December, after some more regiments left aboard ships for Louisiana. Finally, came word that shipping was available to take the regiment to Louisiana. On January 23, 1863, the 49th boarded the steamer *Illinois*, together with a few companies of the 23rd Maine and stragglers from other units, filling the vessel to capacity with around fifteen hundred men. Among the crowd waving goodbye to the troops were Colonel Bartlett's parents. The *Illinois* left New York on January 24 and stopped briefly at Fort Monroe, Virginia, three days later, to receive exact orders about the destination of the trip.[21]

After the *Illinois* rounded Cape Henry and headed south along the coast, the weather got a bit rough and all the way down the Atlantic coast, the ship bobbed up and down the waves. For the country boys from western Massachusetts, this was simply too much. Almost everyone got seasick at one time or another. "Sea-sickness never kills," recalled Henry Johns, but it makes many wish it would." He described how the first bout of sickness would make everyone head for the railing to vomit into Neptune's domain. Then the victim goes to lie down and rest. But as soon as he moves, the nausea in his stomach resumes, but instead of vomiting, he could only "retch," spitting up a little froth. The endless succession of moving and retching continued for hours and hours, making its victim despondent and craving a calm sea. The fact that the fresh beef on board was quickly consumed was forgotten by the hordes of sick soldiers. Fresh water was made by distilling sea water in special boilers, but the quality and quantity was never enough to satisfy the men on board.[22]

Once the *Illinois* passed Key West and headed into the Gulf of Mexico, the weather was better and the sea remained relatively calm. To ensure his men's continued good health, on Sunday, February 1, Colonel Bartlett marched each company onto the main deck, ordered the men to strip, and had them sprayed with salt water, a process which occupied his attention until three in the afternoon; "some grumbled & some thought it nice," wrote Corporal Gamwell. On the morning of February 7, the *Illinois* steamed up to a pier at New Orleans for a brief stop. The men now knew they were in a completely different environment than that of the hills of western Massachusetts. One described it as "a strange combination of green fields, orange groves and slave cabins." The men remained on board and only a mail carrier went into the city to deliver the sack of letters written by the regiment to the military post office. Peddlers besieged the wharf and sold pies, oranges, and other victuals to those fortunate enough to have any money at all. The steamer moved on and went up the Mississippi about seven miles to the village of Carrollton, where the troops debarked on February 10. The 49th was now in the seat of war.[23]

6

"OH, HOW GOOD BERKSHIRE WATER WOULD SELL HERE"

The Department of the Gulf

The 49th's arrival in Louisiana was part of a major reinforcing of the Department of the Gulf. Union troops had seized New Orleans in April 1862 and had moved upriver to occupy Baton Rouge, the state capital. Under the command of Major General Benjamin F. Butler, the Department of the Gulf had solidified Union control of the lower Mississippi valley. Butler, however, a political general from Massachusetts, had earned the scorn of Southerners with his high-handed approach to justice in New Orleans. Although he cleaned up the city, fed the poor, and kept order, his approach to Southern womanhood, as evidenced in his General Orders Number 28, offended Southerners so much that a price was placed on the general's head. Butler also had hanged a man for tearing down the American flag, violated the sanctity of the Netherlands embassy, and was rumored to be making money from confiscated cotton.[1]

As a result of Butler's controversial command, President Lincoln recalled the general and replaced him with Major General Nathaniel P. Banks, another Massachusetts political general. Banks had been in command of troops in the Shenandoah Valley and had the misfortune to be badly whipped at Winchester in May 1862 by Stonewall Jackson, who chased Banks' routed troops all the way to the Potomac River. Banks partly redeemed his reputation by engaging Jackson at Cedar Mountain in August, but was forced to concede the field to the more numerous Confederates. He led a corps during the Second Manassas Campaign but his men were not engaged in that defeat later in August. After temporarily commanding the defenses of Washington, Banks was appointed to replace Butler in November. Banks assumed command on December 17, as reinforcements began pouring into his department.[2]

The troops available for active duty in the Department of the Gulf were known as the Nineteenth Army Corps, a formation created on January 5 by the War Department to allow Banks to better organize the troops in his command. This was the situation when Colonel Bartlett and the 49th Massachusetts arrived at Carrollton on board the *Illinois*. The regiment disembarked on February 9, 1863, and went into camp. Other units were gathering here, including the 31st Massachusetts, a three-year regiment organized at Pittsfield in the fall and winter of 1861–1862 and on duty in Louisiana since March 1862. The newly-arrived 49th found many acquaintances in the 31st and had a pleasant reunion after the 49th reached camp.[3]

Quartermaster Johns took a stroll in the neighborhood soon after arriving to reconnoiter the local wares. He and a companion found an oyster saloon and were charged forty cents each for a stew. Johns commented on the local whites:

> The residents here are mainly Germans. Occasionally you meet a
> native, who, with his fierce eyes, long hair, light-sleeved, short-tail
> coat, closely-fitting pants, and shining black-silk hat, looks as if he
> belonged to another race. Some of these natives have a low, mean
> scowl on their faces, and would be dangerous if their courage were
> equal to their fierceness. They are generally taller, and larger-boned
> than we are. Men, women, and children, are sallow. Any careful
> observe would see that, for real grit, manly defiance, persevering valor,
> we are almost infinitely superior. There *may* be some Southern *gentle-
> men*. I have as yet seen no one that had a right to answer to that call. I
> have seen men of wealth, but they looked like a cross between the
> Spanish brigand and the overseer. Gazing at them is apt to make you
> doubt whether it is possible or desirable to live in peace with them. I
> suppose the chivalry are all in the army. Everybody here looks lazy.[4]

Johns was equally descriptive of the African Americans he met. "Genuine" African Americans had come down the river into Union lines, having run away from their masters. Natives were generally mulattoes and quadroons, many women having nearly white children, leading Johns to theorize that they had no virtues and that "Southern passion was superior to Southern taste." Johns questioned a number of blacks about slavery and learned much in reply, finding none willing to return to the pre-war days. To Johns, as well as numerous other Northerners now face to face with the realities of slavery, the reasons for the war were becoming much clearer. In addition to the Northern desire to suppress the rebellion, soldiers such as Johns, when confronted with slavery and its evils, could easily understand what else needed to be done before the war could end.[5]

The first regimental camp, half a mile from the Mississippi, was quickly abandoned when the regiment received orders to move farther from the river, remaining here for a week. The campground was flat as a board, recalled

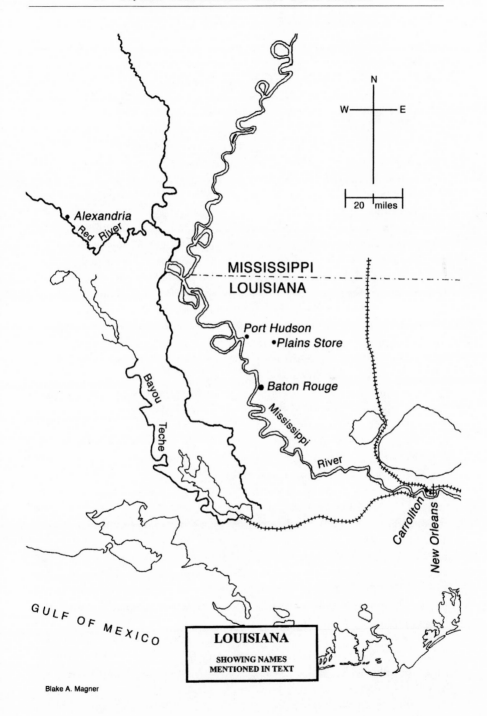

LOUISIANA

SHOWING NAMES
MENTIONED IN TEXT

Blake A. Magner

Johns, and the water table of the ground was only eighteen inches from the surface. This was still the rainy season, and it was not unusual to have several showers each day. This, together with flies and spiders "as large as walnuts," were part of Johns' recollections of the week spent at Carrollton. "The air was so warm," penned the quartermaster, "that many abandoned their under-clothes, a hazardous experiment where the ground is very damp, and the fogs so heavy that the sun does not rise till near noon." With little more than river water to drink, diarrhea quickly spread through the ranks, followed by case after case of typhoid fever. This was a typical problem with Union troops in the deep South, leading to an ever-growing sick list in most units. "Oh, how good Berkshire water would sell here," opined Corporal Gamwell, "and how many lives save!"[6]

The constant rains inundated the regimental camp. Colonel Bartlett's tent, situated on a low ridge of ground, at times appeared to be the only structure above water. "The smallest cloud baptized us, and we obtained a deeper insight into mud than ever before," opined Johns. The regiment's fist death took place on February 17, when a private of Company B succumbed to typhoid fever. But there was no chaplain to read the funeral service; Colonel Bartlett had yet to locate a suitable fellow for the position. A complaint to Governor Andrew about the lack of a chaplain in the 49th stirred the colonel to reply that he would rather not have a chaplain than one who was qualified "both in character and ability." Bartlett pointed out that Sunday was generally a day of rest for his regiment, except the normal routine of inspection, guard mounting, and dress parade. Bartlett himself was known to read a Sunday service in front of his men; "[h]is rich voice was in unison with the richness and majesty of that liturgy, producing so good an effect that we the more earnestly desired to have the labors of a good chaplain," penned Johns.[7]

On February 16, Colonel Bartlett received orders to move his regiment to a transport and head upriver to Baton Rouge. It was dark by the time the regiment was formed and waiting to board, a process that lasted until four the next morning. Frank perched himself on a rail overlooking the gangplank and personally supervised the loading of the regimental baggage, during which he fell asleep. Part of the process of boarding included dispensing a full load of cartridges to each man. This signaled the end of duty in the rear. Johns recalled that "some have shown the symptoms of bullet-fever," after being handed their live ammunition. "Imagination presenting danger in every form, he will find the reality so much less than he feared, that he will not be nearly so apt to be panic-stricken as he who meets the experience for the first time in the presence of the foe.... Dealing out cartridges somewhat strengthens the impression that we are nearing the hour when men's souls and *reputations* will be tried."[8]

The trip up the mighty Mississippi was uneventful, the vessel anchoring off Donaldsonville in a dense fog on the evening of February 17. "Many of the mansions lining the river are all that we have imagined of Southern wealth and luxury," wrote Sergeant Johns. The 49th reached Baton Rouge around midday on Wednesday, February 18, disembarked, formed in line and marched through Baton Rouge. "Not much of a city," recalled Gamwell, "low wooden buildings & narrow streets." The regiment marched to "Camp Banks," situated on high ground about a mile and a half from the river. Sergeant Johns wrote that the area had once been a Confederate campground, and yet showed signs of the August 1862 engagement when Southern troops under former vice president John C. Breckinridge attacked the Union garrison.[9]

Upon its arrival at Camp Banks, the 49th Massachusetts was assigned to the First Brigade, First Division, Nineteenth Army Corps. Major General Christopher C. Augur, the division commander, was an 1843 graduate of West Point, had fought in the Mexican War, and was commandant of cadets at West Point in 1861. Augur led a division in Banks' corps in northern Virginia, where he was badly wounded at the Battle of Cedar Mountain in August 1862. Now he was back in active command, again leading a division under Banks. The First Brigade was under the command of its senior colonel, Edwin P. Chapin of the 116th New York. Chapin had entered volunteer service as a captain in the 44th New York and had been wounded at Hanover Court House, Virginia, in May 1862. In July 1862, he was elected colonel of the 116th New York and sent to Louisiana with his regiment later that year. In addition to Frank Bartlett's 49th Massachusetts, other units in the brigade included the 21st Maine and 48th Massachusetts.[10]

The regiment's arrival at Camp Banks also meant a more rigorous daily schedule, preparing to meet the enemy. "Guards no longer slouch along with unloaded guns, or run to their tents when off their beats, or are careless as to who pass or repass," penned Sergeant Johns. The growing Union troop concentration was surrounded by a cordon of picket posts, and the 49th took its share of this important but onerous duty. The picket line ran six miles in an arc with both ends on the Mississippi River. Every man detailed for such duty had to take along his full set of equipment so he was ready at a moment's notice to rejoin his regiment or engage the enemy. Cavalry patrols scoured the countryside farther from camp to watch for the approach of hostile troops. On February 22, Colonel Bartlett was general officer of the day, which meant that he was in charge of the picket line, taking six hours to ride from post to post and check on the men.[11]

The increased daily drilling and added duties of an active military camp took a strain on Frank Bartlett. "I am glad enough to get to bed at nine o'clock," he wrote on February 24, "and sorry enough to hear the roll of the drum which makes me get up at six A.M." But the young colonel continually

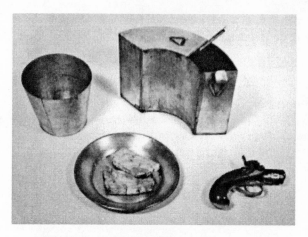

Bartlett used this canvas-covered zinc mess kit while he was colonel of the 49th Massachusetts. The contents included collapsible drinking cups, a small pail and tea kettle, and some small plates and metal boxes. Reprinted with permission from *The Berkshire Eagle.*

worked his regiment, perfecting their drill and making better soldiers of them. He patterned much of what he did on his experience with the 20th Massachusetts, to the point that first sergeants knew when reporting to be wearing unsoiled white gloves or risk being reduced to mere sergeants. "The regiment is improving constantly," bragged Frank. "I keep at work on them all the time. It is consoling to know that I am doing the country such good service as making soldiers for her."[12]

Sergeant Johns agreed with the colonel. "Drill means work now," he moaned. "The company drill in the morning, and the brigade drill in the afternoon, fill up nearly six hours of the day, and the boys wilt under it." The warmer weather than they were used to in Berkshire County, together with bad water and wet weather, led to case after case of diarrhea and typhoid fever. By early March, more than 115 officers and men were on the sick list, with scores more laying ill in their tents. But other Union regiments fared just as bad, a common curse for Yankees campaigning in the deep South.[13]

In spite of such sickness, Frank continued to drill the regiment. On March 4, he provided a full account of it in his journal:

> This morning orders came for a review in "heavy marching order," by General Augur. I cautioned the men to "polish up," and at half past two we turned out, as fine a looking line as you often see. The men stood very steadily, and marched very well. After going back to camp and leaving the knapsacks, etc., I took them out to practice with blank cartridges. At first they were very nervous, and did poorly, but after I had given them a very severe talking to, I tried them again at charging in line, and they did it splendidly. Their fire by battalion was like one gun. I then formed a hollow square and fired from all sides. My horse, inside the square, behaved beautifully. I don't care to see any better drilling than they did after my lecture. After we came into camp I closed column and explained to them that if they would only do as well as that in real action, keep cool, and not fire until they were

sure they had the word from me, no matter how near the enemy approached-when they did fire, aim at their opponents' knees (if near),-there was no enemy in the world that could stand against them, etc.

I hope they will remember all I said. They promised, and were very much excited, and cheered loudly for the drill. There is nothing more important to accustom men to firing, and getting used to the noise. What I taught them this afternoon was of more use to them, and will do them more good than all the brigade drills under Colonel Chapin, with unheard of and useless movements.[14]

Three days after lecturing the regiment, Bartlett received orders to take his regiment as an escort for a foraging expedition beyond Union lines. When ready, the colonel formed his command in column and led it out of camp. First came a troop of Bay State cavalry, followed by seven companies of the 49th and two cannon. Then came the forage train of seventy-five wagons, protected in the rear by the remaining three companies of the 49th. Three miles beyond the picket line lay the thousand-acre plantation of a man named Laycock, a professed Union man who had wood ready for the wagons. Bartlett, learning from a slave that Rebel cavalrymen had been there that morning, looking for Union scouts, deployed his escort to guard the wagons while they were loaded, then formed the column and returned to camp without incident. The lucky soldiers of the regiment managed to obtain molasses and sugar, a great addition to their army diet. Although a relatively unimportant assignment that did not result in any fighting, Frank was proud of his unit's march, good conduct, and in his own overall ability to lead such an expedition.[15]

The Union troops continued to drill as the month of March wore on. By March 13, Banks had concentrated three of his divisions at Baton Rouge. In addition to Augur's First Division, he had the Third Division, led by Brigadier General William H. Emory, and the Fourth Division, under the command of Brigadier General Cuvier Grover. At this time, unknown to the troops, Banks was planning a feint against Port Hudson, a river town north of Baton Rouge, heavily fortified and still under Confederate control. Admiral David G. Farragut was planning an attempt to pass the river batteries with part of his fleet, so he could assist Major General Ulysses S. Grant, in command of the Army of the Tennessee, with operations against Vicksburg, Mississippi. Grant's army was situated north of Vicksburg on the Arkansas side of the river. Grant was continually frustrated in his attempts to get into Vicksburg's rear, and Farragut, with his warships, might be able to help Grant.[16]

Accordingly, once Farragut's ships were ready for action, on March 13 Banks dispatched Grover's division up the road toward Port Hudson, followed by Emory's at daybreak on March 14, then by Augur, whose division

This woodcut, drawn in the 1880s to illustrate The Century Company's "Battles and Leaders" series, shows the Nineteenth Army Corps marching toward Port Hudson on March 14, 1863, as a feint to draw attention away from the Union navy's attempt to run past the Confederate batteries at Port Hudson.

would constitute the reserve. "The morning was cool," wrote Sergeant Johns, "the road was in fine order, — trees, just budding out, and festooned with vines and moss, were on either hand; so for five miles marching was a luxury." By nine o'clock that morning, Colonel Chapin's brigade reached the twin bridges (a pontoon and a plank) over the Bayou Montesano. Here, Bartlett saw General Banks pass by, heading toward the front. "All was silence," recalled Frank. "I could not help thinking of the time, nearly a year ago, when we were marching in the same way, on a road very similar, towards Yorktown...."[17]

When the column halted at noon, fourteen miles from Port Hudson, Bartlett witnessed Union soldiers from other regiments entering and pillaging local farmhouses. He was aghast at the situation. "These marauders not only steal poultry and other live meat, but in some cases even go into the houses and take the food off the table, steal jewelry, and other valuables. I believe in 'living on the enemy's country,' but the beef and other food should be taken by the proper officers and issued to the troops as it is required, not slaughtered recklessly and left untouched to rot." Continued the colonel: "My regiment think it hard that I won't let them go in and plunder when every body else is doing it." The Harvard colonel rightfully mused that if such depredations continued, the army could degenerate into "an armed mob," lawless and ungovernable. That afternoon, the army continued on some distance, with Augur's men marching into a large open field to pitch tents for the night. Having been in the saddle since three o'clock that morning, Frank found it amusing to hear other, able-bodied officers complain of "being all tired out."[18]

Frank waited for the regimental wagons to come up, had his tent pitched by nightfall, found some hay, and fell asleep the moment he touched the ground. "Was awakened at eleven by heavy cannonading at the front, towards the river. It was the gunboats." Earlier that afternoon, Union patrols from Grover's division made contact with the Union navy and informed Farragut that Banks was in place to make his diversion. While Banks waited for nightfall and the navy, he deployed his troops and sent out pickets to cover all the roads from Port Hudson to ensure that any Confederate foray would be detected, Banks believing at the time that the garrison outnumbered his own forces. Sometime between 11:00 and 11:30 that night, Farragut started seven vessels past the Confederate batteries, the naval column covered by an ironclad and six mortar boats. Farragut's flagship, *Hartford*, with the gunboat *Albatross* lashed to it, succeeded in passing the enemy cannon. *Monongahela* and *Richmond* each received damage and dropped back down the river. *Mississippi* ran aground midway past the batteries and was pulverized by the Rebel guns. Her crew abandoned ship and torched the vessel, which exploded with a great roar heard and seen throughout the Union army camps later that night.[19]

At two in the morning on March 15, Colonel Bartlett was awakened with orders to prepare his regiment to march. Colonel Chapin told Frank that the army had been repulsed with heavy loss and ordered Bartlett to take the lead with two regiments and a section of artillery, march to Bayou Montesano, and hold the bridge at that point to prevent the enemy from seizing it and preventing the army from returning to Baton Rouge. One of General Emory's aides told the colonel that the fleet was destroyed and the army cut to pieces. Incredulous, Frank wondered why his regiment did not march to the nonexistent fighting rather than lead the retreat. Such startling rumors, coupled with the noise of *Mississippi's* destruction on the river, panicked many teamsters and their wagons. At the start of the march, Bartlett had difficulty halting the wagons until gaps in the baggage train were closed and an orderly procession obtained.[20]

When Frank reached Bayou Montesano, he found the two bridges still in

Another woodcut from "Battles and Leaders," this scene illustrates General Augur's baggage train crossing the twin bridges over Bayou Montesano on March 14, 1863. During the retreat from Baton Rouge, Colonel Bartlett's 49th Massachusetts guarded this crossing and remained there for several days.

place, with the plank span needing some minor repair. Leaving Major Plunkett with two companies to effect the repair and act as guards, Frank sent another company across the stream to guard against any Rebel cavalry coming from the road toward Clinton. He then intended to march the remainder of the 49th along with the wagon train to Baton Rouge. However, after moving a couple of miles, an order from Banks arrived, instructing him to halt until further orders. Two hours later, another order informed the colonel to continue to Baton Rouge. The tired column of the 49th was almost back at their old camp when fresh orders arrived, hurrying the regiment back to the bayou. "This was rather discouraging," penned the colonel, but he allowed the men to rest an hour, then marched back to the bayou, where he put the regiment into camp. Frank was tired, having been in the saddle more than fourteen hours now. And rain set in, quickly turning the campground into mud. To add insult to injury, an order came in detailing the 49th and 50th Massachusetts regiments to be ready to march on an expedition under Bartlett's command, with the colonel to report immediately to Baton Rouge for specific instructions.[21]

Incensed at this order, Frank knew his regiment was too tired to obey. Sergeant Johns gave an eloquent version of the foot soldier's story of this marching and countermarching when he wrote "While few or none fell out of the ranks in coming to the bayou, fearing the enemy might be behind, yet they returned from the city like scattered sheep, mad at themselves, mad at their generals, and mad at the colonel's horse, which kept up a mad pace, requiring the boys to trot to keep up. They did not keep up, but came in singly or in squads-hot, footsore, and tired."[22]

Disgusted, Frank sent his orderly to General Augur's headquarters to explain his viewpoint. Once the general learned how the 49th had marched back and forth all day, which he had not known, Augur released Frank from this expedition, informing the orderly that he had placed the colonel in command as a compliment to his regiment's bearing. After learning that his regiment would stay in camp, Frank obtained a couple of fence rails to keep him from sleeping in the water, then slept like a log till reveille the next morning. The sun came out hot that day (March 16) and that afternoon, Frank went over to General Augur's headquarters to learn the state of affairs. The general told him that an expedition had crossed the river to march up the opposite shore above Port Hudson and see if Farragut's two vessels could be found. Instead of Bartlett in command, a colonel from New York led the expedition, which found that the levees had been cut, flooding the low ground and making a large-scale expedition impossible. Engineers did manage to observe the Rebel batteries across the river and make accurate sketches of their positions. Banks reinforced the scouting force with a full brigade, but troop movements on the west side of the Mississippi proved to be impossible at this time.[23]

The 49th remained at Bayou Montesano for several days, patrolling the area and watching for Rebels. The hard marching on the fifteenth taxed the colonel's strength. On March 18, he confided in his diary how he felt. "I feel very miserably this morning. It was a struggle to get up. Very weak and dizzy.... I have lost all appetite and only eat because it is a duty, not that I am hungry.... I suffer more in case of an attack of weakness or illness than when I had two legs. It takes all the strength and vigor of a healthy man to drag round this 'ball and chain' of a leg. My leg has pained me more than usual lately. No one shall know it, though." When he awoke the next morning, Frank picked a lizard out of his bed. He could not complain much, though; one of his officers killed eight snakes the previous day, one a big rattler with eleven rattles. Finally, on March 20, the regiment packed up and marched back to its old camp near Baton Rouge.[24]

Once back in camp, the regiment resumed its daily routine of drilling and picket duty. The officers lived well, wrote Frank. On March 21, Frank invited Major George Wheatland of the 48th Massachusetts to dine with him. Frank's cook Jacques went all out to impress the major. Dinner that evening consisted of pork steak, French bread from Baton Rouge, chocolate, fried sweet potatoes, guava jelly, boiled rice, butter, and for dessert, figs, coffee, and cigars, followed by a thimbleful of whiskey. Frank continued to drill his regiment and act as role model for his yet untested soldiers. When the regiment was ordered to dig a series of rifle pits to better protect the camp, the men witnessed their colonel "with spade in hand" to show his men how a proper rifle pit looked when finished. Because of their colonel, wrote Sergeant Johns, the 49th was the banner regiment of the First Division. "Soldiers copy after their officers," wrote Johns. "Neatness is the prominent characteristic of our commander. Who ever saw him looking slovenly? ... The boys grumble at the time and toil this cleanness demands, but are well satisfied when they compare themselves with some of their neighbors, whose officers are careless in their attire." When some men began grumbling because they had to purchase white gloves for use at dress parade, the colonel was known to give a pair of his own gloves to one of the malcontents, which, when learned by other men, stopped the grousing.[25]

While in camp at Baton Rouge, the men erected larger wedge tents to live in and used their shelter halves as awnings to sit under to keep out of the hot Louisiana sun. Late March weather continued cold at night, but as April passed, the men began to realize that the area residents were not kidding when they told the Yankees that it would be harder and harder to keep cool as summer approached. "See us in our thick woollen garments," wrote Johns, "and you would suppose we would dissolve in perspiration, but this is the only climate in which a man can wear flannel next to his skin with pleasure." The food eaten by the regiment while in camp varied, but was generally better than the usual fare given to soldiers. Sergeant Johns complained that fresh vegetables were hard to find for daily use; he also wondered why fish was not issued to the troops instead of meat. Johns observed that their salt beef was generally of good quality, but pork quickly turned "soft, oily, and maggoty" in the hot climate. Still, diarrhea and fevers continued to be a problem, with over one hundred men on the sick list at one time, with others prostrated by illness and not able to do daily duty. As a result, wrote Johns, those on active duty had to contend with picket and fatigue duty more often than normal. Yet, in spite of boredom, sickness, and hot weather, the regiment's morale remained high, primarily due to the colonel's good example and insistence on maintaining a high state of discipline, bringing the regiment to the attention of the rest of the corps.[26]

What Johns did not know at the time as the reason for the rifle pits, was the fact that Banks and much of the Nineteenth Army Corps departed Baton Rouge for active operations elsewhere in Louisiana. Banks, knowing that General Grant planned another strike at Vicksburg, and that he was expected to cooperate by moving against Port Hudson to draw off Confederates from Grant's front, was worried about the safety of New Orleans. Confederate troops west of the Mississippi might drive toward New Orleans when Banks moved north. To prevent this, Banks moved Emory's and Grover's divisions, plus one of Augur's brigades, to Brashear City, located at the end of a local rail line west of New Orleans, to clear the Bayou Teche area of Confederates. From April 12 to April 14, Banks' 16,000 men faced 4,000 Confederates under the command of Major General Richard Taylor at Fort Bisland and Irish Bend; Banks moved cautiously and allowed Taylor to escape, although two Confederate gunboats were burned to prevent their capture.

Banks continued to advance northward along Bayou Teche, reaching Opelousas on April 20. After a short delay here while his patrols ranged across the countryside, securing more than 3,500 bales of cotton and looking for detachments of the enemy, Banks, after communicating with both Grant and Farragut, decided to move on Alexandria, a town on the Red River in order to drive the enemy away and secure his rear once he turned back toward Port Hudson. Admiral David D. Porter, whose naval force was cooperating with Grant at Vicksburg, moved up the Red River with some of his vessels, arriving off Alexandria on May 6, to find the town evacuated by Taylor's troops. Banks' infantry marched in the next day. By that time, Grant had moved downriver from Vicksburg, crossed at Bruinsburg, and was moving to get between the Vicksburg garrison and reinforcements congregating at Jackson, Mississippi's capital. After a delay of a few days at Alexandria, during which time Grant and Banks exchanged messages and discussed strategy, Banks decided to move on Port Hudson. His troops would leave Alexandria and move down the Mississippi to a point north of Port Hudson, then cross the river and invest the city. Augur's two brigades at Baton Rouge would be reinforced by Banks' Second Division, led by Brigadier General Thomas W. Sherman, from the defenses of New Orleans, and move on Port Hudson from the south.[27]

While Banks was campaigning along the Bayou Teche, Augur's two brigades, about 4,500 strong, protected Baton Rouge, assisted by a naval force that patrolled the river. Frank and the 49th continued to drill, perform picket duty, and wait. The weather got warmer, and Frank got sicker. "Never felt worse in my life," he moaned. "Never took so much medicine." The colonel left his tent and moved into a nearby house to be more comfortable. Dr. Frederick Winsor, the regimental surgeon, thought it was an attack of typhoid that threatened the colonel. "Horrible pain in my head all day," penned Frank on May 19. That night, however, orders came for the regiment to pack up and prepare to march at five o'clock the next morning. Dr. Winsor told the colonel bluntly that it was impossible for him to accompany the regiment. "I *must* go. I know the risk is great, but I have got to take it," Frank wrote. "If I get killed, or wounded, or die of fever, people will say it was rash, etc. I know my duty, though, better than any one else. Colonel Chapin has offered me the use of a spring wagon to ride in. I shall go in that."[28]

7

"WE THOUGHT HIM *TOO* BRAVE A MAN TO BE KILLED"

Port Hudson

The officers and men of the 49th Massachusetts received the order to be prepared to march on May 20 with great enthusiasm. "The effect was magical," recalled veteran Joseph Tucker years afterward. "A new cheerfulness beamed on every face, every sick man that was permitted left the hospital. At last we were to reap the harvest of this long, weary cultivation." But, he continued, "this was sadly damped when we heard that the colonel was sick in bed. It was wonderful how the men leaned on him.... Any order of the colonel was to the men law and gospel, they felt it must be right. They had entire faith and trust in his capacity and judgment. He knew this and felt his responsibility very keenly."[1]

The regiment left camp under the command of Lieutenant Colonel Sumner early on the morning of May 20. Only about 450 men were fit enough to head off toward Port Hudson. Hundreds more were still convalescing and were left behind to help protect the camps around Baton Rouge. The first five miles went by the best, for the road wound through a magnificent Southern forest which shaded the road from the rays of the sun. Sergeant Johns noticed that many men were as yet unwell enough to stand the march and began to drop back as the column plodded along. Some time after dark that night, the regiment went into bivouac on the Merritt plantation, having marched sixteen miles. The progress was not rapid because Colonel Dudley's brigade led, with Colonel Chapin's bringing up the rear, protecting the baggage train. Twelve miles into the march, Company G was detached from the regiment and ordered back to Baton Rouge to resume its provost duty, much to the chagrin of its members.[2]

73

Colonel Bartlett had dearly wanted to accompany the regiment. He was also up at five and ready to march, but he could hardly stand. Dr. Winsor begged him not to go. The buggy promised by Colonel Chapin did not appear so the doctor set off to find the brigade commander to see where it was. Once Winsor departed, Frank mounted and started up the road after the regiment. He met the doctor after about a mile; Winsor had discovered that the carriage had broken and would arrive once it was repaired. Winsor prevailed upon Frank to dismount and placed him in a nearby house to rest. Hours went by and then word came that the carriage had mistakenly been sent ahead to join the brigade baggage train. Frank resolved to go on and made it as far as the Bayou Montesano, where he halted and waited at another house.[3]

Around four o'clock that afternoon a man sent by Colonel Chapin appeared with the buggy, under orders not to return without Bartlett. With himself ensconced in the buggy and his servant riding one horse and leading another, Frank finally departed for the 49th's camp, where he arrived that evening. Frank was pleased by his reception at camp. "It all happened very quietly," recalled Tucker, "but somehow it got whispered that Col. Bartlett had once more joined the regiment. The men could not suppress their feeling of joy and a hearty cheer was given. One of the privates turning away was heard to say, 'Well, now I can go to my tent and sleep easy to-night.'"[4]

"Thursday, May 21. Ordered to move at six A.M. I rode in the buggy; kept the horses near, in case I should want them. We had advanced about three and a half miles, when we were saluted by some shells from rebel batteries ahead. I immediately got on my horse Billy. I had to be pretty careful to keep my balance, as I felt very shaky still."[5]

With these few words, Colonel Bartlett described the morning of May 21, when Augur's advance encountered Confederate troops at a small village crossroads called Plains Store, east of Port Hudson. Union cavalry ranging ahead of Augur's infantry column ran into Confederate troops about two miles south of Plains Store. These Mississippians had been placed there to lure the Yankee horsemen north to the crossroads, where a larger force under the command of Colonel Frank Powers, consisting of more cavalry and an artillery battery, lay deployed in the woods just north of the village. The Mississippians fired into Dudley's green regiments before falling back to join Powers. The enemy fire caused havoc in the ranks of the untried rookies which in fact comprised Augur's entire division. This was their first baptism of fire and many soldiers broke ranks and fled into the woods as the enemy artillery joined in.[6]

Dudley managed to rally the troops and form a line of battle across the road near a little country church in a clearing. His artillery unlimbered and began dueling with the Rebel cannon just beyond Plains Store. The colonel advanced three regiments toward the enemy line while deploying a third battery to silence the enemy guns. As the Yankee line neared the smaller Rebel force, Colonel Powers sent his cannon off to the north and fell back, leaving Dudley's troops in possession of the village. His troops moved up and took position around the village, with a battery of artillery placed to command the Bayou Sara road (the road leading north). One section of Battery G, 5th United States, covered the Port Hudson road to the west.[7]

The noise of the first phase of the engagement at Plains Store was what the 49th Massachusetts heard as Chapin's brigade marched up the road. Quartermaster Johns eloquently captured the mood at the time as the men from Berkshire headed toward their first encounter with the enemy:

> Slowly we pressed our way. Soon wounded men and bleeding horses were brought to the rear. Shells shrieked and bursted. Our first battle had begun. A strange sickness came over me. I doubted if it were right for *me* to fight, and was tempted to retreat to the safety of the quartermaster's department. But *that* was no time to reconsider a grave question, so I fell back upon the conclusions I had reached in quieter times, though, in the fear and excitement of the hour, I could not recall the arguments that led to those conclusions and determined I would walk in the path of duty, though it led to the jaws of death. I felt no more fear that day, for *will* triumphed.

Chapin's brigade reached a large field and went into bivouac, the men expecting, perhaps, that this would be their evening encampment. But, just then, the artillery opened anew and the fighting erupted suddenly. Continued Johns:

> The firing was so rapid that the roar was continuous. Oh, it was grand! I never heard any thing half so inspiring. It made the wild blood leap through the veins, and stiffened every muscle. I had heard of the "joy of battle." I understood it then.[8]

The rattle of musketry and roar of cannon announced the arrival of Confederate reinforcements. Major General Franklin Gardner, the commander of Port Hudson, had received word from the Rebels engaged at Plains Store of the oncoming Union troops. Earlier, he had received an order from General Joseph E. Johnston, the theater commander, to evacuate the town and join Johnston at Jackson, the state capital, where he was gathering an army to oppose General Grant's movement against Vicksburg. But now, with Yankees coming up from Baton Rouge and word of more Yankees crossing the Mississippi above Port Hudson at Bayou Sara (this was Banks' main force), Gardner knew he might be cut off and forced to endure a siege.[9]

To help Powers at Plains Store, Gardner ordered Colonel William R. Miles, commander of a legion of Louisiana troops, to take part of his force, accompanied by Captain Richard M. Boone's Louisiana battery, out the Port Hudson Road and engage the Yankees at Plains Store. Miles soon had his four hundred soldiers on the march, sweeping aside Union horsemen as he approached the crossroads. These retreating cavalrymen informed Dudley of the approaching Rebels. Dudley, whose men were tired after marching and fighting, sent his adjutant to Colonel Chapin with a request for help. Chapin responded by sending the 48th Massachusetts, which marched off to support the section of Battery G, 5th United States, on the Port Hudson Road.[10]

As Miles moved east toward Plains Store, Colonel Powers reformed his cavalry and again ordered an attack southward. His drive was halted by Dudley's 174th New York, which moved into position to support the 2nd Vermont Battery, which brought Powers' troopers to a dead stop by firing charges of canister.[11]

While Powers' men were stopped north of the road junction, Miles continued his advance from the west. As his men neared Plains Store, Miles divided his command in half, sending Lieutenant Colonel Frederick B. Brand with three companies to advance south of the Bayou Sara Road, while Major James T. Coleman's two companies moved north of the road. Boone's battery supplied artillery support. Coleman's detachment emerged from a wooded belt and entered an apple orchard on the right flank of the two guns of Battery G, 5th United States. Without hesitation, Major Coleman ordered a charge. The two Louisiana companies let out a yell and surged forward, straight into the flank of the 48th Massachusetts, which was facing west toward Miles' main line. Lieutenant Colonel James O'Brien tried to wheel his regiment to the rear to face the small force of Confederates, but his untested regiment "broke in confusion and disgracefully fled from the firing of the enemy, ..." The Rebels surged forward and managed to seize one of Battery G's guns even as the cannoneers raced off with the other.[12]

As the engagement heated up, Colonel Dudley sent one of his staff officers for help. This officer rode up to Colonel Chapin with an order to send Dudley the 116th New York. But Chapin refused — he retorted that Dudley was not in charge and that he had not received any proper order from General Augur to detach a unit from his brigade. But, even as the 2nd Vermont Battery turned some of its guns to fire at Miles' Southerners, the general appeared and ordered Chapin to send *two* regiments to Dudley's support.[13]

Colonel Bartlett formed his regiment in column of fours and followed Major George M. Love's New Yorkers up a narrow road through the woods southwest of Plains Store. Sergeant Johns recorded that this road "was so narrow that we could see but little in advance of us." As the 49th reached the Bayou Sara road, the 48th Massachusetts broke into confusion and flooded back through the woods, slamming into the 49th as it moved forward. "For a moment, we were in confusion," recalled Private Tucker, "but were quickly rallied." Though some of the 49th's soldiers were swept along by the resulting chaos, most of the regiment remained on the field. The leading companies managed to fire a couple of volleys, but the enemy could not be seen and

Frank ordered a halt to the shooting. Some of Bartlett's men tried to stop the rout of the 48th by collaring fugitives and pointing them toward the enemy. General Augur rode into the fray and helped to steady the troops who remained on the field.[14]

As the situation became clearer, Colonel Bartlett ordered his men to charge bayonets. The men willingly surged forward into the woods, which they found impenetrable, "neither man nor beast could get through there," penned Sergeant Johns. Bartlett withdrew his command, forming them in line back in more open terrain. As the 49th withdrew, the men saw Major Love's 116th New York also charge forward with the same result. General Augur met Frank and ordered him to move the regiment through the open space as Rebel artillery shells "shrieked and bursted over our heads as if a legion of fiends had been let loose." As the regiment approached the edge of the woods, Bartlett ordered the men to lie down. After a short while, the firing died down, so Frank had the men stand and put them through the manual of arms to calm them down.[15]

In the meantime, the 116th New York, at first on the left of the 49th, was fired into its rear by some of Colonel Brand's Louisianians. Major Love turned the regiment to face the hostile fire as bullets tore into his men. Lieutenant Joseph Tucker of the 49th, acting as a mounted aide to Colonel Chapin, was hit in the knee by a solid shot; he survived but his leg was amputated later that day. This same projectile caused Chapin's horse to throw its head back so violently that the animal smacked its rider in the face, covering him with blood and making his face "benumbed and senseless."[16]

The firing went on for some time until General Augur sought out Major Love and asked the major if his men would charge. Receiving a positive reply, Augur gave Love a positive order to attack. After relaying the message to each company commander, Love placed himself in the center of his line and, twenty paces ahead of his men, personally led the attack. Miles' men fell back through the woods, across an open field, and rallied inside another wood, firing back and halting the 116th. However, Love reformed his line and surged forward again, and Miles, realizing he was badly outnumbered, ordered a withdrawal. He had received a message from Colonel Powers, who informed Miles that he had managed to break contact with the Yankees and was withdrawing to the north.[17]

Thus ended the engagement at Plains Store. Though sharp and protracted, the loss on each side was light. Augur reported casualties of fifteen killed, seventy-one wounded, and fourteen missing, a total of one hundred men. Frank's regiment suffered a slight loss of five wounded and one missing. Colonel Miles reported a loss of eighty-nine (twelve killed, thirty-six wounded, and forty-one missing). Miles had done well to slow down the Union advance from Baton Rouge, but the fact was that he had withdrawn from a vastly superior force and allowed the Yankees to control one of the exits from Port Hudson. With Banks' main force coming down from the north, General Gardner's position soon became precarious.[18]

The following afternoon, General Gardner sent out a flag of truce and asked permission to bring off his dead and wounded while the Yankees bivouacked around Plains Store inspected the battlefield and gawked at the shot-riddled buildings at the crossroads. Meanwhile, farther north, Banks moved his divisions south toward Port Hudson while Colonel Benjamin Grierson's cavalry blocked the roads leading east out of the town. Brigadier General Thomas W. Sherman's division, coming from New Orleans by river, disembarked at Springfield Landing and moved northwest toward the southern defenses of Port Hudson. Gardner, meanwhile, set his men to work building fortifications north of Port Hudson; his existing defenses were meant to counter an enemy advance from Baton Rouge, and his men worked feverously, pickets from both sides shooting at each other as Banks' men neared the enemy.[19]

Augur's division finally marched for Port Hudson on Sunday, May 24. As the infantry column plodded along on the dusty road, Rebel artillery opened on the head of the column. Johns, whose regiment was father back in line, heard the firing. After about two hours, the artillery firing ceased. That night, the 49th camped in the woods about a mile and a half from Gardner's entrenched soldiers, "rocked to sleep by a music which is becoming quite familiar to us." The main worry, though, seemed to be the lack of potable water, "which grows scarcer and meaner the further we advance," penned Johns. Wood ticks were also a source of extreme irritation to Augur's New Englanders.[20]

On the evening of May 25, word was passed along the line to prepare for an enemy attack; Gardner might try to break through and evacuate Port Hudson before it was too late. Chapin's brigade lined up at the edge of a wood behind a fence, facing a wide, open space. Artillery rolled into position and was ready to assist the infantry. Colonel Bartlett rode along the line of his regiment. "Be steady!" he warned. "[D]on't fire till I give the command; wait till you can smell their breaths, and then cut them down. If I see any man skulking to the rear I will kill him, just as I would a rebel." Minutes passed into hours, and finally the men were allowed to sleep on their arms. After dawn, the troops went back to camp and made breakfast.[21]

It wasn't until the evening of May 26 that Banks felt confident enough that he had developed the enemy's lines sufficiently to allow for a major assault. Rather than spend time in a lengthy siege, the general hoped to overwhelm the defenders with a massive frontal attack. A siege would require more time to develop better roads and telegraph lines to ensure smooth communications between his divisions. A siege would also need heavy artillery pieces to assist the navy in bombarding the enemy positions. Therefore, Banks hosted his generals at a conference to discuss plans for an attack. Augur, Sherman, and Weitzel apparently opposed an attack, but Banks had already made up his mind, hoping to win a quick victory and then assist Grant at Vicksburg if needed.[22]

Earlier that day, Banks had already issued preliminary orders. General Augur transmitted them to his two brigade commanders, who in turn lined up each regiment in their commands and gave a stirring speech about duty, then asked each regiment to supply a "forlorn hope" to lead the May 27 assault. Colonel Chapin explained that there was a ditch in front of the enemy line, perhaps fifteen feet wide and twelve feet deep. He asked that his brigade supply two hundred men, a field officer, four captains, and eight lieutenants. Unmarried men were preferred, and if more than five men from each company volunteered, five names would be drawn by lot. Half these men would carry fascines to fill the ditch, keeping their muskets slung across their backs, while the other half would charge across the ditch with fixed bayonets. In the 49th, Major Plunkett and two lieutenants volunteered, as did sixty-four men.[23]

Once these volunteers were gathered, they went behind the lines to construct fascines. Each was composed of a bundle of branches and twigs secured with grape vines, and was about eight feet long and weighed from fifteen to thirty pounds. Quartermaster Johns was not impressed with them. "I fear they are too heavy," he worried. "If lighter, they could be carried as shields, if the ground be smooth, which is quite unlikely; now they must be shouldered, leaving the vitals all exposed to the fire of the foe."[24]

That night, Johns penned a letter home, perhaps his last, he quipped. Other men did the same, worrying over the morrow and their chances of survival. Many worried men in blue pondered religious questions. By daybreak, many soldiers had made their peace and were ready to die for their glorious cause, mused Johns. Dawn revealed a beautiful summer day, heralded by the roar of artillery to the north. "There is no swaggering, but a quiet falling back on the fixed will," said Johns. "I would not, for much wealth, miss the grandeur of this hour." By now a full-fledged abolitionist, Johns went on to write that the cause he was fighting for would exterminate the "national curse" of slavery. Johns also by now had heard that African American men in blue were standing ready to assail the Confederate line. Knowing that their cause was just, Johns mused, how could they fail?[25]

The noise of combat that Johns heard was the initial Federal attacks on the Confederate left. General Weitzel's division began its attack around 6:00 A.M., followed by Dwight, Paine, and Grover. The outnumbered Rebel defenders met the challenge however, and repelled every attack. The broken terrain disrupted a coordinated advance, and piecemeal charges were all driven back, some with heavy losses. By 11:00 A.M., Banks' northern attacks had

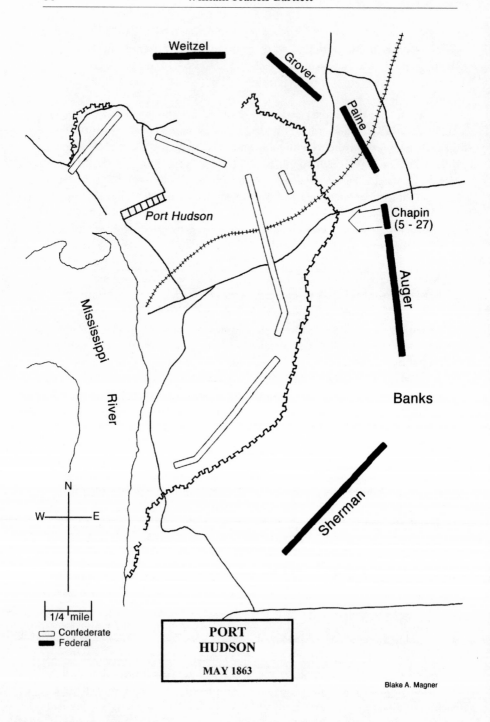

Weitzel

Grover

Paine

Port Hudson

Chapin
(5 - 27)

Auger

Mississippi

River

Banks

N

W———E

Sherman

1/4 mile

Confederate
Federal

PORT
HUDSON

MAY 1863

Blake A. Magner

petered out, the surviving soldiers taking cover among the abatis and dense undergrowth in front of the enemy line, pinned down by a heavy volume of defensive musketry.[26]

Farther to the south, the divisions of Thomas W. Sherman and Christopher C. Augur were in line ready to attack when they received the order to charge. As the fighting started to the north, Union artillery went into position and began to shell the Confederate works. Initially, Confederate guns had the better advantage and pounded the Yankees, but as more Union batteries went into line, their numbers began to tell and soon they had the upper hand. General Banks, mystified by the absence of musketry on his left, arrived at General Sherman's headquarters around noon, to find the general dining and his men still waiting to attack. The generals argued and Banks left, sending his chief of staff to relieve Sherman. But when that officer located Sherman's headquarters, he found the general leading his men forward and so took no action. But Sherman's attack also failed, the red-legged Zouaves of the 165th New York suffering a loss of 186 officers and men in the futile assault.[27]

While the battle raged on the northern front, General Augur followed his orders, waiting for the sound of Sherman's attack before beginning his own. In the meantime, he deployed the 2nd Vermont Battery in front of Chapin's brigade, with a portion of Dudley's brigade in reserve, supporting the guns. Chapin's men were screened from the enemy by a belt of woods in their front as the artillery firing continued. While the men relaxed as best they could in a cornfield, orders came for volunteers to return to their former position to bring up the fascines, which unaccountably had been left behind. "It was one of those mistakes no one is responsible for," opined Johns, but in the resulting confusion, some of those who had joined the forlorn hope went back to get their bundles, and were joined by men who had *not* volunteered for the storming party. When this mass of men reached the front, the attack was gearing up and thus the forlorn hope went forward, now composed partly of men who had not originally volunteered for this dangerous duty. Johns recorded that Lieutenant Siggins and forty-five men from the 49th went forward on this duty.[28]

By the time Johns and the other volunteers arrived at the front, Colonel Chapin had lined up his brigade to advance. Augur added the 2nd Louisiana and part of the 50th Massachusetts to the assault column. The Vermont battery was now firing in "one unbroken roar, stirring up fighting blood as no martial music could do," recalled Johns. "We could feel the ground tremble. The wind from his guns shook our clothes as leaves shaken by the breeze." Then came a lull in the shooting, during which Chapin's men filed into the woods preparatory to the attack. In the hour the men lay there, many began to brood about the upcoming attack. Colonel Chapin climbed a fallen tree that had wedged itself in a crotch of another tree, giving him a clear view of the ground before his men. Men below the colonel heard him gasp "My God," as he scanned the open ground. Chapin saw in the distance the felled trees that formed a natural abatis that would slow his advance. To make matters worse, the Rebels had left the dense undergrowth in place. The fallen trees, when combined with the brush, made an orderly attack almost impossible. It was a daunting task facing the men in blue.[29]

Quartermaster Johns had just carved "49th M" in a tree when he heard someone exclaim, "In fifteen minutes we start." "A mortal fear came over me," he recalled, "and a deathly sickness. It seemed as if I had taken all the emetics and purgatives known to *materia medica*." A swirl of feelings raced through Johns' head until he calmed down. After all, he just had to do his duty, no matter what may come. The assistant surgeon of the 49th, Doctor Albert R. Rice, came along the line, giving each man half a gill of whiskey.[30]

As the men readied for the attack, General Augur strode along the line. "Now, boys, charge, and reserve your fire till you get into the fort; give them cold steel, and as you charge, cheer! Give them New England!" Lieutenant Colonel O'Brien of the 48th Massachusetts was the officer in charge of the forlorn hope. "Come on, boys," he cried, "we'll wash in the Mississippi to-night." O'Brien's comments were echoed by Colonel Chapin, resplendent in his dress uniform and white Panama hat. "You must do your whole duty today," he said to the forlorn hope. "Remember that you do not go unsupported. My brigade will follow close on your heels. Do your duty and we will drink Mississippi water tonight."[31]

Around 3:00 P.M. the order came to advance. Silently the men of the forlorn hope slung their rifles over their shoulders and grabbed their fascines, followed by the 116th New York, then the 49th Massachusetts. Colonel Bartlett knew what was about to happen. "I had seen Rebel fortifications before," he wrote. "I knew it would be almost impossible to get through the fallen trees, etc., even if I was not shot at." And Frank was the only mounted officer in the column, making himself a good target. Mounted on his brown mare Billy, the colonel knew he couldn't go forward on foot. Riding a stirrupless saddle, his crutch strapped behind him, Frank was quite conspicuous in the column of men on foot. "I knew that my chances for life were very small. But I had to go horseback, or not at all. So prayed that life and limb might be spared, and went in."[32]

The column moved up along the west edge of a belt of woods, then turned toward the enemy line. As soon as the attackers came in sight, Rebels popped up from behind their works and opened a devastating fire, supported by several artillery pieces firing grape and canister. A survivor of the 21st Maine recalled that they were met by a "terrific storm of missiles from the artillery and infantry that crowded the Confederate works." His colonel, Elijah Johnson, wrote that the "brave boys advanced with a cheer which would have precluded the possibility of a defeat, had the enemy been in an open field." Johns observed "great volumes and little jets of smoke, as muskets and cannon bade us defiance."[33]

The words of the Down Easters were echoed by Sergeant Solomon Nelson of the 50th Massachusetts, part of Dudley's brigade. "The batteries at different points were pouring in a continual shower of shot and shell," he wrote. "The roar of the cannonading, the wild yell of the soldiers, the whistling minie balls as they flew over and around us, the horrible shriek of the shrapnel, grape and canister, were sounds, to a peaceful citizen like myself, altogether unpleasant, and what made it still more aggravating, not a single rebel head could be seen to fire at."[34]

Colonel Edward P. Chapin of the 116th New York was Bartlett's brigade commander at Port Hudson. Resplendent in a full dress uniform, Chapin was slain during the failed attack on May 27, 1863. Courtesy United States Army Military History Institute, Roger Hunt Collection.

The heavy fire from the enemy created chaos in the attacking ranks. Soon after the charge started, Colonel Chapin was hit in the knee by a bullet. He went down, managed to get up, then was hit in the head and killed. Though Colonel Johnson of the 21st Maine was next in line to succeed Chapin, he evidently did not learn about Chapin's death until later. One of his men remarked that "the work to be done was plain and few commands were needed." The attacking column then reached the abatis and ground to a virtual halt. Johns best expressed the situation:

A deep ditch or ravine was passed, and we came to trees that had been felled in every direction. Over, under, around them, we went. It was impossible to keep in line. The spaces between the trees were filled with twigs and branches, in many places knee-high. Foolishness to talk about cheering or the "double quick." We had no strength for the former, aye, and no heart either. We had gone but a few rods ere our Yankee common sense assured us we must fail. You could not go faster than a slow walk. Get your feet into the brush and it was impossible to force them through; you had to stop and pull them back and start again. As best we could we pressed on; shells shrieked past or bursted in our midst, tearing ground and human bodies alike; grape and canister mowed down the branches, tore the leaves or lodged in trees and living men. Solid shot, sinking into the stumps with a thumping sound, or thinning our ranks; Minie balls "zipping" past us or *into* us, made our progress slow indeed.[35]

Augur's men were opposed by units from Arkansas, Mississippi, and Alabama under the command of Brigadier General William N. R. Beall. As the Yankee attack started, Colonel Miles, in command of the Confederate right flank units, could see that Beall needed help. He immediately detached as many men as he could spare and sent them north along the line, arriving in time to help repel Sherman's division. Then, some of these troops were shifted north yet again to reinforce Beall's men in their fight with Augur. As a result, there were plenty of defenders to keep up a steady fire on the beleaguered Yanks.[36]

The resulting carnage in the Union attack column destroyed any forward momentum that the column might have had without encountering the abatis. As Johns aptly described, the abatis completely disrupted the attack and was the main cause of its failure. Johns managed to wade partway into the abatis before he realized that he was alone. He and four other men gathered behind a fallen tree, but within seconds, Johns was the only unwounded man there. While moving forward, the quartermaster witnessed the wounding of Lieutenant Siggins and the death of the color sergeant of the 48th Massachusetts. Johns realized that the attack had failed; the storming party, especially the men with the fascines, simply were unable to navigate the labyrinth of the abatis to even find the ditch in front of the Rebel works. Without them, any Yankee who reached the ditch would be unable to leap it.[37]

The survivors crowded into the abatis and were pinned down by Rebel fire. After an hour of enduring this, Johns saw Lieutenant Colonel O'Brien suddenly stand and charge forward, yelling for men to follow him. O'Brien was quickly slain and the few men who followed him just as quickly dissipated into the abatis, or at least those who were not killed or wounded. The survivors continued to cower under the abatis, but soon noticed that bullets were flying into them from the rear, where Union soldiers farther from the

Rebel line were firing too low, sometimes hitting their own men as they fired at the distant enemy line. "Fire higher" was heard all throughout the abatis as men tried to yell back to their comrades to stop firing too low.[38]

Johns failed to see what had happened to his own regiment during the assault. He had stood up once after the forlorn hope fell to pieces to look for the 49th, but found it was "not prudent" to stand in the open very long. He thought he had noticed a body of men with a Massachusetts flag off to the right, the line distinctive in their dark blue pants, which the 49th wore in lieu of the regulation sky blue trousers. The regiment, like the rest of the brigade, was repelled long before the majority of the men reached the abatis. Lieutenant Colonel Sumner was hit in the left shoulder early in the attack and was helped off the field. One of the company captains later counted thirty-eight bullet holes in his clothing; he was hit only once, though, in the ankle.[39]

Colonel Bartlett, as he feared, did indeed make a conspicuous target as his rode Billy toward the enemy. When the line faltered, Bartlett seized the colors from the bearer and waved them aloft as he rode Billy closer to the enemy entrenchments, entering the abatis, which slowed Billy and scratched up the animal very badly. Frank's luck finally ran out. As he was yelling for his men to close up on the colors, a bullet slammed into his left wrist, while another hit the outside of Frank's right ankle, glanced downward, and went through the sole of his foot. When hit, the colonel dropped the flag and tried to grab Billy's reins with his right hand. As he leaned forward, Frank lost his balance and flipped forward over Billy's head, landing flat on his back on the ground. Rebel defenders later recalled seeing Frank lying on the ground, waving the regimental colors over his head for a brief time. When help finally arrived to carry him off the field, Frank proudly asked them if they had seen Billy, who, after his rider fell, turned to the rear and jumped over obstacle after obstacle in his haste to find safety. "Did you see Billy?" he inquired. "He jumped like a rabbit."[40]

When some men finally managed to rescue the fallen colonel, they carried him to the rear to the 49th's field hospital, located just out of musket range in a cleared acre alongside a country road. Doctor Winsor and his staff set up their equipment and waited, listening to the roar of artillery and then the rattle of musketry as the infantry assault began. The doctor and his assistants paced back and forth, wondering what was happening. Around 3:30 P.M. some assistant surgeons came back to report that the attack was in progress but the firing was too severe to allow them to bring back any wounded men. Half an hour later, wounded men began to trickle in to the hospital, helped to the rear by their comrades rather than coming in ambulances. Soon it became apparent by the stories told by the wounded that the attack had failed. But what had happened to the 49th, Winsor asked. "Oh, doctor, the regiment's all cut to pieces! The' aint twenty men left 'thout a wound," was one of the replies. Windsor heard rumors of Bartlett's wounding, that Sumner had been hit, and that Major Plunkett was dead.[41]

Soon, though, Winsor heard familiar voices coming his way with the wounded colonel. Thoughts raced through the surgeon's mind as he glanced at Frank's prostrate form. How could he take away another limb? And how would he inform Frank's parents, to whom he had pledged to look after their son? The doctor's words best tell what happened next:

> His clear blue eye met mine steadily, his strong right hand grasped mine firmly, and the voice that could ring along the line like a trumpet had no waver in it as it said, "How are you, doctor? We've had a rough time of it. Now you must do your best for me. I can't lose another limb, you know." I saw that the hurt in the head could be nothing serious; a buckshot had scored the scalp to the bone, and another had done the same for the heel of his one foot. I undid the bandage that bound his left wrist, and examined it. A ball had entered on one side, and lay near the surface on the other. His eyes questioned me, and I replied, "I can soon take that ball out, when you are under ether. That's a very tender place." "But you won't take off the hand?" "I will do nothing without letting you know and having your consent, colonel." So he drank of oblivion and ceased to suffer, but his dream was not of home. "Doctor," he muttered (talking in the ether sleep), "that's my bridle hand, you know. Never can ride at the head of my regiment again if you take that off." In a moment I held the bullet in my hand, and saw with joy that it was round and rather small, giving reason to hope that it had not shattered the bones badly in coming through, which could hardly have been the case had it been conical. No loose bone was to be felt, and I had the great pleasure of telling him, as he returned to consciousness, that there was good reason to hope that his "bridle hand" would by and by hold the rein again. A smile of satisfaction and relief lit up the face which had till then been set in the resolve to bear the worst, and with the simple, hearty thanks which we surgeons had from the hundreds of men that night he was borne off to his blanket side by side with his officers.[42]

Winsor and his staff worked until midnight, operating as necessary and trying to save as many of the wounded as possible. Lieutenant Colonel Sumner came in shortly after darkness had come, "walking bowed and painfully" into the hospital. Doctor Winsor examined Sumner's shoulder and initially could not locate the ball; an hour later, however, one of his assistants probed, located it, and extracted the lead slug from the officer's arm. Later, Major Plunkett came back to see the doctor. Overjoyed at seeing the major, who had been reported dead, Winsor readily agreed to the major's request to issue a whiskey ration to the regiment's survivors. "Forty men's all I can get together of the old forty-ninth," lamented the major. Darkness and Rebel fire had prevented Union stretcher parties from being able to rescue the wounded that lay strewn all over the battlefield. Losses were as yet unknown. Finally, some-time after midnight, Winsor and his assistants lay down to sleep.[43]

That night, while surgeons worked on the wounded behind the Union line, a portion of the underbrush in Augur's front caught fire, lighting up the night sky. Wounded men, unable to move, lay in the blaze's path. But concerned Rebels emerged from their works, dragged men away from the blaze, then extinguished it. Other grayclad men came out with water to comfort their enemies, while others went about collecting weapons and ammunition from the field, taking it back into their works. Once morning came though, artillery firing started again at points along the line. But as the day wore on, it became apparent that Banks would not launch another assault. Beginning at daybreak, Banks and Gardner exchanged messages regarding the rescuing of the wounded men laying between the lines. Gardner, worried about further Union advances toward his lines, resisted Banks' initial messages. An agreement was hammered out and went into effect at 10:00 A.M. but quickly broke down when a Union artillery battery attempted to move into a better position and the navy continued its desultory firing. Finally, at 3:30 P.M., a truce went into effect until 7:00 P.M., allowing the Yankees to remove their dead and wounded.[44]

During one of these truce negotiations, Captain Walter Cutting of General Augur's staff met some of the Confederate officers whose troops had opposed the May 27 attack. "Who was that man on horseback?" some of them asked Cutting. "*He* was a gallant fellow.... We thought him *too* brave a man to be killed, so we ordered our men not to fire at him." Cutting told them Colonel Bartlett's name and the men spoke some more about the brave colonel on horseback.[45]

The truce allowed Banks' officers to tally their losses. Once this was done, Banks realized that he had suffered casualties of 293 killed, 1,545 wounded, and 157 missing, for a total of 1,995. The 49th Massachusetts went into action with only seven companies; Company G was still back in Baton Rouge and two other companies were on detached service guarding supply trains. Frank took only 233 officers and men into the fight, with 76 soldiers killed or wounded. With both the colonel and lieutenant colonel out of action, Major Plunkett was left in command of the survivors. Johns reported that the survivors of Chapin's brigade were "dispirited, having lost confidence in our generals." Johns passed along home the camp gossip that most of Banks' generals opposed the attack but were overruled by Banks. To Johns, a frontal attack without preparation made no sense. The Union brigades should have attacked simultaneously, wrote Johns, with enough skirmishers or sharpshooters out in front to neutralize the Rebels while the storming parties charged forward.[46]

While the burial parties interred the dead and stretcher bearers removed the wounded from the battlefield, Colonel Bartlett was placed in an ambulance and sent on the road to Springfield Landing. Roswell Harris of the 21st Maine saw the wounded colonel lying on the floor of an ambulance next to the wounded adjutant of the 21st, with two other officers on the pull-down cots above them, with yet another pair of wounded officers riding with the driver. The train of ambulances plodded along for six miles over a rough road to the landing, where Frank was transferred to the steamer *Iberville* for the fifteen mile river trip to Baton Rouge.[47]

Once in the hospital at Baton Rouge, Frank continually worried about losing his left arm. Once, he fretted that the doctors who were supposed to examine him did not show up, learning the next morning that one was drunk and the other attended his comrade. On June 13, he penned a hopeful letter to his mother, informing her that his appetite had returned, and his arm was suppurating freely under the application of warm woolen cloths. The doctors, he reported, were all of the opinion that his arm could be saved. Frank admitted that moving his wrist caused pain, and also that his foot was pretty well healed.[48]

Six days later, Frank penned a missive to his father. "If I had been told just how bad the wound was that afternoon on the field, I would have made the surgeon take off the hand without a second thought," he wrote. "The surgeon assured me so positively that I could save the hand, that I didn't think to ask, 'At how great a risk, in how long a time?' I want the surgeons to take it off now, and let me get well, instead of running the risk of inflammation, and losing it *above* the elbow, or worse."[49]

On June 20 Frank wrote a lengthy missive to Doctor Winsor:

> I am not in very good spirits. The doctors here differ so about my arm, and the question whether or not to take it off, that I don't know what to believe. The majority are thus inclined: Don't take it off yet. It looks healthy; the pus is *very* healthy. Small pieces of bone have come out, three, I think, not any bigger than half a bean. That was a week ago, since which no more pieces have come out, but the suppuration has continued *very* freely. A day or two since (the 16th) inflammation, which has entirely subsided, appeared on the outside face of the ulna, spreading up toward the elbow three or four inches. Warm fomentations were changed for cold water again. The inflammation still continues on the outside of the joint, but does not extend up the arm so far as it did. The hand is puffed very full with edema.... The arm is puffed a little, too, at the elbow, and for a short distance above. In a few days, after the inflammation is reduced, they propose to cut open and explore it, and take out the loose spicula of bone. They ask me often "how thoroughly it was explored at the time on the field, and how much bone you took out," questions I cannot answer. The examination will decide whether the arm ought to come off or not; if not, by taking out the bones hurry the healing. If I had known

it was so bad and was likely to be so long and tedious a wound, I should have had the hand taken off that afternoon, without a thought to the contrary....[50]

Colonel William Francis Bartlett with his wounded left arm in a box sling, taken after his return to Massachusetts in the summer of 1863. Courtesy Berkshire Athenaeum, Pittsfield, MA.

The surgeons continued to worry about the inflammation in Frank's arm. Soldiers were detailed around the clock to sit by Frank's bed, dripping ice, drop by drop, onto his wrist to keep it cool and also keep down the inflammation. Soon though, the surgeons decided that the time had come to operate, and went off for their instruments. When they returned it was growing dark, and though candles were lit to provide light, the colonel asked them to delay until morning so they could do the work by proper light. In the morning, they readied everything, then removed the bandages. After examining the wound, they consulted among themselves and decided that the wound looked a slight bit better. They determined to wait till that afternoon for another look, and when they did, they concurred that it was getting better. This process went on for several days, and Frank's wrist actually did improve. However, his wrist was permanently stiffened and he lost full mobility of some of his fingers.[51]

Frank recovered enough in the opinion of the surgeons that he was allowed to leave Baton Rouge on July 19, via steamer for New Orleans. While waiting here in the hot, humid summer heat, three large pieces of bone came out of his arm. Frank wrote in his journal: "It is the way everything is managed or rather mismanaged in this department, which, if Heaven ever permits me to get out of it alive, shall never be troubled by my presence again." On July 23, Frank boarded the steamer *Matanzas*, arriving in New York on the last day of July. Frank went north to Boston, then to his home in

Winthrop. He first reposed in the home of lawyer J. R. Morewood, and was greeted with a serenade by the Pittsfield Leiderkranz. Though his wound had healed quite well, the colonel was still weak and spent the next month resting and enjoying himself.[52]

Meanwhile, the 49th remained on duty outside Port Hudson, occupying the front line as Banks began regular siege operations to reduce the garrison. The regiment took part in the general assault on June 14, losing an additional eighteen men. After receiving word that Vicksburg had surrendered to General Grant on July 4, Gardner opened negotiations and capitulated to Banks on July 9. The 49th then moved south to Donaldsonville, and went out on an expedition to Bayou La Fourche, where the Yankees encountered a superior Rebel force and had to retreat; the 49th suffered a loss of twenty-four men. The regiment spent the remainder of its term of service performing guard duty near Donaldsonville. On August 1, the 49th moved to Baton Rouge, where Company G rejoined the regiment. The men were then sent to New Orleans, but found that the steamer they were intended to board had already departed, so the 49th was placed aboard another steamer and sent north along the Mississippi to Cairo, Illinois. Here, the regiment boarded a train and headed for Massachusetts via Indianapolis, Cleveland, Buffalo, and Albany.[53]

The 49th's train chugged into the Pittsfield station on Saturday, August 22. By prior arrangements, when news was received that the regiment had arrived at Buffalo, bells were to be rung and cannon fired to announce the imminent arrival of the Berkshire Regiment. Thus, by the time the train pulled into the station, throngs of people had crowded into Pittsfield; a Boston reporter estimated the crowd at twenty thousand or more. Flags and banners of welcome could be seen everywhere. Some businesses and residences sported evergreen arches appropriately festooned with words of welcome.[54]

As the regiment formed at the depot, Colonel Bartlett arrived via a loaned carriage. When he reached his men, Frank was able to remount his war horse Billy, which had been brought along home by his men. Lieutenant Colonel Sumner was also at the depot; he had been sent home after his wound healed sufficiently for travel. Major Plunkett moved the column to North Street, where Frank rode at the head of the regiment, which paraded through several streets to Park Square. Three local bands, three volunteer fire companies, as well as aid societies and other groups, led the men in blue. At the square, Mayor Colt launched into a "welcome home" address, followed by a bountiful picnic feast arranged on tables set up throughout the park. The men were then dismissed, with fireworks later that night. The next several days were spent making out the final muster rolls, with the regiment being mustered out of service on September 1.[55]

8

"I MUST DO THE BEST I CAN"

Into the Wilderness with the 57th Massachusetts

Our citizens will be pleased to learn from a special order published in our advertising columns, that Col. Bartlett, the noble young commander of the 49th Reg., is to recruit a regiment of veteran volunteers in Western Massachusetts, No officer could have been selected who would be more universally acceptable. We look to see the ranks of the veteran volunteers speedily filled.[1]

In brief articles such as the above did Massachusetts citizens learn that Colonel Bartlett, though wounded badly at Port Hudson, had decided to continue his military career by accepting Governor Andrew's proffer of the colonelcy of yet another new regiment. Bartlett was mustered out of service as colonel of the 49th Massachusetts and remustered as colonel of the new 57th Massachusetts Veteran Volunteer Infantry. The 57th was one of four new "veteran volunteer" regiments conceived by Governor Andrew, the idea being to entice discharged veterans to reenlist and thus provide the four new units with men of military experience. When President Lincoln announced a call for an additional 300,000 troops on October 17, Governor Andrew decided to credit these four new regiments as part of his state's quota.[2]

Frank was also tasked with raising the entire regiment. The colonel immediately set to work, sending out announcements and contacting brother officers with whom he was familiar to recruit the ten companies needed to make up the regiment. The original captains of his regiment were as follows, showing their prior military service and age:

Company A, John Sanderson, 13th and 51st Massachusetts, age 32
Company B, Joseph W. Gird, 25th and 35th Massachusetts, age 24

Company C, Charles D. Hollis, 46th Massachusetts, age 39
Company D, Edson T. Dresser, 49th Massachusetts, age 24
Company E, George H. Howe, 46th Massachusetts, age 23
Company F, Levi Lawrence, 25th Massachusetts, age 38
Company G, James Doherty, 1st Massachusetts, age 36
Company H, Julius M. Tucker, 25th and 36th Massachusetts, age 23
Company I, Albert W. Cook, 25th Massachusetts, age 21
Company K, Albert Doty, New York regiment, age 23

Bartlett's second in command, the lieutenant colonel, was Edward P. Hollister, age 27, a Pittsfield resident who had once served in the New Jersey militia in 1861 and then with the 31st Massachusetts. But Hollister resigned his commission after only three months because his wife wanted him at home. His replacement was the 24-year-old Charles L. Chandler, who had served with the 1st and 34th Massachusetts. Major James W. Cushing was 38 years old and had also served with the 31st Massachusetts.[3]

Bartlett selected Worcester as the rendezvous place for his regiment. Just south of town was Camp John E. Wool, a camp with wooden barracks and other associated structures that had been erected in the fall of 1862 by the 51st Massachusetts, which was one of the state's nine-month regiments like Bartlett's old 49th. The camp was a bit run down a year later, though. The barracks had been constructed with green wood that had dried out, leaving spacious cracks through which cold winds could blow. There were no beds, only wooden platforms where beds were supposed to be placed. The wooden buildings smelled musty after being unused for a year.[4]

The pace of recruiting for the 57th went much slower than anyone expected. Two and a half years of war had drained most of the initial enthusiasm of 1861 from the entire recruiting process. The return of several nine-month regiments and the tales the former soldiers told further dampened recruiting efforts. The federal government tried to entice men to sign up with a $300 bounty, to which Massachusetts added a $325 bounty. Several towns also added to the incentive to enlist by offering localized bounties. Still, it was difficult to fill up the ten companies of soldiers. In the end, only 245 veterans enlisted in the 57th; 34 of these men came from the 49th Massachusetts, with many of these enlisting in Company D, led by former 49th officer Edson Dresser.[5]

Frank was not present at Camp Wool until mid–February 1864. He was patient enough not to overtax himself while his arm mended and his overall health improved. In late September 1863, Governor Andrew confided to Frank that Secretary of War Edwin M. Stanton had informed him that he was very pleased with Bartlett's military career and promised that as soon as Frank had raised the 57th, he would received a brigadier general's commission. Frank could only write, "This was very gratifying, of course. I hope he will keep his promise." A month later, Governor Andrew queried Frank to see if the colonel would go to South Carolina and take command of the 40th Massachusetts, which was taking part in the siege operations at Charleston. "He wanted someone to straighten it out," penned Frank. "I told him if I was well enough to take the field now, I would."[6]

But Frank was not yet strong enough. In early January 1864, he noticed that the left side of his face was becoming numb. He consulted a physician who informed Frank that his face had become paralyzed. The doctor confined Frank to his house and also said he should not even read while recuperating with an external treatment that he prescribed. "This is the worst of all," moaned the colonel. "Not that I am proud of my face, for it is not at best a handsome one, but to lose all power of expression or motion on one side, and not be able to laugh or eat without distorting it, is rather hard." Frank left Worcester and returned home for three weeks, his face becoming noticeably better over time. His physicians theorized that his affliction had been caused by sitting near an open window, with cold air flowing over him as he worked near a hot stove.[7]

Frank was certainly in Camp Wool by February 12, when he issued under his own name General Orders Number Six from headquarters of the 57th Massachusetts. From that date forward, drilling became more intense as the Harvard colonel tried his best to shape up the regiment. He issued additional orders to keep the camp as clean as possible to prevent outbreaks of disease. Thanks to the efforts of Bartlett and Lieutenant Colonel Hollister, together with prompt medical attention provided by Surgeon Whitman V. White, there was only one death in camp, a man who died from pneumonia on April 3.[8]

When Frank assumed command of Camp Wool, there were only five companies present; the others were still recruiting. The colonel concentrated his efforts on keeping both the camp and its occupants clean and tidy, and in drilling the recruits so they would become better soldiers. By mid–March, he had created "awkward squads" throughout the regiment, these squads composed of the soldiers who were the slowest to learn, careless, or inattentive to soldiering. These men would receive extra attention to move them along in their learning. The changeable New England weather frequently interfered with drilling, but Frank did the best he could, standing on his one good leg in front of the men, as he had with the 49th, showing them how to perform the manual of arms. By February 22, there were seven companies in camp, and finally, on March 17, Frank formed the entire regiment in line for its first regimental dress parade. Though drilling was proceeding smoothly, the 57th Massachusetts would never achieve the tactical drill perfection achieved by the 20th, a fact that always rankled the Harvard colonel.[9]

On March 28, there were 898 officers and men present in Camp Wool, with only fifty-five in the hospital or otherwise unfit for duty. That same day, Colonel Bartlett was given a fine sword by the citizens of Winthrop. Governor Andrew and his staff came out to the town hall for the ceremony. Also present were Lieutenant Colonel Palfrey of the 20th Massachusetts and Colonel William R. Lee, late of the 44th Massachusetts. Frank was flattered to receive such a fine weapon, and responded with an appropriate speech. The colonel pointed out that his new regiment was taking the field to keep the enemy away from Massachusetts:

> You, in this quiet Northern town, know little of the realities of war. If you should some day see a column of troops file into your broad fields' your hay and grain which you had carefully stowed for the winter vanish in a day; your chicken and pigs and cattle killed before your eyes; a rifle pit perhaps dug through your garden, your choice young fruit and shade trees cut down because they obstructed the view. If coffee, or tea, or flour, or salt, were "worth its weight in gold" or greenbacks, and you had neither gold nor greenbacks to buy it with, you would at least suffer inconvenience and prize more highly the advantage of keeping the war at a distance. And you would see that the bitter fruit which the South is to-day reaping, is but the just reward of treachery and rebellion.

Frank was confident that the 57th would add its full share to help suppress the rebellion. The regiment had enlisted for three years, but Frank hoped that the war would end sooner. However, the regiment would be there till the end, no matter how long it took. There would be no peace, declared the colonel, except an honorable one. "You must out forth every exertion" Frank intoned. "You must spend, if need be, every dollar, and send, if need be, every man. You must follow up the blows which you have already struck with others more telling and more terrible, until you have broken down and punished rebellion and *conquered a victorious peace*."[10]

Then followed the presentation of flags to the new regiment. The first such event took place on April 7, when Frank marched the regiment through the streets of Worcester, accompanied by the police force and the regiment's own drum corps. The men were in full dress uniforms, and after a dress parade on the Common, Miss Frances M. Lincoln, on behalf of the ladies of the town, presented a stand of national colors to the regiment. A week later, Governor Andrew appeared at Camp Wool to present state and national colors to the 57th. After a stirring patriotic speech by the governor, the reporter who witnessed the presentation wrote that Colonel Bartlett replied "with a clarion voice and impassioned utterance that must have fired every heart as he turned to his men" to begin his acceptance speech. He extolled the virtue of the national flag and how the traitorous Southerners would pay in the end for firing on the old flag at Fort Sumter. There were those in the South, Frank said, who were waiting silently for the return of the stars and stripes. "Wherever the flag floats, *all men are free.*"[11]

By the time the regiment received its set of colors from the governor, rumors had begun circulating that the 57th would soon leave Camp Wool. After a large detail of men had cleared the parade ground of the snow from a late storm, Frank had the entire regiment formed in line. A paymaster appeared and paid the men their state bounties, after which the colonel announced that Lieutenant Colonel Hollister had resigned. Then, as a final note, Frank told the men that the regiment would leave for the seat of war in two days.[12]

The next two days were a busy time for the officers and men of the 57th, as they packed up their gear in preparation for the move. There was a raft of desertions as some of the "bounty jumpers" and other shady types tried to evade the guards and leave camp. Throughout its time at Camp Wool, one hundred men attempted to desert; sixty-one of them were successful. On the eighteenth, 916 soldiers boarded a train for a railroad journey to Norwich, Connecticut, where the regiment boarded the steamer *City of Norwich*. The vessel steamed south along the coast to Jersey City, New Jersey, where the men unloaded and again boarded a train to Philadelphia. Here, in the City of Brotherly Love, the men were fed at the Cooper Shop Refreshment Saloon on the afternoon of April 19. Then, after roll call, the regiment marched across the city to a railroad station, taking a train for Baltimore, where they arrived on the twentieth. After stopping for lunch, the men reboarded the train, which chugged east to Annapolis, where the men got off, formed line, and marched to a new campsite.[13]

The 57th Massachusetts Veteran Volunteers was now a part of the Ninth Army Corps. This body of men was under the command of Major General Ambrose E. Burnside, who had organized the regiments that originally formed the corps in 1861. Burnside had led many of its troops to North Carolina, where they successfully attacked and occupied much of coastal North Carolina. Then, Burnside had come north with most of his men in the summer of 1862, when the corps was formed. The corps fought at South Mountain and Antietam, then at Fredericksburg, where Burnside led the Army of the Potomac. When Burnside was sacked as army commander, he and his corps were sent to Kentucky, where Burnside was in command of the Department of the Ohio. Some of the corps participated in the siege operations at Vicksburg and Jackson, Mississippi, then went back to Kentucky and marched to Knoxville, Tennessee, which they successfully defended against a Confederate attack in November 1863. In early 1864, the Ninth Corps was sent back east, rendezvousing at Annapolis, from whence it had left for North Carolina in January 1862. Burnside was back in corps command, his troops intended to act in concert with the Army of the Potomac. But because Burnside outranked Major General George G. Meade, Burnside's corps would act as an independent command.[14]

Bartlett's 57th Massachusetts was assigned to the First Brigade, First Division, Ninth Army Corps. Division commander Brigadier General Thomas G. Stevenson had started the war as colonel of the 24th Massachusetts, then was promoted to brigadier general in April 1863. His brigade participated in the operations at Charleston, where Stevenson contracted malarial fevers. He was home on sick leave when he was reassigned to command Burnside's First Division. Like Frank, General Stevenson was young, only twenty-eight. In command of the First Brigade was Colonel Sumner Carruth of the 35th Massachusetts. In addition to his own unit, Carruth's brigade consisted of the 56th, 57th, and 59th Massachusetts, three of the Bay State's "veteran volunteers" regiments. Two Regular Army units, the 4th and 10th United States, were also assigned to the brigade, but were not yet present in the field. Stevenson's Second Brigade was composed of the 21st Massachusetts, 100th Pennsylvania, and 3rd Maryland, under the command of Colonel Daniel Leasure of the 100th. Two batteries of artillery were also assigned to the division.[15]

The 57th was only in its Annapolis camp until April 23, when reveille sounded at four o'clock in the morning. Officers had already alerted the men that the corps would start for the front on this day, so the men were somewhat prepared. Some of the veteran regiments in the corps had assumed that the Ninth Corps would board transports for the North Carolina coast again, but there were no such ships in the river. After roll call, breakfast, and loading camp equipage into wagons, the corps finally got underway sometime after eight o'clock. Burnside's corps contained four divisions, Stevenson's First, Brigadier General Robert B. Potter's Second, Brigadier General Orlando B. Willcox's Third, and Brigadier General Edward Ferrero's Fourth. An independent brigade, reserve artillery, and four regiments of cavalry rounded out the 25,000-man command. Ferrero's Fourth Division was composed of seven regiments of United States Colored Troops, African American soldiers with white officers.[16]

The corps marched fourteen long miles that first day, heading west from Annapolis along the Bladensburg Road toward Washington. Though the ground was generally level, the novices of the 57th Massachusetts experienced a hot, uncomfortable march with all their new equipment. As the unit marched along, more and more men began discarding unwanted and heavy items from their persons. Veteran units following the First Brigade, which led the entire column, had good pickings as their men retrieved more desirable items such as blankets for themselves. When the halt was made for camp, Colonel Frank Bartlett did everything by the book, forming his regiment in line, had the men stack arms, and march by companies to a nearby creek for water. Veterans in adjacent camps were quickly laughing at the new regiments which did everything by the book. When they heard the new men complaining about the hard march, they continued to laugh. Fourteen miles a hard march?[17]

The corps was on the march again on Sunday, April 24, another hot, sultry day. The troops waded the Patuxent River at a knee-deep ford, another dose of real soldiering for the novice 57th. A late afternoon thunderstorm drenched the marching columns, to the relief of men whose throats were parched and canteens were dry. By the time the troops went into camp that night, they had moved twenty miles.[18]

The next day, the troops were on the move early and stopped for dinner at three o'clock that afternoon, three miles from Washington. The men polished their brass and combed their uniforms, then formed in column and headed into the nation's capital to pass in review before President Lincoln. The 57th was first in line that afternoon, as Colonel Carruth followed the custom of rotating regiments so that each regiment received its turn to march in front of the column. Thousands of spectators lined the streets to cheer the corps as it marched through the city. The men were marching in step with drummers beating the cadence as the corps reached Willard's Hotel. Here on its balcony stood the president and General Burnside. Once the 57th had finished its part in the review, Colonel Bartlett "complimented the regiment very highly for their marching when passing in review after such a hard march as we had today," recorded one of the regiment's writers. The corps continued south across the Potomac on Long Bridge and went into camp near Fort Scott, a part of the capital's line of forts near Alexandria, Virginia.[19]

After a day's rest, the corps was underway early on April 27, heading to Fairfax Court House. The men had been issued forty rounds of ammunition and four days' rations, so they knew they were heading for the front. The day's grueling fifteen-mile march under a hot sun also saw the regiment's first casualty, a man who dropped dead from severe sunstroke. April 28 was a cooler day, and sundown found the corps camped near Bristoe Station, on the Orange & Alexandria Railroad. By nightfall on the thirtieth, the 57th Massachusetts, together with the rest of the corps, pitched their tents near Bealton Station, about four miles north of the Rappahannock River. Across the river lay the camps of the Army of the Potomac, stretching for miles over the hills around Brandy Station. On May 1, the 57th relieved the 20th Maine of the Fifth Corps from guard duty at Rappahannock Station, taking over their wood huts that were found to be filthy from months of occupation.[20]

The 57th was destined to remain for only a brief time in its new camp, for on May 3, orders came to prepare to move early the next morning. General Grant had issued orders for the forward movement of the Army of the Potomac and attached units; Burnside's Ninth Corps would follow in the army's rear and be prepared to act as reinforcements as needed. Colonel

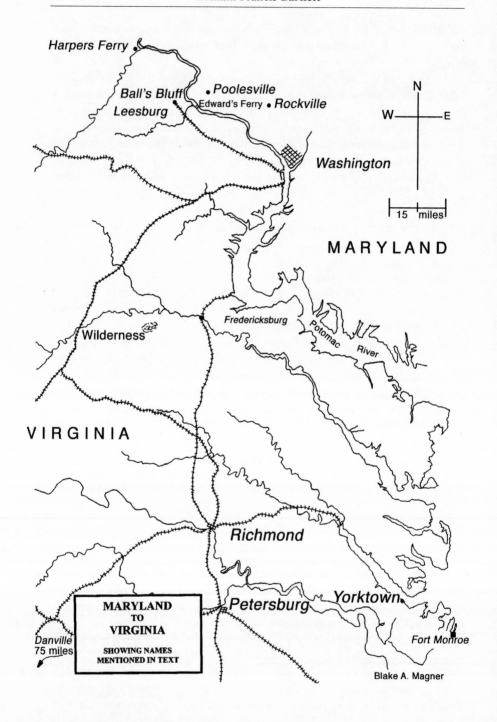

Harpers Ferry

Ball's Bluff
Leesburg
Poolesville
Edward's Ferry • Rockville

N
W——E

15 miles

Washington

MARYLAND

Wilderness
Fredericksburg
Potomac River

VIRGINIA

Richmond

Yorktown

MARYLAND
TO
VIRGINIA

SHOWING NAMES
MENTIONED IN TEXT

Danville
75 miles

Petersburg

Fort Monroe

Blake A. Magner

Bartlett sat down that night in his tent and penned a letter home. "My regiment is in no condition to take into action," he mussed, "but I must do the best I can.... Give me twenty days, and I could make a splendid regiment of this, but man proposes and Grant disposes. Good-by."[21]

Reveille sounded in camp before dawn on May 4. After being issued ammunition and three days' rations, the regiment formed in column and marched six miles to Brandy Station, where the First Division halted shortly after dawn to await further orders. Those orders finally came after a long, slow day of sitting around in the hot sun, when at five o'clock the corps moved off, moving southeast across Mountain Run toward Germanna Ford on the Rapidan River. After dark, a driving rain came down, thoroughly soaking the marching column. Frank suffered immensely during this grueling march. "Hard marching," he wrote in his diary. "Thrown twice. Not hurt. Brier caught in horse's flesh. Marching till four A.M." He failed to note in writing that during the night, the regiment's two wings became separated when the right took the wrong road and became lost. The worn out troops were finally reunited close to dawn. While they made coffee and cleaned their equipment, the 35th Massachusetts was detached from the brigade and sent to Ely's Ford to protect the crossing of the divisional trains.[22]

The Ninth Corps was again moving early on May 5, with Stevenson's First Division in the lead. The men crossed the Rapidan on a wooden pontoon bridge erected by engineer troops, then moved off the road south of the river to cover the crossing of the remainder of the corps. As the men lounged around and watched the other units march by, sounds of battle could be heard off to the south and southeast. Lieutenant Colonel Stephen M. Weld of the 56th Massachusetts "heard cannon and musketry about one o'clock, continuing at intervals during the afternoon." This was the beginning of the two-day engagement known as the Battle of the Wilderness. Grant had hoped to move Meade's troops through this tangled growth of trees and underbrush to more open ground to the south before Lee could react and stop the movement. But Lee quickly had his men moving and elements of both armies began dueling along the region's primitive road system, drawing into action more and more troops.[23]

By nightfall, Stevenson's troops moved about two miles and encamped in open fields of a farm on the west side of the Germanna Plank Road. The two regiments of Regulars had finally caught up with the brigade, bringing Stevenson's effective strength up to about 3,400 officers and men in his two brigades. The men were not destined to catch a lot of sleep that night, for at two o'clock on the morning of May 6, the men were awakened and formed to march. Grant and Meade had decided to bring up Burnside's troops and commit them to battle in the wooded interval between Gouverneur Warren's Fifth Corps and Winfield Hancock's Second Corps, each of which had fought hard the previous day. Grant hoped that Burnside's fresh troops could fall on Confederate General A. P. Hill's left flank and open the way for a successful assault by Hancock's troops westward along the Orange Plank Road. Thus, Burnside brought up his Second and Third Divisions, leaving Stevenson's men as a reserve. Ferrero's Fourth Division was still north of the Rapidan, guarding the army's baggage trains.[24]

Stevenson's men moved along the Germanna Plank Road behind the other two Ninth Corps divisions, then halted near Wilderness Tavern, the headquarters site for both Meade and Grant. The tired and nervous men remained here for two hours as the battle opened in front of them. Wounded were brought back to field hospitals, further unnerving the untried rookies. The noise of the fighting was deafening at times. "It was one continual roll at long intervals broken by the load booming of cannon," penned Weld. Many of Stevenson's men ate breakfast while waiting for orders. Company K of the 57th was detached during this time and sent to the rear to assist the 35th Massachusetts in guarding the division wagon train. While the men waited, the battle ground to a temporary halt. Burnside's two divisions assisted Hancock in driving back A. P. Hill's men at first. However, James Longstreet's First Corps moved up in time to help bring Hancock's attack to a halt. By seven o'clock, after two hours of hard fighting, the battle was stalemated here, so Hancock asked for reinforcements. In response, Grant ordered Stevenson to report to Hancock for assignment in the battle line.[25]

The regiments forming the division quickly moved off to the south along the Germanna Plank Road, edging through crowds of disorganized men in blue, some wounded, some not. When the division reached the intersection with the Brock Road, General Hancock halted Colonel Leasure's brigade and held it in reserve. Colonel Carruth's regiments turned to the right and moved up along the Orange Plank Road, the sound of musketry becoming closer and closer as they marched. Hancock had directed General Stevenson to position Carruth's fresh regiments to the right of Brigadier General Alexander S. Webb's brigade, which was in line north of the Orange Plank Road, facing Hill's Rebels. The regimental color guard led the 57th, moving in front of Colonel Bartlett and the fifers and drummers. Halting briefly to remove and stack their knapsacks and post some guards, the 57th fixed bayonets and moved off through the trees and underbrush to form a line of battle on the right of the 19th Maine of Webb's brigade.[26]

Carruth stacked his brigade in several lines, with the Regulars in the first line, followed by the 56th, 59th, and 57th Massachusetts. They advanced slowly through the thick brush as Webb's line also moved forward. Although General Stevenson outranked General Webb, he apparently deferred to Webb's experience and allowed Webb to control the forward movement. Soon, though, Brigadier General James Wadsworth, whose Fifth Corps division had been repelled and dispersed in the woods, appeared and eventually demanded that he was in command of this sector of the field. As one veteran recalled, there were simply too many generals, all trying to disentangle their troops and reorganize the line. There were troops from the Second, Fifth, Sixth, and Ninth Corps all jumbled together, with generals attempting to provide an overall command and control.[27]

The advancing Federals slammed into A. P. Hill's equally jumbled battle line. Just in front of Carruth were brigades of Florida and Alabama soldiers, who fired at pointblank range as the Yankees advanced. The blue line, already broken by the terrain, now dissolved as men broke into individuals and groups and blazed away at the enemy. As the advance slowed and came to a stop, General Hancock appeared on horseback, ordering Colonel Bartlett to march his regiment to the front over another regiment that was lying prone in front of the 57th, unwilling to advance. "We did it in perfect line," bragged the colonel. Hancock could only remark "Glorious!" as the Bay Staters marched into the maelstrom of combat.[28]

The combat at this point was fierce and deadly. Men on both sides went down at an alarming rate. Smoke obscured everything, but somehow part of the 57th managed to move to within ten feet of Rebel fieldworks before stalling and then falling back a few yards. Color Sergeant Leopold Karpeles mounted a tree stump and waved his silk flag back and forth in an attempt to rally a portion of the regiment. He attracted the attention of General Wadsworth, who joined Karpeles and tried to exhort groups of soldiers from different units to rally on the 57th's colors. In spite of Webb's and Carruth's valiant attack, the Rebels held and managed to force the Yankees to fall back. The attack, which had started sometime after eight o'clock, was over two hours later as the defeated attackers fell back to reorganize.[29]

In the meantime, General Longstreet, perhaps in consultation with General Lee, had devised a plan to attack Hancock's exposed left flank. An unfinished railroad bed allowed Longstreet to send four brigades of troops along it far enough to get beyond Hancock's left. These brigades then faced to the north and attacked sometime after ten o'clock, after Webb's and Carruth's men had fallen back and there was a lull in the fighting. Hancock's front contained fourteen brigades from four different corps. The sudden Rebel attack exploited the difficulties of changing front in the woods, and the Yankee brigades folded like dominos as the Southerners charged forward. While some men actually fled from the attack, other units retired in some semblance of order to regroup farther to the rear.[30]

It did not take long for the troops north of the Orange Plank Road to realize that something was happening to the south. General Wadsworth dispatched General Webb to help rally fugitives, then tried to rally troops to begin an attack on the Confederates in front, who were beginning to advance in conjunction with the flank attack. Wadsworth ordered Colonel George N. Macy to take his 20th Massachusetts and charge the enemy. Macy had his command safely ensconced behind captured Confederate breastworks protected by a ravine in front, so he protested the order. He belonged to Webb's brigade, but Wadsworth prevailed, so Macy reluctantly ordered an attack after Wadsworth himself urged his horse forward to lead the attack. Rebel musket fire decimated the 20th; Colonel Macy went down with a wound, while Major Henry L. Abbott was mortally wounded. Wadsworth's horse became unmanageable and headed toward the enemy. The general was able to turn the animal around, but was hit in the head and fell, mortally wounded, to be captured by the advancing enemy.[31]

By the time the 20th Massachusetts fell back, the entire Union line was dissolving in chaos. Part of Carruth's brigade joined Webb's men in holding off the attacking enemy. Just after taking a sip of water from Sergeant Edwin McFarland's canteen, Colonel Bartlett was hit in the head by a glancing shot that went off his right temple. Stunned, he fell from Billy onto his artificial leg, badly injuring the stump. Members of the regiment placed him back on Billy, his arms around the animal's neck for stability, and led him to the rear as the position collapsed. Lieutenant Colonel Chandler assumed command of the survivors and ordered a retreat before the enemy overran them. Lieutenant Colonel Stephen M. Weld, who had taken command of the 56th Massachusetts after its colonel was killed, spied enemy soldiers moving to their rear, and asked General Webb for permission to retreat. "Get out of there as damned quick as you can!" snapped the general. Webb then ordered his own brigade to "break like partridges through the woods for the Brock Road."[32]

In the end, Hancock rallied the retreating troops, who reformed behind breastworks on the Brock Road and repelled further enemy attacks that threatened to breach the new line. Lieutenant Colonel Chandler gathered thirty-four men of the 57th around Sergeant Karpeles and the colors, which had become tangled in a tree, then had to remain hidden in the brush while the enemy advanced around them. By nightfall, the shattered remnant of the 57th Massachusetts rallied with the rest of the brigade, now under the command of Lieutenant Colonel Weld—Colonel Carruth had been felled by sunstroke and carried off the field. Of the 548 officers and men taken into action, 54 were killed outright, 29 were mortally wounded, 136 wounded, 10 were missing, and 32 captured (20 of these were wounded), for a total of 262. Only five regiments in the entire army suffered a greater casualty total.[33]

While Frank was being taken to the rear, he encountered a stretcher party taking Colonel Macy off the field. The two former captains briefly exchanged news before being taken to hospitals. "Lay there among the wounded and dying till night," Frank wrote, "when there was a falling back, and I was put in an ambulance; ... knocked about all night. I slept a good deal. Morning, lay under some trees near the road to Chancellorsville." That afternoon, Frank was "persuaded" to go on to Ely's Ford, from whence he was moved to Chancellorsville on May 8. While here, Frank was able to locate Macy's ambulance and visited for a while, hearing the sad news of Major Abbott's death. On May 9, Bartlett arrived in Fredericksburg and was moved into a brick house. "My head not bad," he recorded. "Stump painful. A week or two will set me right again." On the eleventh, the colonel started in an ambulance for Belle Plain, where he boarded a transport late in the afternoon. By eleven that night, Frank was in Washington.[34]

Frank remained in Washington for only a single day, but he had the opportunity for a bath and slept in a real bed. He also wrote a letter to his mother, giving her details on his wounding. If it hadn't been for the fall onto his artificial leg, which hurt his stump, Frank wrote that he would have remained with the army, but the fall had prohibited him from wearing the artificial leg. Frank then left Washington and went via Baltimore to New York, where he met his parents. "Cheers when I entered the hotel. Great excitement."[35]

Frank had a medical leave for twenty days when he left for Massachusetts. On May 19, he headed off to Boston, where Governor Andrew undoubtedly informed Frank of his efforts to have him promoted to brigadier general. Andrew had started his efforts that spring when Secretary of War Stanton had promised to have Frank promoted should he succeed in raising a regiment. On April 25, Andrew had written to General Burnside, asking him to write to Stanton in support of Frank's promotion. On May 6, Andrew wrote again to Stanton, reminding him of the earlier promise and asking him to fulfill that promise. As an aside, Andrew wrote that Colonel Bartlett had "peculiar courage and self-possession in action." He was a "young man of fine powers, conspicuous for general mental capacity and of superior culture. He is a graduate of Harvard College." While Frank was in Boston, the governor also sought the support of Henry Wilson, the powerful Republican senator from the Bay State. Finally, on May 30, Governor Andrew again wrote to Stanton, informing him that Bartlett was now healed and ready to rejoin his regiment. Now was the time to promote him.[36]

Frank arrived in Washington on June 3 at the expiration of his medical leave. The next day, he had a brief interview with Secretary Stanton, who "spoke kindly" and assured Bartlett that he had sent the colonel's papers to Major General Henry W. Halleck, General Grant's chief of staff. "I expect that will be the last of it," quipped Frank, expecting to have his nomination buried in red tape and never acted upon.[37]

By the time Frank reached Baltimore on June 11, he had received a letter from his father, who inquired about a letter published under Frank's name in the *Boston Post*. Mystified, the colonel did some investigating and found that the *Springfield Republican* had originated the letter, which was copied by other papers. Whoever wrote the letter signed Frank's name to it. The missive "was a vainglorious, poor affair, full of fulsome praise of the Fifty-seventh Regiment, and of disparaging contrast between it and the other regiments of the Division, and utterly unlike Bartlett in every respect." When Frank read this letter, he was furious. "It is disgraceful, and I will give a month's pay to find out who wrote it. If it was any man or officer of my regiment, I *pity him*." A few days later, the *Post* printed an actual submission by the colonel, who denounced the earlier letter as an "absolute forgery."[38]

Frank had expected to go back to the army, but on Sunday, June 14, as he was getting out of a carriage after church, he was struck by a mysterious pain. While at dinner later in the day, the pain again came and was so severe that he had to interrupt his meal. "I came very near tipping over," he wrote. "I never was so faint before, simply from pain. I was alarmed, as that was a new spot for me to have pain, and I could not account for it. I took off my leg, and in ten minutes the pain had almost entirely gone." A physician who examined Frank theorized that his artificial leg must have pressed on and strained a nerve. He had a couple of additional pains since then, and was advised to use his leg a bit more moderately.[39]

Because of his recent pain, Frank visited Major General Christopher C. Augur, commander of the Department of Washington, and got his pass extended ten days. Augur told Frank that he had heard nothing about his promotion, causing Frank to remark that he would go to the front "in disgust" before his pass was up if he discovered that there was no interest in his nomination. However, there was no need to worry. Late on June 20, Frank's name came up in the Senate and the vote was overwhelming to confirm him as brigadier general. "Thank God!" exalted the new general. He went off to Baltimore and returned to Washington to receive his commission on June 28. He learned that he would be assigned to the Ninth Corps. He was still worried, though, about his health. "My stump gets smaller every day," he wrote. Frank resorted to filling up the space between his flesh and the artificial leg with wads of paper and layers of leather. Before going off to the front, he received a leave and went home to Winthrop and Pittsfield before returning to Washington on July 17, just after General Jubal A. Early's Confederate force had withdrawn to the Shenandoah Valley. After penning a few letters and visiting friends, the new general was ready to depart for Petersburg.[40]

9

"DANGER OF BEING HIT ANY MINUTE"

The Siege of Petersburg

With his new shoulder straps reflecting his new appointment as brigadier general, Frank Bartlett left Washington on July 19 by steamer and arrived at City Point, the main supply depot for the armies operating against Richmond and Petersburg. Upon arrival, he reported directly to Ninth Corps headquarters. General Burnside, happy to see Bartlett, immediately queried army headquarters to ask for an adjutant general for Bartlett's staff. In turn, General Seth Williams, adjutant general of the Army of the Potomac, reminded Burnside that Bartlett should first report to army headquarters for assignment. The new general went through this correct chain of command, and on July 22, Special Orders Number 195 from the Army of the Potomac officially assigned him to duty with the Ninth Corps.[1]

Burnside assigned Bartlett to the First Division of the corps. Frank found numerous changes had taken place in the preceding two months of hard service, during which the division had fought at Spotsylvania, North Anna, Cold Harbor, and Petersburg. General Stevenson had been killed at Spotsylvania. His successor, Thomas L. Crittenden, asked to be relieved and was reassigned on June 9. The current commander, James H. Ledlie, then was assigned to division command.[2]

When Frank arrived at Ninth Corps headquarters, Burnside assigned him to Ledlie's First Division as commander of the First Brigade. Bartlett's opportune arrival at the front in mid–July brought hope to the remnant of the First Brigade that the new brigadier might even replace Ledlie as division commander. New Yorker Ledlie had begun the war as major of the 19th New York, which later that year was transformed into the 3rd New York Artillery with Ledlie as its colonel. The regiment served in North Carolina, and although Ledlie's performance was average at best, he managed to secure promotion to brigadier general in December 1862. However, the Senate failed to act on the recommendation and Ledlie did not receive his star until October 1863. He was in charge of a district in North Carolina until assigned to the Ninth Corps during the fighting at Spotsylvania. Anxious to gain a reputation as a great general, Ledlie sent his brigade forward on May 24 at the North Anna River against Crittenden's orders and it was bloodily repulsed. That day, Ledlie himself was drunk and was of no account on the battlefield.[3]

On June 17, Ledlie's division assailed the Petersburg defenses, initially seizing some prisoners and cannon before running out of ammunition and being forced to retreat by a Rebel counterattack. Ledlie was nowhere to be seen. He failed to lead his troops into battle or to maintain any sense of command and control. Colonel Jacob P. Gould of the 59th Massachusetts, the senior colonel then present, led the attack. Ledlie was found later behind the lines, asleep on the ground in another drunken stupor. Wrote Gould years later, "If I had been older or had more sense, I should have preferred charges against him."[4]

Repelled by the Confederates, Ledlie's survivors attacked again on June 18 as part of a larger effort, and again seized the enemy positions they had briefly carried on the seventeenth. The Rebels fell back perhaps a mile into a new line of defenses; further Union assaults later in the day failed to drive them out. Weary now to the point of exhaustion, both armies faced each other and dug in, creating elaborate systems of forts and trenches. This was the general situation when Frank arrived at the front army in July.

When Bartlett rejoined the Ninth Corps, the First Division had just been reorganized into two brigades. Bartlett's First Brigade included the 21st, 29th, 56th, 57th, and 59th Massachusetts regiments, and the 100th Pennsylvania. The Second Brigade was led by Colonel Elisha G. Marshall and consisted of the 3rd Maryland, 179th New York, 14th New York Heavy Artillery, and the 2nd Pennsylvania Provisional Heavy Artillery. The 35th Massachusetts of the First Brigade was serving on detached duty as acting engineers for the division.[5]

Bartlett's new command was but a shadow of its former self, with perhaps 1,300 men in its seven regiments. The brigade had suffered heavy losses since the fighting had begun in the Wilderness back in early May. His own regiment, the 57th Massachusetts reflected the horrendous casualties associated with Grant's campaign thus far. When the regiment entered the Wilderness, it took 548 officers and men into battle. Now, by late July, less than 100 men were still with the colors.[6]

Frank quickly found himself in daily jeopardy as he went to the front and assumed formal command of the brigade on July 23. Along the front of the Ninth Corps, the two opposing trench lines were closer than in most places along the entire front, with the distance at Pegram's Salient only 125 yards. As a result, the pickets kept up a constant firing all day long and on into the night hours. "Steady firing all the time," wrote Bartlett on July 21. "Headquarters under shell and bullets. Danger of being hit any minute, asleep or awake. I expect I shall get killed as soon as I go down to the lines." The very next day was no different. "As I write, a bullet strikes the tree near the tent. Another goes humming a few feet over. People at home do not appreciate what this army is doing and suffering for them," he wrote.[7]

Along other sections of the siege lines, the pickets generally fired much less and usually gave each other a signal before they opened

The 57th Massachusetts Veteran Volunteers received this national color shortly before the Battle of the Crater in July 1864. During the fighting that day, this flag was captured by a lieutenant in the 61st Virginia. It was returned to Massachusetts in 1905 when all captured flags were returned to their states. Courtesy Commonwealth of Massachusetts, Art Commission.

fire, as much illegal trading went on when the officers were not looking. A Mississippi private in Brigadier General William Mahone's Division described his situation in a letter to his sister:

> The sight of hundreds of Yankees is a common sight. There is hardly a minute in the day or night without a cannon is firing on the line somewhere. The lines are as near as two hundred yards in some places. In our front, they are one thousand yards apart. They are on one side of a field, and we are on the other. We go on picket duty every seventh day. When we stand picket, our skirmishers are one hundred fifty yards on their battle line and one hundred yards from their sharpshooters. Firing has been agreed to by all parties as a senseless waste of ammunition, and we boldly stand and look each other in the face from daylight until night, then listen for each other to advance. We read each others papers in fifteen minutes after the newsboys bring them up from the offices.[8]

But the Ninth Corps pickets were always in danger from their counterparts because of the close proximity of the trench lines. The Confederates maintained a steady rate of fire along most of the Ninth Corps front. As a result, most Ninth Corps regiments suffered a steady attrition rate in late June and July. The 51st Pennsylvania, assigned to Brigadier General Orlando B. Willcox's Third Division, remained at the front for twenty-six straight days until relieved for a day's rest after dark on July 16. Colonel William J. Bolton recorded that the regiment had at least six men killed and five wounded during this time span. His men also expended 171,000 rounds of ammunition. From June 20 through July 30, the entire Ninth Corps lost 1,150 officers and men as a result of the constant musketry and artillery firing.[9]

July 23 was Frank's first day as brigade commander. "Quiet day," he noted in his daily journal. His men were deployed in two lines of battle, each one entrenched and a hundred yards apart. Brigade headquarters was 250 yards behind the second line, with Ledlie's headquarters another 200 yards to the rear. Headquarters tents and bombproofs were protected by wooden stockades to prevent the fusillade of bullets from interfering too much with daily duty. In a letter to his mother written that evening, Bartlett described his surroundings:

> ... We are in pine woods, the trees not very thick. The Headquarters have to be protected by a stockade of logs against bullets, which are constantly coming through here. Four officers of the Fifty-seventh have been hit since I got here, one killed, three very badly wounded, in the second line. Our stockade does not protect us against shells, which fall in front and rear of us, but have not hit the Headquarters yet. Some fall way in the rear of Division Headquarters, and some near Corps Headquarters, which are about one fourth of a mile in rear of Division. We have a stockade to protect the horses, too, but one of the orderlies' horses and one of General Ledlie's were killed the other day. A bullet goes whizzing over my tent every few minutes as I write, and goes thud into one of the trees near, with a sound that makes you think what a headache that would have given you if your head had been where the tree was. The bullets patter like rain at times against the outside of this stockade of logs, the inside of which my elbow touches as I write. It is a continual rattle of musketry, sometimes swelling into a roar along the line, and varied with the artillery and mortars. So you see we are liable at any moment to be struck, even while reading a paper or eating dinner. A bullet went through Dr. Anderson's table as he was eating breakfast this morning. You must be prepared to hear the worst of me at any time. God grant it may not come, for your sake, and for the sake of all I love and who love me at home. But you must *be prepared for it*. It is wearing to body and mind this being constantly under fire. People at the North who are enjoying themselves and thinking of nothing but making money, little appreciate what this brave army is enduring every day and hour for them, and how much more cheerful and hopeful they are than people at home. I wish some of the patriotic (?) ones at home who are making speeches (and money), would just come out here and spend a week, even back here at my Headquarters. The would not care to go down to the lines

where the men are day and night fighting for their security and safety.[10]

Frank went on writing, indicating that he counted eighty-one bullets in the next minute. To enliven his men's spirits, Frank wrote that he ordered the brigade band to play at intervals throughout the day. "The rebs have the benefit of it a much as I do, but I can't help it," he said. "They favor us with a band sometimes. Tell the Nut and Miss Barnett that they just played 'When Johnny Comes Marching Home' and "Faust."" Two more bullets slammed into a nearby tree as Bartlett neared the end of his letter. "How should you like to lie down and go to sleep with this going on all night? I expect to sleep soundly. I have for two nights."[11]

On July 26, starting at eight o'clock in the morning, Bartlett was detailed as general of the trenches for the next twenty-four hours. In brief, this assignment meant that the general had to inspect the trench system occupied by units of the Ninth Corps, make sure everything was in order, and correct any problems. Bartlett's report indicates how he spent the time:

> Hdqrs. First Brig., First Div., Ninth Army Corps
> Before Petersburg, July 27, 1864.
>
> Lieut. Col. Lewis Richmond,
>
> Assistant Adjutant-General:
>
> Colonel: I have the honor to report as general of the trenches for the twenty-four hours ending at 8 A.M. to-day as follows: In the lines of the First Division the policing is very thoroughly done. The work of widening the pits and constructing bombproofs is begun. The enemy's mortar shells for the past two days fallen inside the second line principally; nearer than heretofore to brigade headquarters. In the Second Division the work of widening the pits and constructing bombproofs has been begun; the abatis on the left of the railroad cut being strengthened. Too little attention is paid to the fact that there are sinks for the use of officers and men. In some parts of this line the interior slope is too high for the men to fire over it; directed the tread of the banquette to be raised. The officer of the day of the Third Division reports "the firing was kept up briskly all night, except when rockets were thrown up by the enemy, when they would cease firing for the space of fifteen or twenty minutes. These rockets were thrown up at four different times during the night." He also invites attention to the indiscreet practice of a battery in rear of Roemer's, which almost daily drops shells into our works.
>
> I remain, colonel, very respectfully, your obedient servant,
>
> W. F. Bartlett, Brig. Gen., Comdg.,
> First Brig., First Div.,
> Ninth Army Corps.[12]

In summary, Bartlett commented on the progress of widening rifle pits, constructing bombproofs (reinforced shelters for the troops to take cover in during bombardments), and strengthening the abatis (felled trees with sharpened branches to delay an enemy attack). He instructed some troops to rectify the firing steps in the trenches to ensure ease of fire. The general also noticed, with proper Victorian prose, that the latrines (sinks) were not being used as they should be. Another officer reported that the enemy was firing rockets into the sky at night and that one of the Union batteries in the rear often dropped its shells on friendly troops.

Also on July 26 the brigade was reviewed by General Ledlie. "Did not make a very good appearance. Officers, even of old regiments, ignorant ....," penned Bartlett. He continued in his diary, "Shells burst all around these Headquarters in a very disagreeable way. I pray hourly that I may be spared."[13]

The morning of July 27 brought an order from General Burnside to have all troops not in the front line ready to move at a moment's notice. Burnside's order was prompted by a brief note from General Meade, advising his corps commanders that the enemy might attempt to attack the army's left flank. Therefore, the general wished his subordinates to have a reserve force ready to march to any threatened point in the line.[14]

The reason for Meade's worries over his left flank stemmed from events that had been placed in motion on July 26. That evening, Major General Winfield S. Hancock's Second Army Corps quietly vacated its section of the

siege line on the Union right flank and headed north, crossing the Appomattox River behind the lines of the Army of the James at Bermuda Hundred. Accompanied by two of Major General Phil Sheridan's cavalry divisions as well as the Cavalry Division, Army of the James, Hancock's objective was to cross the James River via the pontoon bridges at Deep Bottom and head toward Richmond's defenses. In Washington, authorities were panicked over General Jubal Early's recent attack on the city's

Bartlett wore this regulation forage cap after being promoted to brigadier general; his new rank was evidenced by the single star on its crown. This cap was manufactured by the Washington, D.C., firm of Shute & Sons. Courtesy Berkshire Museum, Pittsfield, MA.

defenses. Even though reinforcements had been sent, Grant, under pressure to do something, felt that a thrust toward Richmond would both prevent more troops from joining Early and possibly force Lee to recall Early to Petersburg. Hancock's movement north of the James might also influence Lee to send troops from the Petersburg lines to confront the Yankee attack. If Lee did this, Burnside's plan for attacking Petersburg after the explosion of a mine under a Confederate fort might well succeed.[15]

Bartlett's First Brigade was in the second line on July 27 and was thus subject to the readiness order from Burnside. In a letter written sometime that day, Bartlett again commented on the incessant shelling and musketry that kept him and his men on their toes. Thus, when word came to be ready to move, he wrote, "I shouldn't be very sorry to leave this place." When Bartlett rejoined the army, rumors were flying that General Ledlie had tendered his resignation. Colonel Stephen M. Weld of the 56th Massachusetts sincerely hoped the Bartlett's opportune arrival might spell the end of Ledlie's command. Bartlett himself, in his July 27 missive, confirmed these rumors and was seemingly touched by the hopes that he would become the new division commander, "but I think I had rather try a brigade before I venture any higher...."[16]

The troops remained on alert during the next day, July 28. Friday, July 29, was destined to be another warm summer day in Virginia. As General Bartlett waited in his headquarters for additional orders, he received a summons to appear at division headquarters. "We storm the works tomorrow at daylight," he wrote. "Our Division leads. I hardly dare to hope to live through it. God have mercy.... If I could only ride, or had two legs, so I could *lead* my brigade, I believe they would follow me anywhere. I will try as it is. God have pity on dear mother, Agnes, and all loved ones."[17]

The meeting at division headquarters confirmed all the rumors that Bartlett and others in the Ninth Corps had heard about a supposed mine being tunneled under the Rebel entrenchments. Now, Frank Bartlett was about to play a key role in one of the most colorful — and tragic — episodes of the Civil War.

10

"IT WAS PANDEMONIUM LET LOOSE"

The Crater

The origin of the idea to undermine and blow up a portion of the Confederate trenches began shortly after the failed Union attacks on the Petersburg defenses on June 18. Brigadier General Robert B. Potter's Second Division of the Ninth Corps had assailed the enemy lines by crossing Taylor's Creek and charging uphill into the new Southern line of defenses. When the Yankees were repelled, they retreated perhaps a hundred yards at the closest point and began digging in themselves. By morning on June 19, both sides were feverishly entrenching. Burnside's corps occupied the central part of the Union siege lines, with Major General Gouverneur K. Warren's Fifth Corps on its left and the Second Corps, temporarily under the command of David B. Birney, on its right.

After surveying the terrain in his division's front, General Potter suggested to Burnside that the Confederate fort opposite his front, only 125 yards away, could be approached by means of a sap — digging a zig-zag trench protected by portable defensive measures such as gabions — and then successfully assaulted. There is no record of any reply that Burnside might have made to Potter's proposal.[1]

On June 24, Lieutenant Colonel Henry Pleasants came to Potter and made an even stronger suggestion on how to eliminate the menacing Rebel earthwork — undermine it and blow it up. Pleasants was temporarily in command of the First Brigade of Potter's division. His regiment was the 48th Pennsylvania, composed entirely of men recruited in Schuylkill County, located in the southern edge of the state's anthracite coal region. In civilian life, Pleasants was a mining engineer very familiar with tunnels and coal mining. Approximately one hundred officers and men in the 48th were coal miners; one of them had suggested to the colonel that a mine could be run under the Rebel lines.[2]

General Potter liked the mine proposal and forwarded the idea to General Burnside with his endorsement of it. Burnside then asked both officers to come to headquarters and provide more details. Burnside liked the plan and told Pleasants to go ahead with the mine. Thus, at noon on June 25, the colonel assembled his initial team and started a tunnel in a ravine a hundred feet behind the Union entrenchments. The colonel recalled that the biggest problem he initially encountered was how to dispose of the excavated dirt. Confederate soldiers perched in trees behind the lines might spy the fresh earth and report on the suspicious activity. Pleasants detailed men of his regiment to cut bushes and cover up the piles of earth to avoid it being spotted by the enemy.[3]

As the work started, Burnside went to army headquarters to inform Meade of it. The general scoffed at the plan, as did his chief engineer, Major James C. Duane. According to Pleasants, Burnside was told that the mine idea was "all clap-trap and nonsense." No tunnel that length had ever been dug; if it was, the men would suffocate or else the roof would cave in. Even if either of those fates did not occur, the enemy would find out and ruin the plan. Meade informed Burnside that in spite of such reservations, he would pass the idea along to General Grant; in the meantime, said Meade, he would not object to the work.[4]

And indeed the work continued. To conserve timber, the tunnel was kept smaller than normal. It was four feet wide at the base, tapering to two feet at the top, and around four and a half feet in height. Pleasants placed Sergeant Henry Reese in charge of the actual digging. The 29-year-old Welshman was an experienced miner and pushed the work day and night. His men worked three hour shifts to keep the diggers as fresh as possible.[5]

Since Meade and Duane failed to endorse the project, Pleasants was on his own as far as any help was concerned. In January 1865, he recounted the major difficulties he faced:

> ... I had to remove all the earth in old cracker boxes. I got pieces of hickory and nailed on the boxes in which we received our crackers, and then iron-claded them with hoops of iron taken from old pork and beef barrels.... The most important thing was to ascertain how far I had to mine, because if I fell short of or went beyond the proper place the explosion would have no practical effect; therefore I wanted an accurate instrument with which to make the necessary triangulations. I had to make them on the furthest front line, where the enemy's sharpshooters could reach me. I could not get the instrument I wanted, although there was one at army headquarters, and General Burnside had to send to Washington and get an old-fashioned theodolite, which was given to me.
>
> ... I could get no boards and lumber supplied to me for my operations. I had to get a pass and send two companies of my own regiment

with wagons outside of our lines to rebel saw-mills and get lumber in
that way, after having previously got what lumber I could by tearing
down an old bridge. I had no mining picks furnished me, but had to
take common army picks and have them straightened for my mining
picks.[6]

At first the tunnel went smoothly, fifty feet the first day and forty feet
each the second and third days. Then the miners struck some hard clay that
slowed them down. While working through the clay, the miners hit a vein of
marl that threatened the integrity of the tunnel. Marl is soft and slippery, and
it caused the roof to sag until reinforced with more timber. Pleasants ordered
a slight incline to the tunnel and within a hundred feet the miners cleared
the marl, when the tunnel was again straightened and the besmeared men in
blue continued to delve into the red clay.[7]

The summer of 1864 was one of the hottest and driest on record in southern Virginia. The stifling heat and dryness added to the time it took to dig
underground, made all the longer by the increasing distance the men had to
go to dump the excavated earth behind the lines. To provide ventilation for
the miners, Pleasants bored a shaft to the surface from roughly a hundred feet
into the mine, surfacing just behind the Union trenches. At the base of the
shaft was a small furnace which was always kept lighted. Between this furnace and the tunnel entrance Pleasants erected a burlap partition, which forced
the fire to draw oxygen from the tunnel. As the men dug, Pleasants had a
wooden duct, eight inches square, built along the floor. As the furnace drew
air from the mine, it created a draft that started outside in the fresh air, which
it drew into the tunnel via the wooden shaft, all the way to the current day's
progress deep inside, then back down the tunnel and up the air shaft.[8]

On July 17, the tunnel reached a length of just over 510 feet, placing it
squarely under the Confederate fort as Pleasants triangulated the distance. But
at almost the same time the colonel was warned that the Rebels had found
out about the tunnel. Three deserters had come into the Union lines and during their interrogation revealed that their officers knew something was going
on. In fact, Colonel Edward Porter Alexander, one of Lee's artillery officers,
had feared for the safety of the salient fort that Pleasants was digging underneath. Alexander had placed a request for hand grenades to be stockpiled in
the fort, to be used on the enemy when their trenches came close enough;
Alexander believed that the Yankees would use sap rollers (cylindrical baskets
stuffed with tree branches) to move forward toward the Confederates, keeping themselves protected by the rollers as they came within range of the fort
to make a successful attack. On June 30, Alexander visited the fort, to see
that no rollers were visible. The colonel suddenly realized that the Yankees
must be tunneling underground and that the heavy daily firing along the
Ninth Corps front was meant to cover the digging.[9]

While en route to the rear, Alexander was struck in the shoulder by a bullet and hurt badly enough to warrant a furlough. On July 1, before going home, he stopped at Lee's headquarters to advise the general of his concerns about the Yankee tunnel. Lee was absent, but Alexander reported to Colonel Charles Venable, one of Lee's senior staff officers. Francis Lawley, correspondent for the *London Times*, overheard Alexander's report and scoffed at the likelihood of such a tunnel. None over four hundred feet had ever been dug, he asserted, for a longer tunnel could not be properly ventilated. But Alexander answered the Englishman that there were Pennsylvania coal miners in the Union army who were used to such mining and could indeed produce a lengthy tunnel.[10]

General Lee, according to Alexander, only half believed the colonel's report. But he did issue an order for countermining to begin. Vertical shafts were dug into the ground at each end of the fort, with the intention to link them together in hopes of detecting the Yankee mining operation. Tunnels were constructed to the left and right of each shaft, and the crew chief used an auger to drill into the walls of the tunnels in an effort to either break through into the Yankee tunnel or perhaps pick up the noise associated with digging. But the Rebel tunnels were only ten feet underground; it has been estimated that Pleasants' men were perhaps twenty feet under the surface as they finished their excavation.[11]

Having ascertained that there was little danger from the Rebel activities on the surface, Pleasants gave the go ahead for the construction of two lateral galleries, which branched out to the left and right at the end of the main tunnel. The left gallery was thirty-seven feet long, while the right was a foot longer. Each lateral gallery had four magazine rooms, two on each side, where the powder for the explosion was to be packed. To ensure secrecy, Pleasants had all the timber for the galleries and magazines pre-cut and fitted outside the mine, then taken in and assembled by hand, without the use of hammers. The right gallery curved a bit because the colonel heard hammering noise from above and curved the tunnel around the source. These galleries were finished on the evening of July 23.[12]

General Potter promptly informed Burnside that the mine was finished and could be stocked with powder at any time. Since the miners had found several underground springs while constructing the lateral galleries, and had to drain them off, Potter also wrote that the mine should be used as soon as possible before it got too wet for powder or the Confederates located the mine with their countermining operations.

As the mine was being finished, the Union high command was already at work on ideas for offensive operations. On July 23, General Meade made a personal inspection of the Ninth Corps front and the opposing Rebel positions. Meade was worried about a second enemy line on the ridge behind the main line. If there was such a line, and from his reconnaissance, Meade was sure that there was, he reported to Grant that even if the mine was success-fully exploded and the first line occupied, artillery batteries on the second line would dominate the lower ridge in front and jeopardize any attack. Three days later (July 26), Meade examined the enemy line from atop a new signal tower and realized that the enemy had no continuous line on the second ridge, only disconnected batteries. Thus, a successful attack appeared likely.[13]

In the midst of Meade's actions, Grant, on July 25, ordered Meade to go ahead and have the mine charged with explosives. Grant left the time of the explosion up to Meade, but advised Meade that the Deep Bottom expe-dition might weaken the enemy line and make an attack possible. Also, warned Grant, be sure to do it soon after placing the powder.[14]

Once Meade's examination of the Rebel lines were completed and Grant nodded his approval, at 7:45 P.M. on July 26 he sent a note to Burnside, directing him to immediately prepare the mine for explosion. General Henry J. Hunt, commanding the artillery of the Army of the Potomac, would send four tons of black powder to the Ninth Corps front, together with the nec-essary length of fuse. The powder arrived in 25-pound kegs. Each keg was placed in a sack, which a soldier slung over his shoulder and carried to the mine. Then each keg was very carefully taken into one of the eight maga-zines. Pleasants recalled that it took six hours — from four to ten o'clock in the afternoon and evening of July 27 — to completely place the powder kegs. The colonel had wooden troughs laid to connect the mines, half-filled the troughs with powder, then attached fuses to connect all the magazines via the troughs. Pleasants was disappointed that the fuse sent up from Fort Monroe was common blasting fuse, in shorter lengths than desired, which had to be spliced together. And once the powder was in place, Pleasants' men took into the mine perhaps 8,000 sandbags and logs to tamp the mine to ensure that the force of the explosion went up instead of down the tunnel. Ten feet in each lateral gallery was tamped, along with thirty-four feet of the main tun-nel. This backbreaking work took twenty hours to complete; it was finished at 6:00 P.M. on July 28. Pleasants ran three parallel fuses out from the tamp-ing to ensure that at least one of them lit properly and would not burn out along the way at a splice.[15]

While the mine was being finished the generals decided what to do. On July 26, Meade asked Burnside to put in writing any plans he had for an assault once the mine was exploded. In reply, Burnside stated that it would be best, in his opinion, to explode the mine just before daylight or perhaps late in the afternoon. His Fourth Division, composed of United States Col-ored Troops, would then lead the attack. Its two brigades would advance on each side of the crater, the leading regiment in each brigade turning to sweep down the enemy lines to clear away any opposing troops. Meanwhile, the bulk of the division would continue on and occupy the crest of the ridge (called Cemetery Hill by Union commanders) behind the Rebel line. Burnside's other three divisions would attack in turn, reinforcing the African American soldiers and extending the breakthrough.[16]

General Burnside had a very good reason in wanting to use the African American troops to spearhead the assault. His three divisions of white soldiers — those of James Ledlie, Robert B. Potter, and Orlando B. Willcox — were worn down from the constant exposure to enemy fire in the trenches. They had suffered heavy losses during the recent campaign from the Wilderness to Petersburg. Brigadier General Edward Ferrero's Fourth Division, on the other hand, was relatively fresh. During the campaign, it had been detached from the corps much of the time and used to guard the army's supply trains and perform menial labor rather than be used in combat, a reflection of the belief of many general officers that black soldiers were not equal to whites on the battlefield. Burnside had already issued orders to Ferrero that the regiments comprising his division were to start training for just such an assault. Thus, when the mine was ready, Ferrero's inexperienced but eager soldiers were more than ready to show how well they could fight.[17]

Once Burnside was informed that the mine was ready, he rode back to General Meade's headquarters to report the situation. The Ninth Corps commander was very surprised when Meade informed him that he did not approve of placing Ferrero's troops in the first wave of the planned attack. Furthermore, "he did not approve of the formation proposed, because he was satisfied that we would not be able, in the face of the enemy, to make the movements which I contemplated, to the right and left; and that he was of the opinion that the troops should move directly to the crest without attempting these side movements."

Then followed an animated discussion, during which Burnside told Meade about the deteriorated condition of the white troops and insisted that the black soldiers take the lead. But Meade still objected. The black soldiers were still essentially without combat experience, a requirement of such a bold plan. Still, Meade informed Burnside that he had planned a visit to General Grant's headquarters, and would bring the matter to the general-in-chief for his opinion. Burnside left after telling Meade that he would "cheerfully" abide by any decision his superiors would make.[18]

Meade probably informed Burnside at this time that the attack would commence at dawn on July 30. At noon on July 28, Meade had sent a dispatch to Grant, informing him that July 30 was the earliest that the mine could be exploded, since troops would have to be moved into position and other arrangements readied. An hour later, after hearing from Grant, Meade proposed that the mine be exploded at daylight on the thirtieth. Hereafter, the exact chronology of the order to attack on July 30 remains murky because of the lack of existing documents in the *Official Records*. In all probability, when Burnside visited Meade's headquarters to announce that the mine was ready, Meade and Grant had already decided on the July 30 date, and thus Meade would have informed Burnside at this time.[19]

The timing of events on July 29 is also confused. At 10:15 that morning, Meade's chief of staff, Major General Andrew A. Humphreys, sent the following to Burnside:

> I am instructed to say that the major-general commanding submitted
> to the lieutenant-general commanding the armies your proposition to
> form the leading columns of assault of the black troops, and that he,
> as well as the major-general commanding, does not approve the
> proposition, but directs that those columns be formed of the white
> troops.[20]

Burnside had not received this dispatch when he called two of his white division commanders — Robert Potter and Orlando Willcox — to headquarters to discuss the upcoming attack. According to Willcox, the call to headquarters was the first time that Burnside announced the general plan of attack for the next day. At this stage, Burnside assumed that his plan — to have Ferrero's division lead the attack — was still functional, as he had not heard from Meade regarding his inclination to have a white division lead the charge. Burnside candidly informed his two subordinates of Meade's wish to use one of their divisions to spearhead the attack.[21]

While Burnside and his two division commanders were discussing the plan, Meade, accompanied by some of his staff officers and Major General Edward O. C. Ord, commander of the Eighteenth Corps, arrived at Ninth Corps headquarters. Meade informed Burnside that Grant agreed with him that the black soldiers should not be used as the spearhead for the assault. Burnside quickly asked if that decision could be reconsidered. "No, general, the order is final," replied Meade. "You must detail one of your white divisions to take the advance."[22]

Once Meade left, Burnside sent for General Ledlie, and all four officers spent quite a bit of time arguing about whose division would lead the assault. During the course of this discussion, the generals kept coming to the conclusion that it would be better if the Fourth Division would lead as originally planned, but Burnside told them that Meade's order was unchangeable. To break this stalemate, Burnside decided to have the three division leaders draw straws out of a hat. Ledlie drew the short straw and thus was given the task of leading the attack after the mine was exploded.[23]

General Potter recalled Burnside's instructions for the July 30 assault:

> The theory of the attack was, that after the explosion of the mine the
> leading division should advance immediately through the breach made
> in the enemy's works and attempt to seize the crest of the hill beyond,

known as Cemetery hill; General Willcox was then to follow through the breach and deploy on the left of the leading division and attempt to seize the line of the plank road; my division was to pass to the right of General Ledlie's division and form, so as to protect his right flank, on the line of a ravine which ran to the right, and which it was supposed it would be difficult to cross; then the division of General Ferrero, which was composed exclusively of colored troops, was to advance in case we secured a lodgement there, pass over the line of General Ledlie's division, and make an immediate assault on the town of Petersburg.[24]

Sometime later that day, after Meade sent a detailed order to Burnside regarding the July 30 attack. In sum, Burnside was to mass his corps directly in front of the Confederate salient, "prepare his parapets and abatis for the passage of the columns, and have the pioneers equipped for work in opening the passages for artillery, destroying the enemy's abatis, and the intrenching tools distributed for effecting lodgment, &c." General Warren, whose Fifth Corps occupied the line on the left of the Ninth Corps, was to mass the bulk of his corps on his right flank, ready to aid the breakthrough. General Ord, in command of the Eighteenth Corps, would be relieved after dark by troops of the returning Second Corps, and mass his divisions on Burnside's right flank. Hancock's Second Corps would recross the James from Deep Bottom, relieve Ord's men, and be ready to assist in the attack if needed. The Cavalry Corps would cross behind the Union lines and probe the Confederate right flank, thus keeping the enemy pinned inside their entrenchments and prevent reinforcements from confronting Burnside.

Meade's specific instructions continued:

At 3.30 in the morning of the 30th Major-General Burnside will spring his mine, and his assaulting columns will immediately move rapidly upon the breach, seize the crest in the rear, and effect a lodgment there. He will be followed by Major-General Ord, who will support him on the right, directing his movement to the crest indicated, and by Major-General Warren, who will support him on the left. Upon the explosion of the mine, the artillery of all kinds in battery will open upon those points of the enemy's works whose fire covers the ground over which our columns must move, care being taken to avoid impeding the progress of our troops.

In conclusion, Meade wrote that "promptitude, rapidity of execution, and cordial co-operation are essential to success, and the commanding general is confident that this indication of his expectations will insure the hearty efforts of the commanders and troops."[25]

Burnside then issued his own orders to his corps, based on Meade's earlier instructions. To Ledlie, Burnside wrote: "General Ledlie will immediately upon the explosion of the mine move his division forward as directed by verbal orders this day, and if possible crown the crest at the point known as Cemetery Hill, occupying, if possible, the cemetery." Willcox would bear off to the left, Potter to the right, while Ferrero would halt his men within the Union lines until his front was clear. Then, he would follow Ledlie to the crest of Cemetery Hill and continue to advance to the right, occupying a small village within sight of Petersburg.[26]

Once the decision was made to send in Ledlie's troops in the first wave, Burnside sent the general, who was to take along his two brigade commanders, to inspect the ground over which their troops would attack. They reported back to Burnside late in the day that they were ready, and only waited for darkness so their troops could be relieved from the front lines and assembled in the rear.[27]

What words passed between Ledlie and his brigade leaders and their staffs remain a mystery to this day. Ledlie, in his report of the battle, wrote that "I then gave instructions to my brigade commanders to the effect that when the order for the charge was given, the column should move through the breach to be made by the mine and then to press forward and occupy the hill beyond, when the Thirty-fifth [Massachusetts] were to be set at work throwing up intrenchments."[28]

However, when Colonel Elisha G. Marshall, Ledlie's Second Brigade commander, summoned his assistant adjutant general on his staff, Captain Thomas W. Clarke of the 29th Massachusetts, Clarke recalled a different tale than that told by Ledlie:

> The plan as given by General Ledlie to Bartlett and Marshall, and as given by Marshall to his battalion commanders, was to this effect, and it was on this plan that Marshall and Bartlett worked. The Second Brigade was to be formed in column of battalion front. On the explosion of the mine it was to move forward and occupy the enemy's works on the right of the crater, skirting its edge, but not going into it. The First Brigade was to follow with about the same front and occupy the works on the left of the crater, but not going into it. When the lodgment had been made, it was to be secured and connected to our lines by our engineer regiment, 35th Massachusetts. The Second Division was then to extend this lodgment still more to the right, the Third Division was to extend it to the left in the enemy's works by a front attack, and the colored division was then to pass through the crater and assault the hill in the rear. Marshall's distinct instructions were that the security of the lodgment was the prime duty of the First Division and the hill was a subordinate object; and General Ledlie's instructions, as heard, conveyed no other meaning to me, or, as will appear later, to General Bartlett or Adjutant [Horace M.] Warren.[29]

However, Colonel Stephen M. Weld, commander of the 56th Massachusetts, recounted a different tale than Captain Clarke. Weld wrote: "Orders were given, as I now remember them, to push through the gap made by the mine and rush for the crest in rear, which was said to be 400 yards distant. In fact, it was almost a mile."[30]

Clarke and Weld present differing points of view. What this divergence of thought means is that somewhere along the chain of command, Burnside's instructions that the First Division immediately pass through the breach in the Confederate line and assail the higher ground in the rear was garbled. Both Bartlett and Marshall were captured on July 30 and neither officer wrote a report of the engagement. Ledlie's actions in the fighting were never directly questioned; he was not called upon to testify either by the military court of inquiry held shortly after the battle or during the December testimony before the Joint Congressional Committee on the Conduct of the War.

Once darkness fell on July 29, the Ninth Corps was a beehive of activity. Ledlie's First Division held the right flank of the corps line. Sometime before midnight, troops of the Eighteenth Corps finally arrived to relieve Bartlett's and Marshall's men. The two brigades went to the rear, where the men received fresh ammunition, water, and three days' cooked rations for their haversacks. After a brief inspection, the regiments were allowed to rest for an hour or more. Finally, around two o'clock in the morning of July 30, Ledlie ordered his men forward, the officers admonishing the men not to make any noise lest the Rebels notice all the nocturnal movements.[31]

The division marched along a narrow army road that passed behind Fort Morton, a 14-gun earthwork that Burnside now occupied for corps headquarters for the mine operation. Then, the troops turned toward the front, following a zigzag approach known as Willcox's covered way, a wide trench that allowed troops from the rear to reach the front without exposing themselves to enemy musketry. Colonel Marshall deployed his brigade in three lines directly behind the main Union line, still held by part of Potter's Second Division, which was still waiting to be relieved by the Eighteenth Corps.[32]

Immediately behind Marshall's brigade lay Bartlett's First Brigade, six regiments of perhaps 1,300 men. Knowing his incapacity because of his wooden leg, Bartlett divided his brigade into two wings for ease of command. Colonel Jacob P. Gould of the 59th Massachusetts had the Right Wing, deployed as the front line of the brigade, with the 29th, 57th, and 59th Massachusetts, from left to right. Colonel Weld's Left Wing was in the second line, 100th Pennsylvania, 56th and 21st Massachusetts, deployed left to right. Once deployed, the men were ordered to lie down and continue being quiet, waiting for the word to charge. Bartlett himself sought out Chaplain Alfred Dashiell of the 57th Massachusetts so that he could entrust his personal belongings to the chaplain in case he was slain during the coming battle.[33]

Behind Bartlett's lines was Brigadier General John F. Hartranft's brigade of the Third Division; Willcox's other brigade was lined up in the far end of the covered way, as too many troops were already crowded at the front line.

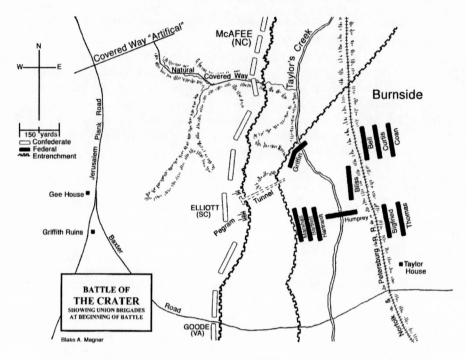

N
W — E

150 yards
▢ Confederate
■ Federal
〰〰 Entrenchment

Covered Way "Artifical"

McAFEE
(NC)

Natural
Covered Way

Taylor's Creek

Burnside

Jerusalem Plank Road

Gee House ■

ELLIOTT
(SC)

Pegram

Tunnel

Griffin

Bell
Curtis
Coan

Bliss

Marshall
Hartranft
Benton

Humprey

Siegfried
Thomas

Griffith Ruins ■

Baxter

Petersburg R. R.

Taylor
House

**BATTLE OF
THE CRATER**
SHOWING UNION BRIGADES
AT BEGINNING OF BATTLE

Road

GOODE
(VA)

Norfolk &

Blake A. Magner

One of Potter's two brigades still occupied its entrenchments; the other was lined up behind the lines. Ferrero's division brought up the rear, resting adjacent to a division of the Eighteenth Corps which was ready to support Burnside.

Also that night, the Second Corps silently moved back across the James River and was ready to support the anticipated breakthrough. And, unknown to the Yankees, a breakthrough was a distinct possibility. Lee, worried about Hancock's maneuvers at Deep Bottom, had sent much of his army to oppose the Yankees at Deep Bottom. On the night of July 29, only three Rebel divisions held the lines at Petersburg. On the left was Robert F. Hoke's Division, its left flank on the James River. Then came Bushrod Johnson's troops. Brigadier General Stephen F. Elliott's brigade of South Carolinians included the sector undermined by Colonel Pleasants' tunneling operation. Finally, Brigadier General William Mahone's division held the Confederate right flank. The Rebels were stretched thin, hoping that the Union troops would not launch any offensives that would expose their weakness. Thus, the mine explosion would prove a golden opportunity for a decisive breakthrough while the enemy troops were at their weakest strength.

Grant had specified that the mine would be exploded at 3:30 A.M. on July 30. Half an hour before the time, Colonel Pleasants knelt down to touch off the three fuses that began burning at the mouth of the tunnel and soon disappeared into the darkness of the shaft. Pleasants had estimated that the ninety feet of fuse would take half an hour to burn before the three fuses reached the troughs of gunpowder, which would then spark and quickly burn along the troughs to the magazines.[34]

Men grew palpably nervous as 3:30 approached. Nothing happened. Burnside dispatched a staff officer to ascertain the state of affairs. Shortly after, two of Meade's staff officers came to see Burnside. The army commander also was wondering why the explosion had not occurred. Both he and Grant were back at Burnside's old headquarters, half a mile behind the lines. Burnside quickly sent a second officer to find Pleasants and inquire what had happened. Two of Pleasants' men, Sergeant Harry Reese and Lieutenant Jacob Douty, offered to crawl into the tunnel and locate the problem, which all three men surmised to be a failed fuse. But Pleasants wanted to make sure that his men would not be blown up if the fuses were still sputtering slowly.

Finally, at about 4:15, Pleasants nodded his assent and allowed Sergeant Reese to crawl into the tunnel. Reese found that all three fuses had failed at the same splice, much to his relief. But Reese had forgotten to take a knife along with him, and he crawled back toward the entrance. He encountered Lieutenant Douty, coming in to check on him. The lieutenant had a knife, and both men returned to cut and repair the fuses, then relit them. They were out of the tunnel by 4:30, and informed Pleasants that the fuse would take no more than fifteen minutes to reach the magazines. Burnside sent his staff officer to relay this news to Meade, who in the meantime had bombarded Burnside with messages, the last of which authorized the Ninth Corps to attack even if the mine failed to work.[35]

Captain John Norris of the 2nd Pennsylvania Provisional Heavy Artillery was speaking with his regimental commander when, at 4:44 A.M., the powder reached the magazines under the Confederate earthworks. "A dull sound was heard and a trembling of the earth felt, and the fearful explosion took place. It was the most awful grand sight I ever witnessed; a mighty mound of earth upheaved with an awful convulsion, apparently rising almost mountain-high, the pent-up flames beneath bursting through the crevices. It seemed to stand in the air an instant and then fell, leaving a cloud of dust and smoke...."[36]

Lieutenant John W. Morrison of the 100th Pennsylvania was equally eloquent in his later description of the explosion. "There was a sullen, subterranean roar and a quivering of the solid ground. A huge mass of earth, timbers, cannon and men, were raised fountain-like into the air, falling slowly back, leaving, where the fort had been, an immense crater.... Simultaneously with the upheaval of the fort, the guns from all the federal batteries opened fire. It was Pandemonium let loose!"[37]

To the soldiers of Ledlie's division, especially the men of Marshall's Sec-

This contemporary woodcut shows the explosion of the Union mine under the Confederate trenches at Petersburg on July 30, 1864. From The Century Company's "Battles and Leaders" series.

ond Brigade, it seemed as if the mountain of debris that was flung into the air would descend on them. Many soldiers broke ranks and began to head to the rear, only to be stopped by their equally nervous officers. Within ten minutes after the explosion, the troops were rallied and the order was given to advance. Smoke was still roiling out of the explosion, but it had dissipated enough for the men to see ahead of them. But no sooner had the explosion taken place than the Yankee artillery —110 field guns and 54 mortars — opened along a two-mile front to further disrupt the enemy and provide covering fire for the attack. The noise was deafening and the massed artillery added its own smoke to that brought about by the mine explosion.[38]

The momentary delay caused by the sheer size of the explosion was finally broken by the shouted command "Forward!" echoed by many officers along the front lines. But the order was easier to shout than it was to obey. According to Meade's instructions, the trenches were to have been prepared to remedy an advance. The obstructions in front of the Union lines were also to have been moved or destroyed to facilitate an advance. Burnside's failure to do so was one of the major indictments against him by the military court of inquiry.

The system of trenches in front of the mine explosion was eight feet deep in places, deep enough so that men could walk upright without constant fear of being hit by sharpshooters' bullets. There was a firing step along the front of the trenches to allow soldiers to fire at the enemy. Thus, when Major Charles B. Houghton of the 14th New York Heavy Artillery of Marshall's Second Brigade gave the command to advance, there was some delay as the men looked for ways to get up over the top. Some of the men jammed their bayonets into the side of the trenches and held them against their hips or on their shoulders as their comrades climbed up these makeshift ladders. Once on top, many soldiers stopped and helped pull others up. Major Houghton tried placing his men in line as they worked their way out of the trenches, but Colonel Marshall ordered the major to simply take the men he had and charge the enemy. The primary sources agree that there was no orderly advance by Marshall's brigade, but rather a haphazard advance as groups of soldiers came out of their trenches and headed for the smoking hole blown by the mine.[39]

The trenches had not been prepared for an advance and neither had the Union abatis been cleared. Here the sources disagree as to their effectiveness in disrupting the Union attack. General Willcox wrote that his pioneers had removed much of the abatis in front of his division (to the left of the Crater) that night. The general recalled that "there was really little left to move that night, certainly none that obstructed the passage of troops for a moment. It had nearly all been shot away." Willcox further stated that to clear more away than was done would have attracted the attention of the enemy pickets. There simply was no time to accomplish such a task thoroughly, said Willcox. The orders for the attack were issued only the day before, then Meade changed Burnside's plan at the last minute. Since General Ledlie had been in division command only a few weeks, opined Willcox, such last-minute changes materially affected anything he might have done to enhance the chance for success.[40]

William Powell, in his *Battles and Leaders* article, wrote that nothing had been done in Ledlie's front to prepare the works for an advance. Such an undertaking would have been extremely hazardous because of the line's proximity to the enemy. On the other hand, Powell also stated that the enemy's abatis in Ledlie's front had been buried by the explosion, and thus presented no obstacle to the advancing Union troops. Colonel Weld recalled things differently, however. He wrote that there was surviving abatis in front of the Confederate line, all connected with wires to prevent a surprise Union attack. But the wires were sliced through and whole sections of abatis swung forward to create gaps through which the Yankees charged.[41]

Thus, an unorganized mob of advancing Union soldiers, led by company and regimental officers of Marshall's brigade, swarmed forward as the smoke still billowed out of the exploded area in front of them. Lieutenant Powell eloquently penned what the soldiers found when they reached the scene of the explosion:

THE CHARGE TO THE CRATER. FROM A SKETCH MADE AT THE TIME.

Union soldiers of the Ninth Corps charge toward the Crater in this woodcut from The Century Company's "Battles and Leaders" series.

Little did these men anticipate what they would see upon arriving there: an immense hole in the ground about 30 feet deep, 60 feet wide, and 170 feet long, filled with dust, great blocks of clay, guns, broken carriages, projecting timbers, and men buried in various ways-some up to their necks, others to their waists, and some with only their feet and legs protruding from the earth....

The whole scene of the explosion struck every one dumb with astonishment as we arrived on the crest of the debris. It was impossible for the troops of the Second Brigade to move forward in line, as they had advanced; and, owing to the broken state they were in, every man crowding up to look into the hole, and being pressed by the First Brigade, which was immediately in rear, it was equally impossible to move by the flank, by any command, around the crater.[42]

Colonel Weld put it more succinctly when he wrote that "the moral backing of an organized body of men, which each one would sustain by his companions on either side, was wanting." Marshall's brigade, as a result of the lack of preparedness for the advance, degenerated into a mob of sightseers, officers and men alike gaping at the smoking debris-filled hole created by the explosion of the mine.[43]

The explosion had initially stunned the Confederates manning the trenches in front of the Ninth Corps. The blast destroyed the four-gun battery in Elliott's Salient, virtually annihilated that portion of the 18th South Carolina on duty around the battery, and sent survivors running for their lives. Elliott's Brigade and Captain Richard Pegram's battery lost 278 men killed and wounded in the explosion, and for the moment, the sudden, awe-inspiring explosion had rendered the survivors stunned into silence as the Yankee infantry surged forward.[44]

Colonel Marshall's brigade thus lost all semblance of any order it might have had. Many soldiers climbed down into the debris to dig out their half-buried enemies. Bodies were everywhere, some buried, some barely sticking out of the ground. Lieutenant Colonel Benjamin G. Barney managed to get much of his 2nd Pennsylvania Provisional Heavy Artillery into line and led it forward, crossing through and around the Crater, heading for the ridge which was supposed to be the division's objective. The regiment actually advanced 150 yards beyond the Crater but ran into Confederate return fire, and being unsupported by any other troops, fell back.[45]

No sooner had the Second Brigade advanced than the soldiers in the First Brigade heard General Bartlett call out, "First Brigade, forward!" The individual regimental and company officers echoed the general's stentorian order and the men of the brigade rose up and began climbing out of the trenches and into the dead space between the lines, following Marshall's troops. Recalled George Barton, a soldier in the 57th Massachusetts: "General Bartlett commanded the Brigade, he was perfectly splendid, and led us in the charge on foot." Adjutant Thomas W. Clarke of Marshall's brigade recalled seeing Bartlett "hopping along very cheerfully, aiding himself by a stout malacca cane with an ivory cross handle."[46]

The advance of Bartlett's men was similar to that of Marshall's. The effort to get out of their own trenches was eased somewhat by using piles of sandbags that previous soldiers had erected, but the forward advance also disorganized the brigade's formation. As the brigade swept forward, Bartlett steered it to the right of the Crater, instead of moving off to the left as planned. The regimental historian of the 57th Massachusetts blamed the general for misinterpreting Ledlie's order to branch out to the left and occupy the enemy trenches there. Bartlett seemed to think that Ledlie's instructions meant moving to the trenches on the *Confederate* left of the Crater, rather than the straightforward left as meant in the Union view of the enemy line.[47]

Ledlie himself did not accompany his troops forward. He was apparently at the front line when Bartlett's brigade began to advance. "Good luck to you General," Ledlie called as Bartlett's troops moved off. Then, Ledlie was seen to turn toward one of his aides and inquire, "Where is a good place to see the fight?" With Ledlie out of the way, comfortably situated out of imminent danger, his two brigades were left to fend for themselves.[48]

So, the jumbled mass of the First Brigade veered to the right of the Crater, even as individuals and groups of soldiers stopped to take in the sights of the explosion. Part of Marshall's brigade had already moved into the enemy line to the Crater's right, but found the going slow. The Yankee soldiers discovered that the Rebel lines were much like theirs. In addition to the main line of trenches, the area behind the front line was a confusing array of other trenches — covered ways, traverses, bombproofs, and connecting trenches — a veritable rat's warren that made maneuvering impossible and forward progress slow.[49]

Behind Ledlie's division came the other two white divisions of the Ninth Corps. Potter's Second Division moved off right after Ledlie's men cleared their front, heading off to the right of the Crater as planned. His troops managed to slowly move north, seizing perhaps two hundred yards of enemy trenches before coming to a stop against stiffening Confederate resistance. The remnant of Elliott's South Carolinians rallied in a ravine in back of the Crater and managed to turn back the 2nd Pennsylvania Provisional Heavy Artillery, while other portions of his brigade were reinforced by some North Carolinians and managed to bring Potter's advance to a halt.[50]

Willcox's Third Division began to move up on the left of the Crater. Brigadier General John F. Hartranft's First Brigade came to a halt just behind the Crater when the general discovered the milling troops of Ledlie's division in the hole itself. The head of his brigade was at the Crater while the tail remained in the Union trenches. Hartranft's delay effectively blocked Willcox's other brigade until Willcox sent it off to the left to attack, which succeeded in seizing some of the enemy trenches south of the Crater. The infantry were assisted by the fire of two captured enemy fieldpieces, which artillerymen from the 14th New York in Marshall's brigade had dug out, found some ammunition in a magazine, and supplied gunners, who, along with volunteers from Hartranft's brigade, began firing at the enemy troops south of the Crater.[51]

All this while, as the Ninth Corps painfully deployed and tried widening the breach, Confederate artillery began to go into action. A four-gun battery on the crest of Cemetery Hill fired both shell and canister into the Union troops in front of the Crater, while mortar batteries behind the Rebel lines began to range in on the Crater. Other batteries began to assist the beleaguered Confederate infantry, dropping shells into the massed Yankees in the Crater and causing the casualty list to keep climbing upward.[52]

When it became apparent that the attack had bogged down and Cemetery Hill was still in Confederate hands, General Meade became concerned and pestered Burnside for more and more details on the fighting. As the morning wore on and the fighting intensified around the Crater, the two generals both became irritated at the lack of progress. Burnside, under pressure from Meade, ordered both Willcox and Potter to forget about widening the breach and instead to attack toward the high ground. He also sent orders to Ferrero to take the Fourth Division and charge the hill. Ferrero's men had remained idle behind the front line, their front still clogged by other Ninth Corps troops. The division commander had ensconced himself in a bombproof nearby, where he joined General Ledlie of the First Division. When the generals convened their court of inquiry, two of the witnesses called were surgeons, one of whom stated that General Ledlie claimed to be hurt by a spent ball and that he gave the general stimulants to help revive him. When pressed for details, the surgeon revealed that he gave both generals — Ledlie and Ferrero — rum to revive them.[53]

At any rate, Ferrero finally left the bombproof when he received more orders to send his troops into the fray. His two brigades advanced slightly to the right of the Crater, some of his men spilling over into the crowded pit. The black soldiers manfully charged ahead, through the white soldiers and pitched into enemy units attacking Potter's regiments. The initial attack garnered several hundred prisoners and a battle flag before the attack ran out of steam in the confused labyrinth behind the main Confederate line. A second attack ran headlong into an impetuous Confederate counterattack by reinforcements from William Mahone's Division. The Southerners, enraged at having to fight blacks, fought a vicious hand-to-hand combat with their adversaries and finally drove the black soldiers back into the trenches and Crater. Scores of panicked blacks fell back into and over the white troops huddled in the earthworks, leading to the formation of later stories that the blacks had not done their duty at all.[54]

The panicked retreat of Ferrero's two brigades destabilized the fighting north of the Crater. Blacks crowded into the trenches and Crater, making resistance all but useless in many areas; the Union troops were so tightly packed in places that they were unable to fire at the approaching enemy troops. Fleeing blacks disrupted a division of the Eighteenth Corps that was beginning to advance north across the interval between the lines of trenches, forcing it to retreat and regroup. The retreat enabled more Southerners to the north to fire into the massed Yankees in the trenches, causing a pell-mell retreat into the comparative safety of the Crater. Those soldiers who chose instead to head back to the main Union line ran the gauntlet of deadly fire sprayed across the area by Southern riflemen north and south of the Crater as well as the fire from enemy cannon.[55]

The Confederate reinforcements were two brigades of William Mahone's Division, which held the right flank of Lee's army. When word of the explosion reached Lee that morning, he sent one of his aides directly to Mahone with orders to bring two brigades to seal the breach. Mahone chose to take his two right-most brigades to avoid arousing suspicion on the Fifth Corps front that the Confederate trenches were being weakened. When he reached the covered way and ravine in rear of the Crater, Mahone quickly realized that he would need more troops, and sent back for a third brigade to join him. Mahone's old Virginia brigade, now led by Colonel David Weisiger, was the force that slammed into Ferrero's troops and hurled them back. Matthew Hall's Georgia brigade attacked toward Hartranft's men but was repelled by heavy Union musketry.[56]

When General Meade saw from a distance the retreat of Ferrero's men, he decided that the day was lost and at 9:30 A.M. sent an order for Burnside to cease the attacks and pull the troops back to the main Union line. A half hour later, Meade sent Burnside another message, informing the Ninth Corps commander that he could use his own discretion in withdrawing the troops until it could be done safely. The army commander surely lost his last chance for success at this moment. Mahone's reinforcements had indeed repelled Ferrero's division, but if General Warren had attacked with all or part of the Fifth Corps, his men would have found a weakly held trench system in front of them. But fate was not smiling on the Union army this day. As Warren prepared to attack, some of Willcox's men pulled out of their gains south of the Crater, which influenced Warren to notify Meade that he could not attack successfully.[57]

The confusion inherent in the faulty advance of the Ninth Corps makes it well nigh impossible to effectively document the movements of the Union troops on July 30. Many regiments were completely mixed up and companies were separated during the advance and never rejoined their regiments until after the battle. The 100th Pennsylvania, for example, apparently split into two wings during the advance, leaving later historians and veterans to attempt a description of the regiment's actions during the fighting.

Bartlett's First Brigade acted much like the 100th Pennsylvania. The general himself seems to have gone into the Crater personally and remained there during the battle; a number of eyewitnesses mentioned him in their reports and post-war memoirs. Chaplain Dashiell, worried about the general's fate, repeatedly inquired about the general as wounded men of the 57th Massachusetts were carried back to the Union lines. "He is bully sir," replied one of the returning wounded. "He is in the mine, leading the boys with his cane."[58]

Colonel Weld collected a number of men from the three regiments of his wing and led them into action to the right of the Crater, where they became mixed with Potter's advancing division. Then, when Ferrero's division was driven back in confusion by Weisiger's attack, Weld's troops also disintegrated in the mass confusion. There were simply too many soldiers crowded together in the trenches when the Rebels made their final attack that recaptured the trenches to the right of the Crater. Weld himself sought refuge in a bombproof with a captain and a black soldier. When summoned to surrender, the three occupants emerged. The black soldier was promptly killed by the enemy, who grabbed Weld's sword and hat, then hustled him and the captain to the rear. As they crossed the parapets and headed to the rear, Union bullets struck the ground among and around the column of prisoners.[59]

At some point during the fighting, a shell exploded near Bartlett and knocked a piece of clay onto his wooden leg, crushing it and essentially rendering him immobile. Still, the general seemed to be active in trying to direct the defense of the pit. The explosion had created a hole around thirty feet deep, with steep sides and a rim formed from earth and clay thrown up by the explosion that was perhaps as high as twelve feet above the ground. Burnside had wanted to use eight tons of powder in the mine, but Meade would only allow four. Burnside's reasoning was that a larger explosion would create a crater with less steep slopes than a four-ton explosion. And he was right. Men inside the crater could barely scale the earth walls. It was almost impossible to fire a musket from the walls; a soldier had to load by bracing himself with his back against the wall, then turn around and dig himself into the wall to remain steady while firing. Any man hit rolled down to the bottom.[60]

As the morning wore on and the Federal attack stalled, the front became crowded, especially after the Confederates began their counterattacks. More and more men crowded into the Crater as the Rebels recaptured the trenches on either side of the hole. The hot July sun also made itself felt, and the men in blue soon began to run out of water. It was not easy to bring water from the Union lines either. Men in the Crater volunteered their lives to run the gauntlet across the no man's land between the lines, a space swept by enemy musketry and artillery fire. Man after man was killed trying to bring water to their beleaguered comrades, but the amount of liquid brought over to the Crater was not nearly enough for the men inside.[61]

When the Rebels drove the last remaining Yankees out of the trenches on the right, Bartlett redoubled his efforts to ensure that the Yanks kept their hold on the Crater itself. He appointed Captain Theodore Gregg of the 45th Pennsylvania as brigade officer of the day with instructions to rally every man he could find to defend the position. Wrote Gregg:

> General Bartlett and one of his aides-de-camp, a very gallant and
> trustworthy officer, did everything in their power to rally the troops
> on the inside the crater, but found it to be impossible, as the men
> were completely worn out and famished for water. He succeeded in
> rallying some twenty-five or thirty negroes, who behaved nobly, keep-
> ing up a continual fire of musketry, thereby holding the rebels on the
> right of the fort at bay and keeping them from entering it.[62]

Captain Freeman S. Bowley, a company commander in the 30th United States Colored Troops, witnessed Bartlett's heroic actions. Heavy Rebel fire down the length of a trench to the right of the Crater threatened the stability of the Union position. Bartlett directed that a breastwork must be built across the trench to deflect Rebel fire. A detail of black soldiers was put to work, throwing in chunks of clay and equipment to erect a breastwork, but the heavy enemy fire dropped men left and right. "Put in the dead men," someone suggested. The workers capitalized on the idea and began piling up bodies to protect themselves from the incessant musketry. When workers fell dead, their bodies were dumped on the growing pile of dead flesh.[63]

At 12:30 P.M., one of Burnside's messengers managed to reach the Crater and deliver a note from the corps commander to generals Hartranft, Griffin, and Bartlett, the three ranking officers in the struggling mass of humanity there. Burnside had notified his division commanders of Meade's peremptory order to withdraw, and ordered them to ascertain the state of affairs in the Crater area from the generals on the scene, and advise him of the time of evacuation. Bartlett's handwritten note on the back of this order echoed Hartranft and Griffin: "It will be impossible to withdraw these men, who are a rabble without officers, before dark, and not even then in good order."[64]

The battle continued into the afternoon as the Yankees tried their best to hang on to their tenuous position in the Crater. Mahone's two brigades had attacked and driven back the Yankees, but were not strong enough to push their opponents out of the Crater itself. The third brigade Mahone had sent for then arrived on the field. Led by Colonel John C. C. Saunders, it was the Alabama brigade formerly led by General Cadmus M. Wilcox. Attrition had decimated its five regiments so that only around 630 men followed the colonel into line of battle in the ravine to the southwest of the Crater. Mahone ordered Saunders to charge and not stop or fire until his men reached the brow of the Crater. Otherwise, they might be cut to pieces by Union artillery and musketry. To further arouse the men, Mahone told them that General Lee himself was watching from the Gee House up on the ridge behind them. There were no other troops on hand; if the Alabamians did not succeed, they would attack again, with General Lee to lead them in person.[65]

As soon as a signal gun was fired, the Alabama brigade arose with fixed bayonets and charged forward, "in perfect alignment" as one survivor recalled, but as the brigade reached the trench complex ahead of them it broke their alignment. The men continued on, however, raising the Rebel Yell as they closed with the Crater. The Yankee soldiers along the top of the Crater heard the Alabamians coming and opened a ragged volley at them, but most of their shots flew harmlessly overhead. Saunders' men came on and halted just under the rim of the Crater, where Union artillery could not see them, giving them time to reform and catch their breaths.[66]

General Hartranft saw the Alabamians advancing and decided that it was time to retreat regardless of the outcome. When the mine was exploded, it created one large crater but because of the location of the two lateral galleries, the explosion also created a small ridge at the point where the galleries diverged from the main tunnel. Hartranft and Griffin were in the left, or smaller, section, with Bartlett apparently in the right, or larger, section. When Hartranft gave the signal to retreat, he sent an aide to locate Bartlett and inform him that the men in the left section of the Crater were falling back. But in the din and confusion of battle, the word to retreat was not heard by everyone. Soldiers closer to the enemy were already engaging in combat. Alabamians found abandoned muskets on their side of the rim and threw them harpoon-like over the top at the massed Yankees, who responded in kind. Soldiers on both sides threw pieces of artillery shells at each other as well as hard lumps of clay.[67]

When the Alabamians had rested sufficiently, one of their officers ordered some of the men to place their hats on ramrods and raise them high. The appearance of hats coming over top of the rim caused many of the Union soldiers to fire, and before they had time to reload, the Alabamians jumped over the top and a savage hand-to-hand melee broke out.[68]

At about the same time, Confederates had been creeping closer to the rim around the northern circuit of the Crater. Bartlett wrote that "their flag within seven feet of ours across the work. They threw bayonets and bottles on us, and we returned for we got out of ammunition." Before the final attack began, Bartlett was still trying desperately to save what men he could. The general ordered that a traverse be cut through the rim of the Crater facing the Union lines so that water bearers could come and go at less risk, but the detail working on digging must not have been done when the enemy charged over the top.[69]

Once notified by Hartranft that his men were retreating, Bartlett, sitting on a pile of logs somewhere in the northern section of the Crater, quickly informed the men around him that those wishing to try to reach the main Union line could now do so if they wished. Shortly thereafter, the enemy charged over the top and hand-to-hand fighting took place. As soon as he heard the Rebel order to advance echoed across the rim, Bartlett ordered his men to surrender, knowing full well that they would be outmatched, even if they outnumbered their foes. The noise drowned out Bartlett's call, and as the Rebels came over the top, some men tried to surrender, while others continued to fight. When it was seen that some of the enemy were killing black soldiers who had surrendered, Yanks who had already thrown down their guns picked them up and continued the fight. Some Rebel officers tried to intervene to stop the fighting before it got out of hand. "Why in the hell don't you fellows surrender?" said one officer in gray. "Why in the hell don't you let us?" was the reply.[70]

Once an understanding was reached, the fighting quickly was over. Among the bag of prisoners were both of Ledlie's brigade commanders—Frank Bartlett and Elisha Marshall. Bartlett was very laconic in his diary of his fate: "I surrendered to General Mahone." Two Alabamians from Saunders' brigade remembered seeing Bartlett after his capture. John Featherston noticed that the general was "lying down and could not rise. Assistance was offered him, but he informed those who were assisting him that his leg was broken and so it was, but it proved to be an artificial leg, made of cork." George Clark of the 11th Alabama was also taken in by the general's "injury." When Clark encountered Bartlett, the general was using two inverted muskets as crutches. "I could see no evidence of physical pain in his face, and remarked to him that he must have nerves of steel, as his leg was shot away. He smiled and replied that he had lost his real leg at Williamsburg two years before, and the leg he had just shattered was a cork leg."[71]

The Ninth Corps casualties in the Battle of the Crater were severe, with one of every five men on the casualty lists. A divisional breakdown shows the following:

	Killed	Wounded	Missing	Total
First Division	65	239	350	654
Second Division	92	354	386	832
Third Division	106	354	199	659
Fourth Division	209	697	421	1327
Artillery Brigade	1	2	–	3
Corps total	473	1646	1356	3475

Turner's division of the Eighteenth Corps reported 323 casualties, making the Union total for the day at 3,798. Confederate casualties were tallied as 1,612 minimum (588 in Mahone's Division, 894 in Johnson's, and 70 in Hoke's, with 60 artillerymen reported as casualties).[72]

Within days of the failure at the Crater, General Meade insisted that a court of inquiry be formed to investigate the failure and ascertain which officers, if any, were primarily to blame for the Union defeat. On September 9, the court presented its findings. The blame was placed on Generals Burnside, Ledlie, Ferrero, Willcox, and Colonel Zenas R. Bliss, one of Potter's brigade commanders. Meade's purpose for asking for a court was to clear his own name of any misdeeds on July 30 or in the planning for the attack. Burnside went home on leave and never held another command. Ledlie also went home and resigned in January 1865. Ferrero was rotated out of the Ninth Corps and ended the war commanding the troops stationed on the Bermuda Hundred front. Bliss, the colonel of the 7th Rhode Island, was relieved from brigade command in late August by another colonel senior to him; he also never held another such command. Willcox escaped relatively unscathed and remained in divisional command till war's end.[73]

In December 1864, the Joint Congressional Committee on the Conduct of the War began to examine several witnesses about the Crater fiasco. The committee, certainly no admirer of Meade from the beginning, blamed the army commander for the failure on July 30. He changed the attack plan, failed to provide support troops, and in general provided Burnside with little or no cooperation during the entire planning and execution of the mine. The committee blamed Burnside for choosing Ledlie's division by drawing straws.[74]

Ledlie's two brigade commanders did not receive any censure for their heroic actions on July 30. Bartlett and Marshall were both captured and thus could not provide either court with information on their movements and commands that day. From the surviving accounts, it appears that both men did their best to prod their troops forward. Bartlett might have been misinformed by Ledlie about the exact objectives to be gained by the First Division, which, if true, played a large part in the failure of the troops to move out of the Crater area. Still, the labyrinth of trenches behind the main Confederate line doomed any successful Union attack unless the troops were firmly under control of their officers and in a manageable battle line. The afternoon attack of Saunders' Alabamians demonstrates that troops could maneuver through such obstacles, but only if they were not opposed by a steady line of troops. Only a bold initial attack by the Ninth Corps had a chance to succeed. Without overall direction from above, that was not possible. As a result, officers and men alike became trapped in the Crater area and the entire corps formation was disrupted. Within an hour of the mine explosion, the Union assault had failed. The rest of the battle became an exercise in futility on the part of the Union high command. Meade quit too early and failed to send in Warren's Fifth Corps. Burnside's men were sacrificed to the inevitable Confederate counterattack without the benefit of support from the rest of the Union army. For Frank Bartlett, July 30, 1864, marked the end of his active military career.

11

"A HORRIBLE DREAM WHICH I CAN NEVER FORGET"

Prisoner of War

"The past few days seem like a horrible dream which I can never forget. The misery I have suffered is more than I can ever tell," wrote a dejected Frank Bartlett on August 3, four days after being captured in the Crater. By the time the general penned these words of misery, he was more than 150 miles from Petersburg, incarcerated in a prison hospital far from the battlefields of Virginia.[1]

When Bartlett was captured in the Crater, he was escorted behind the Confederate lines, where, that night, he tried to sleep in a field of stones, with no covering at all. All those captured, white and black, officers and men, were mixed together in that field. At least the night was not cold, but the prisoners had nothing to eat. In the morning, the captured Yankees were lined up in march formation, rows of blacks and whites alternating, and hustled through Petersburg by their guards, to the delight and jeers of the crowd of civilians who gathered to watch the procession. Contrary to some contemporary accounts, General Bartlett, the highest ranking officer captured on the thirtieth, was not mounted on a mule and subject to ridicule by the jeering civilians. "I was carried in an ambulance," he wrote. "My belt taken from me by Captain Porter, Provost Marshall Hill's corps, the thief."[2]

Continued the general: "Put on a small island near the South Side Railroad depot. No shelter or food. I drink too much water. Thirst makes me crazy. We wouldn't treat cattle as we are being treated. Slept on some straw to night; delirious all night. Very weak. I cannot touch the food — raw bacon." Keep in mind that the general's artificial leg had been smashed during the fighting and it was with difficulty that he could move at all. The prisoners were ridiculed as they marched through Petersburg. The presence of black prisoners enraged both Southern soldier and civilian alike. As a result, the prisoners were treated more shabbily than usual, deprived of decent food and shelter as they were marched away from the front lines.[3]

The following morning — the first of August — the prisoners were herded up and crowded onto "dirty freight cars" of the Richmond and Danville Railroad for the 145-mile trip to their new home — the Confederate military prison in Danville. The prison dated from late 1863, when General Lee suggested the site as a way to ease the crowded condition of Richmond's prisons. Confederate authorities utilized six existing three-story tobacco factories to create the Danville prison complex. These brick or wood buildings were stripped of all furnishings and used to house the prisoners, officers and men being segregated, as well as white and black captives. Those lucky enough to be in the buildings that faced south could look across the Dan River and see North Carolina, as well as the Smoky Mountains far in the distance.[4]

The prisoner-laden train pulled into Burkesville Junction around nine that morning. Here, the men in blue were unloaded and forced to wait all day "in heat and dirt" for another train. "Am getting weaker every hour," recalled Bartlett as the hours dragged by. Finally, the expected train arrived and was underway sometime after nine in the evening. The train was crowded to overflowing. The unlucky general had to ride on the narrow platform of the last passenger car, which was the conductor's, who was mean enough not to allow the general to enter and ride in better comfort. So, accompanied by Colonel Marshall and Captain Amory, Bartlett endured "the most horrible night I ever passed. Could not sleep, all cramped up. Humane treatment of a prisoner of my rank, sick and wounded. Southern chivalry!"[5]

The prisoner train steamed into Danville early on the morning of August 2. Bartlett said:

> Carried in a dirty wagon without any cover to the prison, a filthy place, an old warehouse and stores. We were on the first floor, about three hundred, as thick as we could lie. No ventilation. I saw the Doctor in the morning; he said he would send me to the hospital. I could not eat anything; am feverish and so weak. No crutches. I have to be partly carried, partly hop along, when I move. Ration issued, corn bread, thick loaf, and bacon. I can't touch either; still drink water. If I do not get away from here very soon, I never shall. Wagon came for me about six, an open wagon or cart, used to carry bacon in, all covered with dirt and grease; gravel spread on the bottom to cover the grease; ride over rough road to hospital; am in a tent, old and ragged, but airy; good breeze.[6]

Information is lacking to indicate which of the six prison buildings the general was briefly placed. Colonel Weld agreed with the general about the horrible conditions. "We were placed in tobacco warehouses," wrote Weld. "We have very poor quarters and rations, being thrust into a lousy, dirty room, badly ventilated, and with no conveniences for washing, etc." On August 3, Weld remarked that "General Bartlett went to the hospital yesterday. He seemed almost worn out. He is no better to-day." The hospital to which Bartlett was sent had been established in January 1864, as a result of a small-pox epidemic that had spread through both the city and the prisons. The tents comprising the hospital were located on a small knoll south of town. As more and more infected men succumbed to the disease, they were interred in a new cemetery created just for prisoners.[7]

General Bartlett was placed in one of the hospital tents, where he slept on a bed of straw that night. In the morning, the weak general managed to obtain some milk. Using an old pocket watch, Bartlett resourcefully traded an old pocket watch for Confederate money, which he gave to the physician to buy him a toothbrush and the milk. Then came the wagon to take the general back to prison. Bartlett demurred; he was far too weak to survive in prison, so he sent a note to the commandant to that effect. The officer in charge at this time was Major Mason Morfit, whom one prisoner described as "a deserter from our regular army .... If but one-half of the enormities prac-ticed upon helpless prisoners, under his orders, could be told with decency, the vile odors of those Danville stables, where we were kept, would be fra-grance to the stench of his memory." But this time the major performed an act of random kindness, for he allowed Bartlett to remain in his ragged hos-pital tent.[8]

Bartlett woke up on the morning of August 5 "no better." This day he managed to write a letter to General Lee and Confederate Secretary of War James A. Seddon, asking for an exchange or parole because of his condition. Bartlett also lamented the departure of the remaining captured officers at Danville for the prison in Columbia, South Carolina, leaving him alone as the only officer captured at the Crater. Bored, the general located a couple of old popular magazines, together with some books, which he eagerly perused to pass the time. He also exchanged $50 United States currency for $200 Confederate currency so he could purchase needed items. Remember that the general had secreted some money in his false leg; though that had been crushed, he apparently brought it with him because of the currency deposit therein. Frank even took time during the fifth to pen a letter to his mother, informing her of his plight, asking for a box of foodstuffs, tea, and coffee. "Don't be worried about me," wrote the general, "I shall be well soon."[9]

Frank Bartlett must have sensed that he was now getting well and would survive when he wrote to his mother. His bowels still pained him on August 6, but he purchased a dozen eggs and reflected on "a week of misery" since his capture. On Monday, the eighth of August, the doctor placed a mustard poultice on his bowels in an attempt to reduce the swelling and pain. But the general did not think highly of the prison doctor, who "couldn't know anything about his business, and doesn't care. Keeps giving me pills." To supplement his fare, Bartlett this day purchased a pint of brandy for $25, "miserable stuff," as it turned out. "Apple brandy, tastes like burning fluid."[10]

Tuesday, August 9, was a "long, long day." His bowels hurt less, but he continued to bleed freely. Sleep came in fits because of the pain and bleeding. Three local gentlemen visited Bartlett, leaving him some tomatoes to eat, but he could not yet eat anything. "If I could only live to get in *our* lines or to Baltimore, I would die contented. Mother would be there."[11]

On August 10 a Confederate officer visited General Bartlett and offered to take the general's recent letter he had written to Robert Ould, the Confederate commissioner in charge of negotiating exchanges with his Union counterpart. After this "General Young" departed, he sent a brief note back to Bartlett:

> Danville, Va., August 10, 1864.
>
> Brig.-Gen. W. F. Bartlett, U.S.A.:—
>
> General,— I am directed by General Young to say to you that he will take great pleasure in handing your letter to Judge Ould in person, and that he will use every means in his power to procure you an exchange, or parole of honor, immediately. If he should fail, General Young will do everything in his power to alleviate your pain, or to promote your recovery.
>
> You will hear from General Young as soon as he has seen Judge Ould.
>
> I am, General,
> Very respectfully, your obedient servant,
> I. Pinckney Thomas,
> Lt. & A.D.C.[12]

In spite of such cheerful news, it seems the general had a physical relapse, for his daily journal indicated such:

> Friday, 12th. No better, no sleep after 12. Some milk porridge this morning. My tongue is fearfully coated, brown. Dr. Hunter just glanced at it and said, "Oh, yes, your tongue looks better." I said I did not agree with him.
>
> Saturday, 13th. Worse and weaker to-day. No surgeon, no medicine, no food suitable.... It is hard to die here without a single friend, not even an officer of our army, to hold my hand and take my last words. I hardly dare trust my body or anything else getting home.
>
> Sunday, 14th. Felt a little better after sat up this A.M.; have got a prayer-book, great comfort in it; have been reading it all morning. Seventieth Psalm, fourteenth day lesson. It is well they do not know how miserable I am. Have been taking comfort from this book all day; have been praying for forgiveness and help. I feel a little better to-day. God is very merciful. I shall never forget this day. I believe I shall be a better man if I live....[13]

The general's physical ailments began to improve, with Saturday, August 13, the turning point. "I can hardly account for the change. Mouth not so awfully dry as it has been. God is very merciful and has heard my prayers." A bottle of "blueberry wine" procured by Dr. Hunter proved to be of little use, so Frank ingested some calomel and opium pills with some whitebark solution. With his health beginning to improve, the general was now becoming impatient at not hearing from General Young about his chances for an exchange or parole. A few days of rain did not help matters; Bartlett's ragged tent was so open that it blew down, soaking the general and his bed.

While waiting for news of his pending exchange, Bartlett whiled away the hours reading and making rings from peach stones. On August 19, he walked a few steps on some crutches for the first time. "I have an egg for breakfast now, with some toast, and clover or hay tea; for dinner, boiled rice which has to be *examined*; for supper, baked apple and tea." Major Morfit, who examined Bartlett's occasional letters home, sent the general some sheets of notepaper with his compliments after noticing that his prisoner was using whatever scraps of paper he could find.[14]

Frank continued to get better as time went by. He smoked a cigar on August 21, noting that his appetite had returned. He read whatever he could lay his hands on, which included an occasional Richmond newspaper. His friend "Jones" brought him some beans for dinner in return for some extra sugar that the general possessed. Bartlett also played chess and checkers with another unidentified inmate, who beat him regularly. He conversed with others as he could, hearing some interesting tales from a West Virginia prisoner. "If I had paper I would write down things that I hear and see from day to day. It would make a very interesting book. I must try to remember them all. I fear I shan't do justice to some of them." But he did find the time to compose an epigram that used Major Morfit's name.[15]

And then, on August 26, just after breakfast, the hospital steward came in and told Bartlett that he had orders from Major Morfit to send the general to his office so that he could be taken to Richmond. "Can it be exchange? If so, God has quickly heard and answered my prayers." An excited Bartlett quickly gathered up his belongings — a cotton haversack containing some hard bread and tea, his

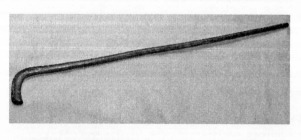

While convalescing in Southern prisons at Danville and Richmond, General Bartlett used this cane as an aid for walking. It measures 35 inches high. Courtesy Berkshire Museum, Pittsfield, MA.

cane, and his wooden foot. The "same old wagon" took Frank to the major's office, from which they departed as seven o'clock that evening, went to the depot, and Bartlett, accompanied by a single guard, was placed on the train for Richmond.[16]

The train was in Richmond by nine the next morning. Commissioner Ould met Bartlett and informed him that he was to go north by the first truce boat available. In the meantime, the general would be remanded to Libby Prison, his home until the boat arrived. Unbeknownst to the general, his release had been planned for several weeks. Back on May 20, a fierce combat had taken place around Ware Bottom Church on the Bermuda Hundred peninsula east of Petersburg. Confederate troops led by P. G. T. Beauregard attacked to drive back Union General Benjamin F. Butler's Army of the James farther into the peninsula so that the Rebel lines could be straightened out. After some initial success, the Confederate assault bogged down in the face of a Union countercharge that regained much of the lost ground. Southern reinforcements arrived and attacked, but the uncoordinated offensive was repelled. During this latter fighting, Brigadier General William S. Walker accidentally rode into the Union lines and turned to flee. He refused to surrender and was shot from his horse. Walker was seriously wounded in the ankle and his foot later was amputated by Union surgeons. After Bartlett's capture, it was decided that Walker would be exchanged for him.[17]

Libby Prison was one of Richmond's best-known jails. Before the war this three-story brick building (actually a series of three connected structures), located on the James River waterfront, was used as a tobacco warehouse. It was appropriated for use as a prison in 1861 and generally was reserved for officers. In February 1864, 109 inmates escaped via a tunnel they had excavated under an adjacent street and up into a fenced yard across the street. By late 1864, the prison was again filled with Union officers captured during the continuous fighting since May.[18]

So Bartlett was transferred to the hospital in Libby Prison to await the truce boat. Among a group of prisoners delivered to Libby the next day (August 28) was Lieutenant Colonel Francis A. Walker, assistant adjutant general on Major General Winfield S. Hancock's staff, who was taken at Reams' Station a few days earlier, had attempted to escape, but was recaptured. "Walker was dressed in rags and filth, but how undisguisable the gentleman is," noticed an elated Bartlett. Walker hailed from Massachusetts and had been a member of the old 20th Massachusetts. Walker filled the general in about the fate of others in the regiment, including its current colonel, George N. Macy, who was badly injured in the recent fighting.[19]

Bartlett's stay in Libby was far superior to the hell he endured at Danville. His improving health, though, meant a lot. The imminent exchange also meant that the general would be treated better by his captors. Dinner his first night in Libby consisted of roast mutton. "I am treated with marked consideration just now for some reason or other. The surgeon marked for me *good* diet." Bartlett passed the time reading and playing chess. On August 30 he received a welcome letter from his mother, dated August 3.[20]

The final day of August brought joyous news for Frank Bartlett — the truce boat had arrived! The general also learned that Arthur Curtis was upstairs and had a joyful reunion with him. On September 1, General Bartlett gave Arthur everything he had and was escorted out of Libby with twenty other officers on "ambulances of boards." The general even was on board the vessel, ready to go. But then, unexpectedly, an order came from Judge Ould. "*I cannot go.* It is a bitter, bitter blow after getting so far. I must go back to prison. Ould says General Walker was not sent up.... My heart sinks at coming back here. I must wait patiently and believe *He* doeth all things for the best. Poor mother, if she only knew!"[21]

"Sunday, 4th [of September].... To-day I was to have been in Baltimore and comfort and freedom, but here I am still in misery, a prisoner. I have so much to be grateful for, it would be base to murmur at my lot." To pass the interminable hours of idleness, Bartlett learned cribbage to supplement his chess games. Rebel papers passed to the inmates of Libby helped them keep abreast of outside developments, such as the nomination of General George B. McClellan as Democratic presidential contender to vie with Lincoln in November, the fall of Atlanta, and other war news. On September 9, Bartlett had a recurring attack of typhoid, for which he was given quinine. The truce boat came again on the 10th and departed on the 12th with thirty officers, but without Bartlett once again.[22]

In spite of the continuing disappointment with having to remain in Libby, Bartlett wrote on September 12, "I am more contented than I was the last time. Arthur being here makes it very pleasant. We play cribbage, talk, smoke, and study Spanish together; the time passes very quickly." The two friends also gathered others and played poker into the night. "Beautiful moonlight nights now," penned the general on the 14th, "too bad to be shut up within prison bars. I hope the next moon I shall see on *salt water*. I am tired of seeing it reflected on this river and canal. My leg pains me a great deal today and to-night. We play poker — six."[23]

On September 20, Bartlett composed a lengthy letter to Francis W. Palfrey, providing details on the disappointment at not being exchanged when he was supposed to. After all, the surgeon at Danville had recommended him for an exchange, writing that "if I recovered would not be fit for duty for many months." Having Arthur around helped the general's spirits. Bartlett admitted to Palfrey that Arthur was feigning illness so he could remain in the hospital instead of being sent back upstairs in Libby. The general hoped to send this very informative missive by an officer going on the next boat, concealed from prying Rebel eyes because of all the information it contained.[24]

On Wednesday, September 21, Bartlett received the welcome news that the truce boat was again docked at a Richmond wharf, and would leave again for Fort Monroe on Friday. "I shall hope to go," he wrote that day. But would he? Erasmus Ross, the prison's clerk, told the general that he would indeed be going this time, but Frank "shall not feel certain till I am under the flag." Friday arrived and the boat did not go. But when the roll was brought in for those exchanged to sign, the general's name was at the top of the list. The poker players were all there save Arthur, who would be left behind. On this last night in Libby, the general was struck with a bad case of diarrhea, "up all night, very weak."[25]

> Saturday, 24th. Off again. I am so ill I can hardly stand. Bade Arthur good-by–left him my chain, etc., again. On the *Allison*. I expected every moment a summons to go on shore again. Off at last, twenty minutes before 10 A.M., down the James. Ashore at Varina. A grasp of a friendly hand, Major Mulford. A short ride, and there floats the old flag. My I never lose sight of it again. I am too ill to eat. Comfortable bed and state room — lie at landing all night.[26]

The boat trip continued next day, arriving at Fort Monroe at 5:30 in the afternoon. Along the way, Bartlett learned he had been exchanged in early August. but was held up because of General Walker. When the vessel docked, brother-in-law Charles Manning was there to greet the general and catch him up on family news. Mother Bartlett was waiting in Baltimore, where she joyfully greeted her son on September 26. Although Frank ate a good breakfast, "can't stand it." Doctor Buxley arrived and examined the patient — "must go on very low diet. 'With care can get well in *six months!*' Pleasant prospect, still I am in God's country once more, and that is everything. Mother tells me all about Agnes; three letters from her, one from Winthrop. Dear Agnes."[27]

On Wednesday, September 28, after a "long, weary, trying ride," Bartlett reached New York City, where an aunt and uncle took him in. Agnes came that evening. "I saw her in the little dining-room. It almost repays one for the misery and pain, this meeting." She came again in the morning, sitting beside his bed, with Frank too weak to get up. "Many callers and cards." Agnes remained in the city until she had to go home on the first of October. Finally, three days later, the general was well enough to travel farther and the family left for Boston, arriving there on the afternoon of October 5. A carriage arrived and took the emaciated veteran to his family's home. "Shown to my room — should not know it, beautifully furnished and adorned. Bookcase and desk from Agnes.... My swords hung in trophy." Finally, the two-month ordeal was over and Frank was at home, surrounded by his family and the woman he loved. Now he could begin to fully recuperate from his ordeal.[28]

12

"I Think It Would Be Hard to Find Two Happier People"

War's End

"This being at home again is delicious; comfort and rest," wrote Frank Bartlett on October 7. "May I never be separated from it again by such an impassable barrier as that line of hostile bayonets!" While recuperating in Boston, Frank was the center of the family's attention. He received numerous cards and letters, but was unable to write himself, explaining that his eyes shared "with the rest of my system a prostration which is something quite new to me." His surgeons informed their patient that he must have "perfect rest and quiet, with careful treatment, diet, etc., for *six* months, and predict very unpleasant things otherwise. I propose to disappoint them in regard to time."[1]

Frank actually went into Boston on October 12 on a shopping trip, but shortly thereafter a spate of rainy weather set in, which, together with frequent headaches, kept him confined to home. His general health was still uncertain, and he was not able to wear his artificial leg very well, necessitating the purchase of a replacement. Frank spent a lot of time with Agnes, who became his fiancée sometime before the end of 1864. The formal announcement of their engagement was made on January 16, 1865. Her father Robert Pomeroy announced the news at his estate in Pittsfield, on the day of his own silver anniversary. But Frank was still weak throughout the winter of 1864–65, thanks to the dysentery he had contracted while in prison. He applied for duty in mid–April, but received no reply. Frank wrote again on May 23, enclosing a surgeon's certificate of disability to account for his absence from active duty. The general indicated that he wished to be assigned to the Ninth Corps if possible.[2]

On June 9, Frank received orders to report without delay to Major General John G. Parke, the commander of the Ninth Army Corps. An elated Bartlett was in Washington by June 13 and then reported to Parke, who on June 17 assigned him to the command of the First Division, which was located at Tenallytown, Maryland, northwest of Washington. Frank took command of the division on June 10, replacing Brevet Major General Orlando B. Willcox, who moved up to corps command when Parke went on leave on the seventeenth. Division headquarters was in a "lovely oak grove" situated next to the Tenallytown Road, and was

This marble bust of the general shows him with a major general's shoulder bars and the moustache that he grew shortly after the war. A July 1865 image of the general with his divisional staff officers clearly shows that he had not yet grown the moustache. **Courtesy Berkshire Athenaeum, Pittsfield, MA.**

composed of tents, which Frank preferred, though he confessed there was a house nearby if he wanted it. The general much preferred the shade of the grove when compared to the "fiendish heat" of the nation's capital. "I was there a week before I came out here," he wrote, "and it nearly killed me."[3]

The First Division was composed of three brigades. The First, under the command of Colonel Samuel Harriman of the 37th Wisconsin, consisted of the 37th and 38th Wisconsin regiments, 109th New York, 51st Pennsylvania, and the 17th and 27th Michigan regiments. Colonel William Telford's Second Brigade included the 1st Michigan Sharpshooters, 2nd and 8th Michigan, 46th New York, 50th Pennsylvania, and 60th Ohio. Brevet Brigadier General Napoleon B. McLaughlen's Third Brigade consisted of the 3rd Maryland, 100th Pennsylvania, and 29th, 57th, and 59th Massachusetts.[4]

Frank was appalled at the condition in which he found his command:

I found the command in rather a slack state of discipline. No attention paid to guard-duty or drill. It is natural that men should feel, now

that the war for which they enlisted is over, that there is no further
need of discipline, and that the strict performance of guard-duty any
longer is needless.... In this they are encouraged by a certain class of
officers,— you well know what I mean if I say the Le Barnes school,-
and this feeling of expectancy and uncertainty about getting mustered
out is prejudicial to discipline.

I had all the regimental and brigade commanders here the other
night, and gave them a lecture of an hour and a half. You would have
smiled to see me laying down the law, surrounded by about twenty of
these old birds. I fancy it woke them up, for I have been pleased to see
a marked change for the better already.[5]

Still, Bartlett realized that there was no incentive for the men to drill,
perform guard duty, and other related daily work. "You feel that the object,
the aim, of this discipline is gone. You cannot feel that next week, in the presence of the enemy, we shall reap the benefit of this drill and training." And
when General Parke informed Bartlett that most of the troops in the Department of Washington were no longer needed and would be mustered out of
service, Frank wrote a letter to the adjutant general and asked to be relieved
from command. On July 14, Frank received written orders that relieved him
from his Ninth Corps assignment and sent him home, from whence he was
to report to the adjutant general.[6]

Though sad to leave active duty, Frank realized that the war was over
and the men were restless to go home. He also understood that his health was
not yet good enough to enable him to be on active duty. "I am very glad that
I came out here and satisfied myself," he wrote to Frank Palfrey, "otherwise
I might have always regretted that I had left the service, and been restless and
discontented.... There is always more or less of a feeling of pride and pleasure in having a number of men under your control. But I have not been quite
so well as I was at home, and I really suppose it would be better for me to be
further north this summer." Thus, it was with mixed feelings that Frank
Bartlett left the Ninth Corps and went north to his parents' home in Boston.[7]

Frank arrived in Boston in time to take part in the July 21 "Commemoration Day" at Harvard College. This event was a formal welcome home to
all the college men who had served in the war. After the concluding dinner
that night, the college president introduced General Bartlett by alluding to
an "ancient picture of a warrior maimed and deprived of an eye, on which
was the inscription 'The heart is left.'" Frank rose to reply and said that he
did not wish to delay the audience; all the eloquence in the world could not
reflect his feelings at this joyous event. As the general hesitated, Colonel Henry
Lee rose and remarked: "As the Speaker of the House of Burgesses of Virginia
said to Washington, Sit down, sir, your modesty is equal to your valor, and
that surpasses the power of any language I possess." The audience exploded
with applause and Frank sat down.[8]

Not long after returning home, Frank penned a lengthy missive to Secretary of War Stanton. The general had stopped in and paid his respects to the secretary before he left Washington; Stanton had told Bartlett that he would be glad to do anything he could for the general in the future. Thus, Frank wrote to ask Stanton's advice. Some of the general's friends suggested that he should visit Europe before being mustered out of service. He had recently spoken with the Canadian adjutant general, who also thought it was a good idea to visit England. Frank asked the secretary for his views rather than formally requesting a six-month leave of absence to leave the country for Europe.[9]

Stanton quickly approved a six-month leave of absence without pay to enable Bartlett to leave the United States. The secretary also forwarded to Frank an appointment to brevet major general, effective from March 13, 1865. This brevet rank conferred no benefits such as higher pay but merely allowed the general to be addressed and respected as an officer of higher rank. A month later, upon further reflection, Frank queried Stanton about postponing his leave of absence to begin October 18, following his upcoming marriage; Stanton immediately approved the new date.[10]

Frank's October 14 marriage to Mary Agnes Pomeroy took place in Pittsfield at the Pomeroy residence. The Reverend E. Livingston Wells, presiding rector of the Episcopal church in Pittsfield, conducted the service. Four days later, the newlyweds, accompanied by eight members of the Pomeroy family, steamed from New York on the Cunard steamer *Paris*, bound for England. To Frank, his first voyage was complete with a couple of days of seasickness. Agnes bragged about how her husband fooled those on ship by walking very well on his wooden leg; the passengers who heard that the young general had lost a leg simply couldn't believe it. "I think it would be hard to find two happier people than Frank and myself anywhere in Christendom," she wrote Frank Palfrey.[11]

Once in England, the passengers debarked and spent a few days getting their land legs. Most of the family rented a house in the Oxford Terrace section of London; one of Agnes' cousins insisted that the honeymooners stay with him in a house on Westbourne Square. Frank spent some time looking around London. After closely scrutinizing the guards in front of Buckingham Palace, Frank commented that they "neither marched well, nor came about well, nor carried their pieces well." The general went out on a fox hunt and proudly wrote to Palfrey that he survived well because of the English habit of riding with the foot in the stirrup all the way to the instep, which served his wooden leg well. Their tours of the English countryside, the dining and country life, impressed Frank very much. His impression of English soldiers went up after witnessing the changing of the guard at St. James' Palace. The general spent much time with several English officers, touring barracks, watching the soldiers, and visiting various sites in London.[12]

Then followed a trip to Brighton. From there, Frank went down to Alder-shott on December 13 to visit with Lieutenant General Sir James Scarlett, who requested to see the American officer. The Crimean War veteran was a division commander who invited Frank to visit his command of some 4,500 soldiers. Frank rode out in a carriage to see the troops march in review. Sir James then formed his division for an advance across the rolling hills. Preceded by skirmishers, his troops advanced to a creek, where engineers laid a pontoon bridge. Frank was impressed as he watched the cavalry, infantry, and artillery maneuver against an imaginary enemy. After touring their barracks, Frank and his party returned to Brighton.[13]

By New Year's day, Frank was in Paris, where his leg flared with pain. This outbreak did nothing to help his low opinion of French theater, though the general was impressed by the celebration of Mass in the Chapel of the Invalides. The chapel was crowded with grizzled veterans, sitting under battle-stained flags. "Martial music always affected me," he penned, "but here to sit

among the old heroes of the first empire, under the very flags they had fought over and won, under the same roof where lie the ashes of emperor and leader, was to me intoxicating, overpowering, and I cried like a child." The newlyweds visited the Louvre and other tourist sites before leaving the city. Their journey took them south to Marseilles, followed by a week in the Nice area, where Frank found the warm Mediterranean air invigorating after the fog of London and rain of Paris. Bartlett described their travel method to his friend Palfrey:

This photograph of Mrs. Bartlett was published in 1909 upon her death in February of that year. Courtesy Berkshire Historical Society, Pittsfield, MA.

You have no idea the comfort of having a good courier....

You get up in the morning, and after a good breakfast, go down and get into your comfortable carriage with four smart horses, find a lunch waiting for you at your halting-place, and at sunset are shown into your parlor where the table is ready and in your room your portmanteau unlocked and open, everything at your hand. It is the poetry of travel. We are fortunate in having a very good man. We give him the purse, and he does all the rest.[14]

After visiting Marseilles and Nice, the party went on to Italy in early January 1866. To Frank, French soldiers presented a better picture than Italians, who did not look so neat and trim. Frank's pen gushed with elaborate words as he described their journey through the Alps that took them to Genoa, Pisa, and Florence. In Genoa, they stayed in an old ducal palace, with rooms so large that it was quite a walk from one end to the other, mused Frank, with ceilings so high that "you felt as if you were out doors." The general was also impressed with Genoa's city walls and the chain of forts on surrounding heights. "The women wear for bonnets white lace or tarlatan veils, pinned over the head and falling around the shoulders. With a pretty face it is very becoming; but pretty faces are what you do not see often in Italy." Their short stopover in Pisa included a trip to the famous leaning tower, but Frank was very disappointed when he laid eyes on the landmark. The cathedral, however, was very impressive to the Americans.[15]

The party spent a week in Florence, though Frank remarked that a visitor needed six weeks to see everything in the city. "I am not fond of old paintings," he quipped, "but some of Murillo's and Raphael's and Andrea del Sarto's and Titian's are very *persuasive*." Upon arrival in Florence, Frank found an invitation from Garibaldi to come visit him on his private island of Caprera, which Frank planned to do after their trip to Naples. From Florence, the party went to Leghorn and thence by sea to Civita Vecchia, and then on to Rome, arriving in time to witness the great carnival from their apartment on the Corso. On George Washington's birthday, Frank found himself at a breakfast for Americans in Rome, during which he made a speech. Then came a trip to Naples, including stops at Pompeii, Sorrento, and Capri.[16]

Frank left for Sardinia on March 10, leaving his wife in Italy because of the fear of rough seas. Frank first landed at the harbor of Maddelena on Sardinia, where customs officers searched his valise before one of Garibaldi's sons located Frank, who took him to a small rowboat for the three-mile jaunt across to Caprera. Garibaldi had purchased part of this island, located between Corsica and Sardinia, in 1855. In 1860, Garibaldi had organized a force of volunteers and had taken Sicily, then crossed and seized Naples, after which he held elections and proclaimed Victor Emanuel king of Italy. Garibaldi then retired to Caprera. In early 1862, President Lincoln, acting on advice from a number of Americans, offered Garibaldi command of the Union army, but withdrew the offer after the Papacy protested. Later that year, Garibaldi again tried to march on Rome, but his forces were defeated, he was imprisoned, then released and granted amnesty by the king. Even as Frank Bartlett stepped ashore on Cabrera, Garibaldi was yet again planning another excursion to the mainland to continue his quest for Italian unification.[17]

Frank arrived at Garibaldi's house just minutes before the veteran came in from one of the fields, "with outstretched hands, his face beaming with the same bright, kindly smile that I had carried in my memory for thirteen years." Garibaldi inquired about Frank's family, then the two men talked briefly before Bartlett went to a room prepared for him to rest a bit. He met the other occupants of the house — an English colonel and his wife and one of Garibaldi's daughters and her children. The Italian then asked Frank to walk with him, and off they went, discussing the recent war in America and how all liberty-loving people in Europe were glad that the North had finally won. He then showed Frank his vineyards and orange trees, then the different shrubs in the area. A one o'clock dinner followed, with Frank seated at Garibaldi's left. "The dishes are regular Italian ones. A soup, thick with rice or maccaroni; a stew, with olives cooked in it, figs, oranges, cheese, and wine from the island." Garibaldi translated into Italian everything he said to Frank, so that his other visitors, some of whom had just arrived from Sardinia, could understand. Frank carefully noted the hero, sitting there in "his usual costume, a poncho of dark woollen stuff over the red shirt, a small fez or smoking-cap on his head when in the house, and presiding over all with the grace and dignity of a king. I never knew before what a superb face he has, and what a glorious voice; when he would get warmed on any subject, it would ring as clear and sweet as a bell."[18]

After a six o'clock supper, the guests sat around drinking tea and discussing various subjects before Garibaldi bid his guests good night and went to bed. Frank sat up talking to Colonel Chambers before retiring. Frank returned to the mainland the next day, after which his party went back north through Italy, across Switzerland, to Strasbourg. Frank took delight in walking to the Rhine bridge and crossing into Germany, making particular note of the different uniforms at each end of the bridge. By the time that the party reached Paris, Frank was not feeling well with some symptoms of typhoid, but he quickly recovered. His six month leave was nearing an end, but he had written to Secretary Stanton to request a two-month extension, thus giving them time to return to America. By the time they reached London, England was in the midst of a bank panic after one of the largest banking companies failed. The only good money seemed to be American securities, which no one would part with. "Rather a let-down for people who were sneering at our bankruptcy two years ago, and disposed to facilitate it. Serves them right; and the men over here who have been true to the North, and backed her by putting their money in her stocks, are now reaping their reward."[19]

The Bartletts returned to the United States in early June 1866. On the fourteenth, Frank addressed a brief note to the adjutant general's department to notify Colonel Townsend of his arrival. On July 18, General Bartlett was mustered out of service and returned to civilian life.[20]

13

"UNITED WE ARE INVINCIBLE"

The Postwar Years

When the newlyweds returned from Europe, they at first made their home at The Homestead in Pittsfield, thus allowing Frank to decide what his postwar employment would be before settling on their own home. While Frank entertained offers, their first child, named Agnes, was born on September 16. Frank was very relieved that his wife made it through the pregnancy, something with which husband Frank was not at all familiar. Baby Agnes was "strong, healthy, and *pretty*," penned Frank to his friend Palfrey. All in all, Frank was happy that baby Agnes was healthy, though it seems that some in the family were hoping for a boy so that Frank could pass along the family name.[1]

Palfrey wrote that Frank at first thought of entering the diplomatic service, but nothing came of his inquiries. Uncle Edwin suggested to his nephew that business was a more preferable way to make a living. While Frank looked for employment, he turned down the offer to be the Collector of the Port of Boston, with its salary of at least $12,000, a princely sum in those days. Though it was tempting, Frank thought the post itself would not agree with him. Judge Josiah Abbott, the late Henry Abbott's father, agreed with Frank that he should turn down the collector's job. Frank was constantly asked to serve as a delegate at political conventions; his name was brought up too often without his consent. Hearing that former Union general Benjamin F. Butler was attempting to return to Congress, Frank thought that if Butler was successful, his post as militia general in Massachusetts would become vacant. "If so, we must think about that."[2]

The Bartletts continued to live at The Homestead into the year 1867. Frank continued to consider various employment opportunities — president of a new life insurance and savings company in New York and United States marshal for the District of Massachusetts among them. But Frank was hesitant to have to move to New York City for the insurance company presidency. Although the salary was high ($10,000), the cost of living in the city meant to Frank that it would only be worth $5,000 in Massachusetts. Therefore, Frank composed a letter to his contact in the city and respectfully declined the opportunity. "One of the principles of my life," he wrote, "is never to undertake anything that I cannot give my whole heart and mind to." Frank wrote that if he accepted the position, he would have to give his whole heart and soul to the work, and thus have to pass up a more suitable employment should it be offered.[3]

This oil painting shows Frank Bartlett in a nice suit and with groomed moustache, the trappings of a postwar businessman. Courtesy Berkshire Athenaeum, Pittsfield, MA.

Finally, in June 1867 he decided upon the management of a paper mill in the nearby town of Dalton. Frank and his family moved into a "snug little house" which he nicknamed "The Box," and started to work hard on his new business. Then in September came the death of his uncle Edwin Bartlett, which Frank took very hard. "I thought we had got accustomed to death,— we could lose comrades and brothers in war, and be calm and stoical. But this is all new to me. I have never lost a near relative before, one whom I knew well.... My uncle was nearer to me ... that is, I went to him more freely for advice, ... and now I feel as if I had lost everything." Uncle Edwin was childless, and his will left his Miramonte estate on the Hudson River to his wife, and on her death to his nephew Frank, "in consideration of his gallantry and devotion to his country in her late struggle for self-preservation." His widow also received $100,000, with the residue to two friends in trust to have appraised. Of this remainder, one-third went to his wife and the rest to Frank Bartlett. The appraisal meant that Frank would inherit about $200,000 in property. But

Frank felt that his aunt should have the money, so he drew up a paper instructing the appraisers to retain the property left to him and pay the income to his aunt. Frank reasoned that his aunt needed the extra money to continue the standard of living to which she was accustomed. Besides, Frank's own business interests promised to earn his family a good living, and it was for these reasons that he declined the provisions of his uncle's will.[4]

Frank continued to live and work in Dalton until early 1868, when the family moved to Pittsfield because Frank accepted the position of treasurer and general manager of the Pomeroy Iron Works, located in West Stockbridge, a town west of Pittsfield. He left his brother-in-law, Colonel Walter Cutting, in charge of the paper mill in Dalton. Frank threw himself into the iron business with his usual energy and attention. As a result, by the end of May he could write that his furnace showed "the best week's work yet made at that or any other furnace in this country."[5]

But Frank's hard work had an adverse impact on his already frail health. In January 1868, he suffered a bilious attack that was accompanied by fever. His health did not improve immediately, and his sufferings continued into February, by which time his bowels and back were constantly sore. Frank's family physician thought that dysentery from his 1864 prison experience contributed to his current illness, and suggested that he avoid prolonged exposure and fatigue. But Frank ignored his doctor and worked hard at the iron business all summer. By early fall his health was again failing. He was very thin, and since his stump lost some flesh as a result, his artificial leg chafed and led to pain in his lost foot. Colonel Palfrey observed that Frank presented a cheerful disposition to the world, and thus his contemporaries did not know how hard he actually suffered behind his outward disposition.[6]

In September, Frank was asked to serve as commander of the Massachusetts delegation to the Soldiers' and Sailors' Convention in Philadelphia. The general's reply shows his lack of interest in politics, but also illustrates his view toward the defeated South:

> I am no politician. If I were to be classed at all, I suppose it would be as a "War Democrat." And having been a War Democrat during the war, now that the war is over I most certainly desire peace. A peace that we so steadily fought for; a peace that we so fairly won. That peace would seem now to be threatened, unless the men who surrendered unconditionally at Appomattox are allowed to dictate terms to the men who taught them, through four bloody years, that the way of rebellion is hard. I believe in the utmost liberality and magnanimity towards a fallen foe, and I would extend the hand right heartily in token of forgiveness and friendship.[7]

Frank's health continued the same into 1869. However, there was joy on February 17, when Caroline was born, the couple's second child. Agnes, however, was worried about her husband. "It would go to your heart to see him," she wrote. "He looks nearly as emaciated as when he came home from the Libby." Frank's health improved somewhat during the summer, but by September he was confined to bed with bowel congestion accompanied by ulceration. The iron business began to decline later in the year, but Frank kept himself occupied in planning a house that would be constructed near The Homestead in Pittsfield.[8]

By the spring of 1870, Frank's health was worrisome to everyone. His family decided that a trip to England might help restore his ailments. But Frank resented the "conspiracy between the doctor and the rest of them" to get him out of the country, no matter how restful the trip might be, because he "do not yet see how I can possibly leave my affairs." The general hoped that his stay in England would not last any longer than necessary, perhaps as short as the arrival and departure of his vessel. In spite of Frank's complaints, he sailed to England in June. He stayed about twenty miles from London, giving himself "over to complete *laziness*," doing little in the way of going out to dinner and the theater. Frank went to London at least once a week,

This is a nineteenth century view of Wendell Hall, the magnificent Pittsfield home that Frank Bartlett built for his growing family in 1870. Located at 31 Wendell Avenue, the home was sold after the general's death when Mrs. Bartlett moved elsewhere in the city. The large structure, shown here on the left, became an inn, then was converted into apartments in 1928. Courtesy Berkshire Historical Society, Pittsfield, MA.

and took many leisurely carriage rides through the lovely countryside. Although his health did not improve for at least two weeks after his arrival in England, Frank admitted later that he was much better and looked forward to a restful voyage home. Frank wrote to his friend Palfrey that this voyage confirmed his belief that "the oftener you leave home for this side, the better satisfied you will be that with all her faults America is the place of all the world to live in. The more you see of other countries, the better you will *love* your own."[9]

Frank returned to America and immediately resumed his workaholic ways. In October, Agnes wrote that her husband's long work hours in the iron furnace had led to inflammation of the bowels. Because Frank threw himself into everything he did, he would frequently exhaust himself, then would not take the time to step back and rest. As a result, his already frail constitution steadily got worse. In addition to physical stress, Frank worried too much about his business affairs; Agnes seems to have constantly worried when she would hear Frank mutter that he longed for the "rest of heaven."[10]

Still, by the end of 1870, Frank moved his family into their new Pittsfield house, "a source of great enjoyment to himself and his wife." But Frank put a brave face on his health, and was constantly entertaining and visiting family and friends. The year 1871 was spent mostly in working, though in August he went on vacation to Nantucket for two weeks. On November 26, his first son was born, christened Edwin after his late uncle.[11]

In January 1872, Frank was appointed a colonel on the staff of the Massachusetts governor. Still, his health was "so, so" as he described it, which meant a delay of a proposed trip to Virginia on iron business. With his health a bit better, Frank journeyed south across the Mason-Dixon line for the first time since the end of the war. The trip involved travel by canal in the Lynchburg area as Frank met possible business associates in a search for new sources of iron ore.[12]

By early April, Frank was back in Pittsfield. Although he was not very politically minded, Frank followed with interest a growing dissatisfaction with the presidency of Ulysses S. Grant. Personally honest and hard-working, Grant proved that although he was an outstanding soldier, he was not nearly as able in the nation's highest office. Few of his cabinet officers were capable, while many of those he appointed to office were more interested in lining their own pockets than in running an honest administration. Grant proved that he was not a good judge of men when out of uniform, and the scandals that rocked his administration had begun to anger a number of Republicans. By the time 1872 dawned, there was a definite upswing of opinion that Grant had to be defeated that fall.

Frank was hardly back in Massachusetts when he was surprised to read a brief article in the *Springfield Republican* that General Bartlett had been

Shown here is a modern view of the old Bartlett home in Pittsfield. It now houses professional offices and has been shorn of its many distinctive Victorian-era architectural features. Courtesy Donna Kasuba.

selected to represent western Massachusetts at the Republican convention in Philadelphia, and would vote for Grant's nomination for a second term. The April 10 edition of the paper contained Frank's brief reply. He was adamant in stating that "I am *not* to be counted on to go for Grant, if that means, as I fear it does, blind allegiance to the group of politicians under whose control General Grant has unfortunately placed himself, and whose solicitude seems to be greater for the Republican party than for the welfare of the country." Rather than Grant, Frank publicly proclaimed that Charles Francis Adams was the best choice for president. The son of former president John Quincy Adams, Charles Francis had been the American ambassador to England during the Civil War and was primarily responsible for keeping the British from siding with the Confederacy. A scholar from an elite Boston family, Adams was someone with whom Frank Bartlett could identify with ease.[13]

The liberal Republicans who had begun to break away from Grant espoused civil service reform, a reduction of the tariff, lower taxes, an end to land grants to railroads, resumption of specie payment, and a better reconciliation with the South that included an end to federal intervention in local affairs. In January 1872, Missouri liberals issued a call for all like-minded men to meet in Cincinnati in May to nominate a presidential candidate. The resulting assembly consisted of a wide range of anti–Grant people — true reformers, free traders, pre-war anti-slavery veterans, and others who aspired to the presidency. A number of attendees aspired to be president–Senator Lyman Trumbull, governors John M. Palmer of Illinois and B. Gratz Brown of Missouri, New York *Tribune* editor Horace Greeley, Supreme Court Justice David Davis, and former ambassador Charles Francis Adams, who was hesitant about the entire situation and left for Europe after indicating he would accept if nominated.[14]

Frank was one of those interested in seeing that Grant was defeated in November. By the time Frank had returned to Massachusetts in April, he was already heavily involved in the movement to defeat the president. At first, he was not enthusiastic about joining the opponents who had called for a convention in Cincinnati. Together with Henry A. Barnum (commander of the New York Grand Army of the Republic), and former general Hugh Judson Kilpatrick, Frank issued a circular letter dated April 15, 1872, that was sent out to many prominent veterans. The three signers requested the recipients to call for a convention of veterans which would call upon the upcoming Republican convention in Philadelphia to nominate someone other than Grant. This man would also unite the party and ensure victory that fall. Replies were disappointing and it was apparent very quickly that Grant would indeed be nominated. It was also clear that the party was splitting over his nomination.[15]

Frank was disappointed. "We have had four years of a soldier, I think we need four of a statesman," he penned to Massachusetts Adjutant General William Schouler. Frank vacillated about personally going to Cincinnati to make the Massachusetts delegation stronger. "I can neither afford the time nor expense, and travelling is very disagreeable to me, to say nothing of my dislike of taking any active part in political meetings," he wrote, "but I just feel that it is my duty to make the sacrifice for the purpose of assisting in the accomplishment of the nomination of Mr. Adams." Frank theorized that a ticket consisting of Adams and Trumbull would be unbeatable, but he was suspicious of those assembling in Cincinnati. He correctly knew that Adams had no great following, and if he was to be elected president, then those who would vote for him would need to rise above "personal considerations" and have an honest desire for "better things."[16]

The Cincinnati convention certainly had its twists and turns. German-born Carl Schurz, a former Civil War general and one of the primary organizers of the convention, had engaged in secret negotiations with Democratic National Chairman August Belmont to unite both parties behind an Adams-Trumbull ticket. But there were other backdoor meetings as well, and in the end, Horace Greeley emerged as the nominee with Missouri governor Brown as his running mate. Indeed, Adams had not garnered much support in Cincinnati. He was described as the "greatest iceberg in the northern hemisphere." His potential running mate Trumbull was also too intellectual for the politicians of the day to accept as a serious contender. Greeley was seen as acceptable in the South because of his calls for a more acceptable reunification than the present harsh policy toward the former Confederate states. In fact, Greeley was one of the men who had posted the bond that freed Jefferson Davis from jail.[17]

Frank Bartlett was not at all pleased with the results of the Cincinnati convention. After coming so near "a glorious success," the nomination of Greeley left him disheartened. "I suppose I shall recover from it in due time, but I am still 'sick,'" he wrote on May 20. He thought that Greeley would gather a large number of votes, but not as many all over the country as Adams would have done. Later that summer, Frank stood behind Greeley as the man to unite the country. He brushed off another article that stated he was behind Grant, not bothering to publish a reply.[18]

The Republican Party reacted to Greeley's nomination by using its influence in Congress to pass a number of bills crafted to undercut the Greeley platform. In July, the Democratic National Convention lined up behind Greeley in hopes of upending the Grant administration. The Republicans nominated Grant for a second term. When the November election came, Grant carried every Northern state and garnered 55 percent of the national vote, the largest majority in any presidential election between 1836 and 1892. Lamented Greeley, "I was the worst beaten man that ever ran for that high office." In Frank's home state of Massachusetts, only 10 percent of the voters cast their ballots for Greeley, belaying Bartlett's earlier opinion that Massachusetts "is as sure to give Greeley a large majority as the sun is to rise."[19]

But Frank did not have the time nor the inclination to take an active interest in politics. On May 27, the iron works at West Stockbridge burned to the ground after an accident started a lethal blaze. As one of the owners as well as the superintendent, the general was greatly disheartened. The works would be rebuilt, but it would take time and the loss of the works cut into Frank's business earnings.[20]

Thus, Frank threw his seemingly boundless energy into a business venture that took him back to Virginia, where his developing interest in the Powhatan Iron Works led to his becoming treasurer and manager of this respectable company. A group of Northern businessmen had purchased this company and had infused it with new capital; Frank would manage the company to ensure its success.[21]

Frank was back in Pittsfield in mid–September. Here, on September 24, the town dedicated its impressive Civil War monument. The general was

Frank Bartlett topped off his work to erect a monument to Pittsfield's Civil War veterans when he spoke at the monument's dedication on September 20, 1872. This view along North Street shows the crowd assembled to watch the procession, which can barely be discerned as shadows move along the street. Courtesy Berkshire Historical Society, Pittsfield, MA.

chairman of the committee that raised the money and designed the monument, and he also wrote the inscription that was chiseled into the base. On that September day, Frank also gave the dedicatory speech in which he transferred the monument to the town. The speech was a mode of patriotism, as evidenced by the following excerpt:

> [The artist] has taken for the subject, not the private soldier nor the commissioned officer, but a greater hero than either,-the man on whom so often hung the fate of battle, the man on whose self-forget-

ting bravery and unflinching firmness the steadiness of the whole line depended, the man who bore the colors. And, comrades, was there ever any flag half so well worth fighting for, half so well dying for, as the flag we followed? As I look upon your faces that I have seen amid the smoke of battle, and remember how you closed up on the gaps made by the fall of those whom we honor to-day, I am conscious that to you also belongs a share of the honor, but with this difference: their fame was achieved and secured by dying heroic deaths,-yours must yet be maintained and preserved by living blameless lives.[22]

Following the Pittsfield dedication, Frank moved his family to Richmond so they could all be together. The general found that the Virginia climate was much better on his health than that of Massachusetts. His vigor brought on by hard work kept him busy almost every day. Agnes thought that this time period was generally kind to her husband:

Frank was very hopeful ane very busy that winter and spring, getting things ready to start the furnaces, making excursions up the canal into the ore districts, going down into mines, and doing things a *whole* man would have shrunk from,-making contracts for ore, getting leases of some very valuable beds, and in every way busy, and working with bright hopes and a hearty faith that all was going well and that the Virginia enterprise would be a complete success.... He was better than

This view shows the Soldiers Monument in the park in Pittsfield. The monument was sculpted by Launt Thompson, who also executed several other statues and busts. Courtesy Berkshire Athenaeum, Pittsfield, MA.

in 1871, when he had that dreadful congestive chill, and also better
than in 1872, when he had the severe attack of pleurisy which laid him
up for so long a time.

Frank's family remained in Richmond until May 1873. As the weather
began to turn hot, they returned to Pittsfield until October, when they again
came back south to Richmond.[23]

The year 1873 was initially a good one for the Powhatan Iron Works. In
early June, Frank managed to gain control of a major iron ore bank, worth
$50,000 to the company, he bragged. "It has taken diplomacy and money. I
have bought up and paid off the various claims and liens, and now have
absolute possession of the place for ten years." But there was disaster loom-
ing on the horizon. In September, Jay Cooke and Company, one of the nation's
largest banking firms, collapsed because of its failure to market millions of
dollars in railroad bonds. A financial panic soon swept across the banking system. Many banks and brokerage houses failed, businesses laid off workers,
and the stock market temporarily suspended its operations. By the end of 1874,
nearly half of existing iron furnaces had suspended operations.[24]

The Panic of 1873 surely affected Frank's health. "[H]is distress of body,"
wrote Palfrey, "was aggravated by the distress of mind which attended his
business failure and the pressure of narrowing means," a reference to the fact
that Bartlett's money was tied up completely in the iron businesses in Massachusetts and Virginia. In February 1874, Frank caught a cold while in Virginia. The attendant cough never left him. Still, he was generally happy, for
on March 20, twin sons Robert and William were born. Frank continued to
gravitate back and forth between Pittsfield and Richmond, ever watchful over
the two iron works.[25]

On June 23, 1874, Frank Bartlett was on hand at his alma mater for the
dedication of Memorial Hall, Harvard University's splendid tribute to her students' part in the Civil War. June 24 was Commencement Day; the dinner
was served in Memorial Hall. On this day, Frank was the grand marshal for
the ceremony. The building was more crowded than normal for such an event,
which took place on a usual summer day in New England. After a number
of speakers and tributes, General Bartlett finally was introduced and stood to
deliver his address. Palfrey was at his best as he described the situation:

> [W]hen Bartlett arose, and the first words uttered by his deep and
> manly voice were heard, and the audience became aware that they
> came from the shattered soldier whose tall and slender form and
> wasted face they had seen at the head of the procession as he painfully
> marshaled it that day, a great silence fell upon the multitude, and he
> continued and finished his speech in the midst of silence, except when
> it was broken, as it was more than once, by spontaneous bursts of
> cheering. When he took his seat, enthusiastic cheering followed, and
> all felt that an event had taken place. It is within bounds to say that it

is many years since any speech made in New England has produced so great an effect.[26]

For Frank, this speech would later define much of what he would be remembered for. His words would not have been possible without his recent pleasant experiences in Virginia. As a War Democrat who had Southern friends but cast his lot emphatically with the Union, Frank understood more than most people the sacrifices both sides had made during the Civil War. His Harvard speech, then, was quickly noted in newspapers far and wide. Frank began by noting the sacrifices of Harvard students that Memorial Hall commemorated. He quickly noted that another orator had noticed that most Southerners were not bitter over the results of the conflict. The occasional "firebrands" who continued to stir up sectional hatred were not in step with the majority of Americans, but merely stirred up trouble for their own selfish ends. These people, Frank noted, were not those who actually fought on the battlefields.

> Take care, then, lest you repel, by injustice, or suspicion, or even by indifference, the returning love of men who now speak with pride of that flag as "our flag." It was to make this a happy, reunited country, where every man should be in reality free and equal before the law, that our comrades fought, our brothers fell. They died not that New England might prosper or that the West might thrive. They died not to defend the northern capitol, or preserve those marble halls where the polished statesman of the period conduct their dignified debates! They died for their country — for the South no less than for the North. And the southern youth, in the days to come, will see this, and as he stands in these hallowed halls and reads those names, realizing the grandeur and power of a country which, thanks to them, is still his, will exclaim, "These men fought for my salvation as well as for their own. They died to preserve not merely the unity of a nation, but the destinies of a continent."[27]

In March 1875, Frank received an invitation to speak at the April 19 commemoration at Lexington, Massachusetts. He was at first inclined to turn down the offer because his talk would again be about North-South relations, which "cannot be discussed from any point of view without criticizing severely the action of the President and the administration party, who are in a great degree responsible for the unfortunate situation." And since President Grant was to be the guest of honor on April 19, Frank reflected that "to say anything in the slightest degree offensive to him would be a breach of taste and hospitality." But his friends continued to urge him to go to Lexington, and finally, on April 15, he replied favorably that he would be there to "say a few words at their dinner."[28]

Frank continued to debate how he would write his brief speech so that he would say something of importance to the whole country. He detested politicians for their divisiveness, placing their party and themselves ahead of their country. When April 19 arrived, the day was bitterly cold, but Frank drove from Boston and was announced after the eighth toast, "The North and the South." In spite of the weather, there was an immense crowd on hand to hear the invalid general rise. His entire speech follows:

> Mr. President,— When I opened the letter from your committee ask-
> ing me to come from five hundred miles away, and say a few words
> here to-day, it seemed impossible. But as I read further your desire
> that I should speak on the "relations of the North to the South," and
> your assertion that, as an unprejudiced observer, what I might say
> would help to restore fraternal relations between the two great sec-
> tions of our country, although knowing how greatly you overrated the
> value of any poor words of mine, I felt that, if they could lend the
> least aid to the result you described, inclination and the cares of busi-
> ness must yield to the voice of duty; and I came. But sir, I am not an
> "unprejudiced observer." On the contrary, I have a prejudice, which is
> shared by all soldiers, in favor of peace. And I think I may safely say,
> that, between the *soldiers* of the two great sections of our country, fra-
> ternal relations were established long ago. I have a strong prejudice
> against any man or men who would divide or destroy or retard the
> prosperity and progress of the nation, whose corner-stone was laid in
> the blood of our fathers one hundred years ago to-day. Moved by this
> prejudice, fourteen years ago, I opposed the men who preferred dis-
> union to death. True to this prejudice, I to-day despise the men who
> would, for the sake of self or party, stand in the way of reconciliation
> and a united country. The distinguished soldier who is your chief
> guest to-day never came nearer to the hearts of the people than when
> he said, "Let us have peace." And, sir, the only really belligerent peo-
> ple in the country to-day, north and south, are those who, while the
> war lasted, followed carefully the paths of peace. Do not believe that
> the light and dirty froth which is blown northward and scattered over
> the land (oftentimes for malicious purposes) represents the true cur-
> rent of public opinion at the South. Look to their heroes, their lead-
> ers,— their Gordons, their Lees, their Johnstons, Lamar, Ransom, and
> Ripley,— and tell me if you find in their utterances anything but
> renewed loyalty and devotion to a reunited country. These are the
> men, as our great and good Governor Andrew told you at the close of
> the war, these are the men by whom and through whom you must
> restore the South, instead of the meaner men for whom power is only
> a synonym for plunder. As I begged you last summer, I entreat you
> again: do not repel the returning love of these men by suspicion or
> indifference. If you cannot in forgiveness "kill the fatted calf," do not
> with coldness kill "the prodigal." When the Fifty-fourth Massachu-
> setts Regiment made its gallant attack on Fort Wagner, in July, 1863,
> it lost, with hundreds of its brave men, its heroic leader, and its col-
> ors. A few weeks ago, that flag was gracefully returned to the Gover-
> nor of Massachusetts by the officer who took it in action, with these
> noble words:—

"Under the existing state of things, I deem it decorous, if not a positive duty, to promote the oblivion of animosities which led to, and were engendered by, the war. I prefer to look upon such trophies as mementoes of the gallant conduct of the men who, like Shaw, Putnam, and other sons of Massachusetts, sealed with their lives their devotion to the cause which they adopted, rather than as evidences of prowess on the one side of the other. The custodians of such a memento should be the authorities of the state served by these gallant men; and I therefore transmit the flag to your Excellency for such disposition as the authorities of Massachusetts shall determine.

"Respectfully, your obedient servant,
"R. S. Ripley."

No one but a soldier can know how he would cling to a trophy that he had taken in honorable battle. No one but a soldier knows what it would cost to give it up, unless compelled by the loftier motives of chivalrous patriotism. And when General Ripley wrote that letter, he thought not of self, not of South Carolina nor of Massachusetts, but of a restored and a united country, and his heart embraced a continent. There are tattered flags in that sacred hall in yonder Capitol, around which, in the shock of battle, I have seen dear friends and brave men fall like autumn leaves. There are flags there that I cannot look upon without tears of pride and sorrow. But there is no flag there which has to-day for us a deeper significance or that bears within its folds a brighter omen of "Peace on earth, good will to men," than that battle-stained emblem so tenderly restored by a son of South Carolina, whom here, in the name of the soldiers of Massachusetts, I thank and greet as a brother. And I am proud that he was an American soldier. As an American, I am as proud of the men who charged so bravely with Pickett's Division on our lines at Gettysburg, as I am of the men who so bravely met and repulsed them there. Men cannot always choose the right cause; but when, having chosen that which conscience dictates, they are ready to die for it, if they justify not their cause, they at least ennoble themselves. And the men who, for conscience' sake, fought against their government at Gettysburg, ought easily to be forgiven by the sons of men who, for conscience' sake, fought against their government at Lexington and Bunker Hill.

Oh, sir, as Massachusetts was first in war, so let her be first in peace, and she shall be forever be first in the hearts of her countrymen. And let us here resolve that, true to her ancient motto, while in war *"Ense petit placidam,"* in peace she demands, not only for herself, but for every inch of this great country, *"sub libertate quietam."*[29]

Frank left the speakers' platform immediately after speaking and went back to Boston. He recorded in his journal that "The British certainly had their revenge on us to-day," in reference to the inclement weather of the nineteenth. The next day, Frank penned that all the papers had printed his speech and that he was receiving many compliments as a result.[30]

Perhaps the highest compliment to Frank and his reconciliation speech came on his return to Richmond later that month. Virginians in general applauded Frank's speech and a number of prominent citizens decided to gather and pay their compliments to the general. On the evening of April 28, a large number of former Confederate soldiers, ranging from privates to generals, assembled in Richmond's Capitol Square. Accompanied by the First Regiment Band, the throng marched up the street to Frank's residence at the southwest corner of Grace and Sixth streets. Ladies from the crowd streamed onto porches and balconies of adjacent houses as the band played "Hail to the Chief." When Frank came out on his porch, former Rebel general Bradley T. Johnson came up the steps to shake his hand and then give a brief speech, thanking the former Yankee general for his Lexington speech. Johnson briefly spoke about the mutual respect shown by the men in blue and gray at Appomattox, and how "You and men like you have kept the original faith and understanding, and we claim that we have done likewise." After a rousing tribute to the sons of Massachusetts and Virginia, Johnson said that it was "all for one and one for all" with the United States.[31]

The band played "Dixie" before Frank made a brief reply. He admitted that he had only spoken the truth to the crowd at Lexington. "I only spoke the hopes and feelings of my people. The chord of love and harmony was there, and only waited for the touch." Frank quoted from a recent address before the Lee Memorial Association to show that he was not the only speaker who touched upon the subject. He noted that the "chief defect in the great fabric of our Union, which, while it existed, rendered a perfect harmony of interests impossible, has been rudely swept away, leaving a structure more permanent, more full of glorious possibilities, than our fathers dared to hope for." The main task was now to cement the new Union and defeat those who kept the old enmities alive. Frank exhorted the former soldiers in the audience to lead this crusade to make America a better place for all. In conclusion, "The war through which we passed developed and proved on both sides the noble qualities of American manhood. It has left to us soldiers — once foes, now friends — a memory of hard-fought fields, of fearful sacrifices, of heroic valor; and has taught a lesson to be transmitted to our children-that divided we were terrible, united we are forever invincible."[32]

The Associated Press ensured that Frank's speech was read all over the country. He noted that Massachusetts papers were nominating him for all sorts of offices, which he really did not care for because, as he wrote in his journal, "I shall take the opportunity to prove that the satisfaction of doing one's duty so as to win the applause and approval of good men, is a reward greater than any office, as I am already repaid."[33]

Frank was a bit bemused to realize that his name was now more popular than in the past, mainly as a result of his Lexington speech. But underneath it all, he was not the happiest person alive, as he recorded in his diary on June 6, his thirty-fifth birthday:

> I hope I live to see another that affairs will look more promising. Business looks very blue. I wish I were out of it. I never ought to have gone into it. I ought to have stayed in the army, or else accepted some of the salaried positions that were offered me. Or even if I had begun to study law at the end of the war, I might be better off now. But God knows best, and we are in his hands. How little we know what he has in store for us! He has been very indulgent and merciful to me in spite of my many shortcomings.[34]

Shortly after writing this entry in his journal, Frank moved back to Massachusetts, evidently worn out in both body and soul. The Panic of 1873's effects were still evident throughout the iron industry, which was also plagued by coal strikes in Virginia. He went to the annual Commencement dinner at Harvard and made a brief speech, but he was not happy with it, commenting in private that he would not do it agin. "They ask me to *represent* those who died in the war. I sometimes feel quite ready to be *sent* as ambassador to them." Frank knew pretty well by this time that his days were numbered. His health was always questionable, and he knew the end was approaching. He fretted that his eldest son Edwin, not yet five years old, would not remember his father after he was gone.[35]

In spite of his declining health, Frank continued to stay busy. He was still active in the iron industry, and spent most of the months of July and September in Richmond attending to business. He was back in Massachusetts in time to attend the annual reunion of the 49th Massachusetts on September 9. In a brief speech to his old comrades, the colonel praised their submission to discipline and reminded them how effective they became because of it. Eight days later, Frank commented that he weighed 123 pounds without his artificial leg but with thin clothes.[36]

Frank's name continued to be popular in his home state. In September, the Democratic party offered to nominate him as their candidate for lieutenant governor. However, Frank was under the impression that Charles Francis Adams might receive the Republican nomination for governor, and thus he declined the offer in deference to his admiration for Adams. Still, the Democrats went ahead and nominated him at their state convention. Before Frank had a chance to reply, the Republican state committee proposed to nominate him for governor! The general was then in a quandary. Though Democrat in political leaning, he had come to believe more in the true Republican sense of politics. Still, did the Republicans nominate him to head off an Adams run for governor? In the end, Frank declined all political offers after much soul-searching.[37]

Rather than get involved in politics, Frank had more personal matters to worry about. The declining fortunes of the iron industry kept him preoccupied. The furnace at West Stockbridge was in danger of shutting down on November 1, and if it did, Frank was worried about supporting his family. Back in Richmond by October 1, Frank was equally worried about his future there. The furnace was struggling and his partners had left its management to him, which weighed Frank down heavily. On top of his business worries, Frank's health was not in top form. Still, he was in demand as a speaker. On November 11, he was the principal speaker at the dedication of a new free library in his hometown of Haverill. On the 27th, he introduced Carl Schurz to a Pittsfield audience. Then, on December 22, he replied to a toast at the annual dinner of the New England Society.[38]

In order to regain his health, Frank decided to go to Europe again, but became severely ill in early 1876, forcing him to postpone his plans. His will was further sapped by the continuing business decline of the Tredegar Company, which had never really recovered from the Panic of 1873. Tredegar's problems affected the entire Virginia iron industry, and the Powhatan company was no exception. Frank had invested his own money in the company in order to be able to obtain credit from local banks. The Tredegar problems meant that Frank's company also suffered, with himself as the primary creditor. After taking care of as much business as he could in Richmond, Frank was back in Pittsfield by late February.[39]

Bartlett departed New York for Liverpool on board the steamship *Russia* on March 1. This time, the voyage was far from smooth, the worst the ship's crew ever saw, they told the general. That spring was unusually cold and raw in Europe. "Since I landed," Frank wrote on March 23, "the weather has been simply atrocious. It has actually snowed every day until to-day, and I would not give odds that it won't yet, though the sun is trying to get out." For a time, Frank seemed better. He wrote that the "dreadful pain" in his lost foot was gone. His appetite was better, "for I do not loathe the sight of food as I did for weeks." After a brief trip across the Channel to France, Frank was back in England in early May, then set sail for America on May 27, arriving on June 7.[40]

Frank was glad to get home, and reported that his doctor said that he was "*decidedly* better than when I went away." He was glad to be away from his business worries, and wrote to Palfrey that even if there had been business letters awaiting his return, he would not have opened them. "The break from that worry is complete still, and I don't mean to take it up till I am much better able to." As late as June 26, Frank could write cheerfully that "I am gaining under the lovely June skies, and am looking forward to going down to Cohasset about the 10th July."[41]

However, Frank never recovered enough to make the visit to Cohasset. His cough worsened, as did his appetite, which, together with his chronic diarrhea from which he suffered ever since 1864, meant a slow death. By early September, Frank was spending most of his time sitting in bed owing to his lack of strength. Colonel Palfrey wrote that his friend's breathing "was audible and rather quick, and his face and throat were pitifully thin." In a rare moment of happiness, Agnes delivered a daughter on September 24; they named her Edith, after Frank's deceased sister.[42]

"For the rest of his life he was simply waiting," penned a mournful Palfrey. On November 6, Edith was christened in Frank's room. Thereafter, Agnes spent much of her time with her failing husband, who often talked about his affairs and what he wanted Agnes to do after his death. Frank's mother was also present and relieved Agnes from time to time. "Death from consumption is a long and sore trial," wrote Palfrey. "In his case, the burden was made heavier by the physical pain which followed the loss of his leg, and by the distress of mind which flowed from his misfortune in business." Frank worried greatly that his death would leave Agnes and the children destitute, but several of Frank's friends banded together and raised funds that would see Agnes through the coming months.[43]

On December 20, 1876, Frank Bartlett was buried in Pittsfield Cemetery under this memorial boulder on a site he had chosen before his death. Courtesy Donna Kasuba.

Death came to Frank Bartlett on Sunday, December 17, 1876. Palfrey wrote that "he called his family and nearest friends around him, spoke words of comfort and encouragement and farewell to them all, and then passed peacefully away." His body was worn away by consumption, with tubercles detected in his lungs prior to his death. The funeral took place on December 20 in the St. Stephens Episcopal Church in Pittsfield. All business in town was suspended during the service. Members of all three Massachusetts regiments were present, as were representatives from state government, and Harvard University. Reverend L. K. Storrs of New York, former rector of St. Stephens conducted the service in the church, assisted by Reverend Arthur Lawrence of Stockbridge, one of Frank's Harvard classmates. Reverend Lawrence's address was unusual for an Episcopalian service. The reverend told the crowd that the same service was read whether the mortal body had been rich or poor, lowly or great. "But there comes, now and then, a time when the world is not content to let a hero pass from its sight without a word of farewell." After eulogizing Frank's exemplary life, the reverend ended his remarks by stating that if Bartlett could speak, he would have said, "I have fought a good fight; I have finished my course; I have kept the faith. Henceforth there remains for me a crown of glory, which fadeth-yes, which fadeth not away."[44]

After the church service, Frank's coffin was taken out for the trip to Pittsfield Cemetery. Among the pallbearers were his good friends Frank Palfrey and Colonel Sumner of the 49th Massachusetts. In spite of severely cold weather, a large crowd assembled at the graveside, where the current rector of St. Stephens, the Reverend William McGlathery, presided. Frank was laid to rest on Sunset Slope, in a plot he had personally selected. A boulder of rough stone stood over his grave, while a bronze shield on the grave was inscribed as follows:

> A Soldier undaunted by wounds and imprisonment,
> A Patriot foremost in pleading for reconciliation.
> A Christian strong in faith and charity.
> His life was an inspiration.
> His memory is a trust.[45]

14

"NO GREATER OR PURER HERO"

Frank Bartlett's Legacy

When news of Frank Bartlett's death reached the outside world, newspapers all over the country printed obituaries. The *Boston Advertiser* praised him as "a hero of the type of the early knights. He had hardly reached the prime of life, but the world had no honor to confer greater than he had already won.... His death closes a pure, noble and heroic life — a life without fear and without reproach." "No greater or purer hero lives in the pages of history or romance," said the editor of the *Boston Daily Globe*, "and there could be no better illustration of the patriotism and heroism which illuminate the period of our country's greatest trials.... [H]e represented at once the courage and the magnanimity of the patriot soldier." "The most searching criticism but reveals its innate nobility and brings its pure quality into bold relief," proclaimed the *Rochester Democrat*. The Richmond *State* noted his death with sadness. "The many friends he made shall mourn him long, and Virginia joins with Massachusetts in lamenting a loss not only to the two states, but to humanity."[1]

Tributes to the dead general contin-

Herman Melville, shown here in an 1860 photograph taken by Pittsfield photographer Dewey, moved to Pittsfield during the Civil War and kept track of Bartlett's military career. His poem "The College Colonel" commemorated Frank's career. Courtesy Berkshire Athenaeum, Pittsfield, MA.

ued to appear in print. On February 7, 1877, the officers of the Military Order of the Loyal Legion of the United States, Commandery of Massachusetts, met to pay tribute to one of their distinguished members whose death affected them all. "We contemplate with pride his brilliant military career, which entailed heavy sacrifices and sufferings upon himself, but did not end till the war ended. Imprisonment, illness, and repeated wounds were alike powerless to shake the absolute tenacity of purpose with which he followed and upheld the Flag.... Wherever he went, he enforced discipline, diffused the soldierly spirit, cared thoughtfully and wisely for his men, led them with conspicuous gallantry, shared all their privations, and thought always first of their welfare and of the welfare of his country.... Four years of fighting raised him to high rank in the army, and won for him a great name, but they left him with a shattered constitution and a crippled frame, at the age of twenty-five." The tribute went on to describe his career as a citizen, businessman, and devoted father and husband. "With proud and tender recollection, we record our testimony to our belief, that he was one of the noblest of soldiers and citizens whom Massachusetts has numbered among her sons."[2]

Frank's death was also commemorated in a number of contemporary poems. The general had already been the subject of a poem by one of America's greatest living authors, Herman Melville. The Melvilles had moved to a farm near Pittsfield before the war had started. During the conflict, Herman's wife Elizabeth was a member of the Pittsfield Ladies' Soldiers' Relief Association and thus helped to support the war effort. Herman often drove into town to participate in patriotic events such as parades and fundraisers, and to watch the troops drilling at local camps. In September 1862, the Melvilles rented a home on South Street to make it easier for Elizabeth to perform her work. The move also enabled Herman to take a closer view of the military activities in the area, especially the establishment of Camp Briggs and Frank Bartlett's drilling of the 49th Massachusetts that fall.[3]

Melville was on hand to witness the return of the 49th Massachusetts in August 1863. The result of his perceptive eye was a tribute to Colonel Bartlett that was included in his *Battle-Pieces*, published in 1866. Entitled "The College Colonel," Melville's poem captured a crippled Frank Bartlett proudly riding at the head of his men as they paraded through Pittsfield that summer day in 1863:

> He rides at their head;
> A crutch by his saddle just slants in view,
> One slung arm is in splints, you see,
> Yet he guides his strong steed-how coldly too.
> He brings his regiment home-
> Not as they filed two years before,
> But a remnant half-tattered, and battered, and worn,

Like castaway sailors, who — stunned
By the surf's load roar,
Their mates dragged back and seen no more —
Again and again breast the surge,
And at last crawl, spent, to shore.
A still rigidity and pale —
An Indian aloofness lones his brow;
He has lived a thousand years
Compressed in battle's pains and prayers,
Marches and watches slow.
There are welcoming shouts, and flags;
Old men off hat to the Boy,
Wreaths from gay balconies fall at his feet,
But to *him* — there comes alloy.
It is not that a leg is lost,
It is not that an arm is maimed,
It is not that the fever has racked —
Self he has long disclaimed.
But all through the Seven Days' Fight,
And deep in the Wilderness grim,
And in the field-hospital tent,
And Petersburg crater, and dim
Lean brooding in Libby, there came-
Ah heaven! — what *Truth* to him.

Melville must have penned a finished version after the war came to an end, when it was known that Frank had been wounded in the Wilderness and captured at Petersburg, learning the truth of war. The 1866 publication of Melville's *Battle-Pieces*, seventy-two poems that encompassed the entire breadth of the Civil War, gave some national fame to Frank Bartlett.[4]

Haverhill native and renowned poet John Greenleaf Whittier also commemorated Frank's death with a brief poem.

A soul of fire, a tender heart
Too warm for hate, he knew
The generous victor's graceful part
To sheathe the sword he drew.
Mourn, Essex, on thy sea-blown shore
Thy beautiful and brave,
Whose Failing hand the olive bore,
Whose dying lips forgave.[5]

Another American author, Bret Harte, also saw fit to write a very Victorian poem to pay tribute to Frank Bartlett's memory. Harte was a Boston resident at the time and was laboring to produce new work for money after the huge publishing contract he had signed with the *Atlantic Monthly* had been revoked.[6]

Soon after Frank's death, his good friend and former commanding officer,

Francis W. Palfrey, borrowed the general's letters and journals and began working on a more substantial tribute to Frank's career. The result appeared in
1878, the 310-page *Memoir of William Francis Bartlett*, published by
Houghton, Osgood and Company of Cambridge, Massachusetts. Palfrey covered Frank's military career in 159 pages, then devoted the remainder of the
book to his civil career, including his many postwar speeches that received
press attention. General A. G. Sedgwick reviewed Palfrey's *Memoir* for *The
Nation*. Sedgwick quoted from the book and waxed eloquently about Frank's
career and his noble character. "As the noise and confusion produced by the
war dies away, and we think more and more of what we really gained and
what we lost by it," wrote Sedgwick, "the lives of the men who, on the field
or in civil life, showed themselves equal to what the occasion demanded will
more and more strongly present themselves as the most priceless possessions
we can hand down to our children; and among these, if we are not mistaken,
General Bartlett's name will hold a very high place."[7]

But Sedgwick was mistaken about Frank's wartime legacy that would
increase in popularity. Sedgwick had noted in his review that because Frank
was so often wounded, he never had the opportunity to show any skill at handling large numbers of soldiers that would have been his prerogative as a general officer. Still, Sedgwick surmised that as time went on, Frank's name would
grow more popular. But that did not happen when compared to other heroes
of the war. After Palfrey's *Memoir*, it appears that Frank Bartlett was the subject of only two major articles, both of which appeared in 1899. One was the
written version of a speech given by James L. High to the Military Order of
the Loyal Legion in 1893. Entitled "My Hero," High's article was essentially
taken from Palfrey's *Memoir* and was a general biography of the general. The
second article, written by Mrs. H. Neill Wilson, was a brief biography that
appeared in one of the Berkshire Historical and Scientific Society's publications.[8]

Frank's comrades also kept his memory alive for a long time. In 1881,
the Grand Army of the Republic established the General W. F. Bartlett Post
99 at Andover, Massachusetts; this post survived until 1930. Far across the
continent, Union veterans in Los Angeles banded together to form another
post named after the general. On Memorial Day 1891, the Bartlett post in Los
Angeles dedicated a monument in the city's Evergreen Cemetery that bore
the general's name. The cornerstone was laid on April 26. Mary Agnes Bartlett
sent a number of items to be placed in the cornerstone, including a copy of
Palfrey's *Memoirs*, a button taken from one of the general's uniforms, newspaper clippings about his death, and a copy of the inscription over the general's grave. She also sent some of the ivy from Frank's grave that would be
planted at the California site.[9]

Frank's wartime colleague in the 20th Massachusetts, Oliver Wendell

Holmes, described Frank's Civil War career during his now-famous 1884 Memorial Day speech at a Grand Army of the Republic post in New Hampshire. Holmes, who at the time was a rising lawyer and a member of the Massachusetts Supreme Judicial Court, made the theme of his speech an answer to a question over why Memorial Day was observed. Holmes did not mention any names of the officers of the 20th Massachusetts, but his vivid descriptions left no question as to who the dead soldiers were. Holmes said of Bartlett:

This photograph shows the 1891 monument erected in the Evergreen Cemetery in Los Angeles by two GAR posts, one of them named after Bartlett. Courtesy Glen Roosevelt, W. S. Rosecrans Camp 2, Sons of Union Veterans of the Civil War.

There is one grave and commanding presence that you all would recognize, for his life has become a part of our common history. Who does not remember the leader of the assault of the mine at Petersburg? The solitary horseman in front of Port Hudson, whom a foeman worthy of him bade his soldiers spare, from love and admiration of such gallant bearing? Who does not still hear the echo of those eloquent lips after the war, teaching reconciliation and peace? I may not do more than allude to his death, fit ending of his life. All that the world has a right to know has been told by a beloved friend in a book wherein friendship has found no need to exaggerate facts that speak for themselves. I knew him, and I may even say I knew him well; yet, until that book appeared, I had not known the governing motive of his soul. I had admired him as a hero. When I read, I learned to revere him as a saint. His strength was not in honor alone, but in religion; and those who do not share his creed must see that it was on the wings of religious faith that he mounted above even valiant deeds into an empyrean of ideal life.

Holmes' description of Frank was only a part of his longer oration. The most famous part that has been quoted in numerous publications includes the following: "Through our great good fortune, in our youths our hearts were touched with fire. It was given to us to learn at the outset that life is a profound and passionate thing.... But above all, we have learned that whether a man accepts from Fortune her spade, and will look downward and dig, or from Aspiration her axe and cord, and will scale the ice, the one and only success which it is his to command is to bring to his work a mighty heart."[10]

In the fall of 1878, Harvard University drew up plans to memorialize their now-famous graduate. The Association of Alumni of Harvard University announced that it had formed a plan "to place in Memorial Hall a likeness of General Bartlett, in bust or medallion, with a tablet commemorative of his services." Should the committee raise more money than was necessary for the memorial, the excess would be donated to Mrs. Bartlett. The committee, chaired by Henry Lee, also included J. G. Abbott, Francis W. Palfrey, John Quincy Adams, and John C. Ropes among its members. The committee hired noted sculptor Daniel C. French to execute a lifelike bust of General Bartlett, with a commemorative tablet describing his services. This tablet included a line from Chaucer: "He was a veray parfit gentil knight." The tablet was unveiled in time for the 1883 commencement services. Mrs. Bartlett received $1,850 to help support her children.[11]

Bartlett's home state of Massachusetts decided to honor their fallen son in 1901, when the legislature voted $20,000 to erect a statue of the general on the state house grounds. Three years later, Mrs. Bartlett requested that the statue of her husband be placed inside the state house. The legislature acquiesced and voted to place the statue in Memorial Hall. Daniel Chester French was hired to produce the Bartlett statue. It was made of bronze, was seven feet, nine inches in height, and rested on a pedestal of green Greek marble; the New York firm of Bonney-Bonnard cast the statue. A contemporary newspaper report described the statue as "excellent. It represents the soldier with his hat in his hand 'saluting the colors.' The erect carriage, the bared head, and old army overcoat thrown back and the high boots and belt and sword of a mounted officer, makes the statue an impressive piece of sculpture." On the base of the statue was a silver tablet inscribed as follows:
William Francis Bartlett

A Volunteer in the Civil War
A Major General at the Age of Twenty-four
Foremost to Plead for Reconciliation Between North and South
Born 1840 Died 1876[12]

The statue unveiling took place on May 27, 1904, in Memorial Hall. It was the forty-first anniversary of the charge at Port Hudson. A large crowd gathered in the hall well before the 2:30 P.M. start of the ceremony. Mary Agnes Bartlett, son Edwin, daughters Edith and Agnes, as well as other family members, arrived to applause and were conducted to a balcony overlooking the statue. At the appointed hour, Governor John L. Bates led a procession to the temporary platform set up for the day. Among the dignitaries who followed the governor was Lieutenant Governor Curtis Guild, Jr., who led James Dwight Francis, one of Frank's grandsons, to the platform.[13]

A bugle call, "to the colors," began the ceremony. Lieutenant Governor Guild then took the lectern and delivered a brief address that covered the history of the legislation that resulted in the Bartlett statue. Turning to Governor Bates, Guild presented the statue to the commonwealth of Massachusetts, "a memorial of one whose sheer, consummate heroism in war was as much a matter of course as his modesty and generosity in peace, a Massachusetts ideal incarnate of an American officer and gentleman, William Francis Bartlett." As Guild spoke the general's name, his grandson pulled the cord on the large

American flag that covered the statue. The flag fell away to the cheers of the crowd as a band struck up the "Star-Spangled Banner." Governor Bates then made a brief acceptance speech.[14]

The crowd then followed the dignitaries into the hall of the House of Representatives. After a prayer by the House chaplain, Brigadier General Morris Schaff delivered a 45-minute oration. Schaff was an 1862 graduate of West Point, after which he served in the Army of the Potomac as an ordnance officer. He resigned from the army in 1871 and turned to a civil career. Schaff was appointed a brigadier general in the Massachusetts militia in 1880 and at the time of his oration had worked twenty-

The Daniel Chester French statue of William F. Bartlett that stands in the Massachusetts State House. Courtesy Commonwealth of Massachusetts, Art Commission.

six years for the State Gas and Electric Light Commission. Schaff's address included a detailed biography that traced Frank's military career and his post-war speeches that advocated reconciliation with the South. "It was a great achievement to overcome the rebellion," said Schaff, "it was a vastly greater achievement, one that history will not forget, for the battle-scarred genera-tion that wore the blue and the gray to be on terms of mutual respect and friendship before leaving the stage.... If there be garlands for generations, and ours wears one, we owe it to Grant and Bartlett more than to any others, for, having won the victory, they wooed peace back to the land."[15]

Following Schaff's address, Edward F. Hamlin, secretary of the execu-tive council, arose to read two tributes from two former Confederate soldiers who could not be present for the statue dedication. One came from Jonathan S. Wise, son of former Virginia governor Henry Wise, the other from Cap-tain W. Gordon McCabe, who had served with a Virginia artillery battery in the Army of Northern Virginia. "In the contemplation of an heroic life," wrote McCabe, "which, tried by both extremes of fortune, was found equal to the trial, and rounded at the last with the sleep which he giveth his beloved, selfish sorrow dares not raise its wail." In his letter, McCabe provided details on the reception Frank received in Richmond after his April 1875 Lexington speech. After these two tributes were read to the approving crowd, "America" was sung and then a benediction given, which ended the afternoon's cere-mony.[16]

Sculptor Daniel French presented a plaster replica of the bronze statue in the State House to Berkshire County. The plaster statue was sheathed in bronze to help give it a long life. There was some debate on where to place the statue. After realizing that there was not enough space in either the local museum or the Berkshire Athenaeum, the decision was made to place Bartlett's statue in a recess in one of the halls of the county courthouse. The dedica-tion took place on December 7, 1904. The organizing committee invited the general's grandson James Dwight Francis to again pull the cord and unveil the statue. Accepting the statue on behalf of the county, Mr. Wood gave an oration that praised Berkshire County's most famous Civil War soldier. "Mea-sured by any standard of citizenship General Bartlett was a model — in peace an example of the good citizen; in war alert and fearless; in all duty faithful," he said. "His only foes were the enemies of the flag which to him was as the rays of a beautiful and beneficent sun; and a union preserved and the con-quered forgiven were the Christian precepts for which he most eloquently spoke. The lesson of his life is worthy of all heed, of all following, and Berk-shire has no name or fame more deserving of monument."[17]

Frank's statue in Pittsfield then had a varied history. As the courthouse grew, the statue was moved to the Pittsfield Armory. By 1928, the statue was in disrepair — parts of the hat, coat, sword, and face had been damaged by flying basketballs and other accidents. The statue was patched and rebronzed, but in 1946, the statue was removed by the state, which spent more than $150 on conservation and another $70 to ship it back to the county courthouse. Eventually, it was transferred to the Berkshire Community College.[18]

Son Edwin Bartlett died in 1913 and was buried near his parents in Pittsfield. His wife was buried alongside him. Courtesy Donna Kasuba.

Frank and Mary Agnes had six children, born between 1866 and 1876. Agnes, the oldest, married Henry A. Francis in 1894. Their son, James Dwight Francis, was the grandson who unveiled Frank's statue in 1904. Caroline, born in 1869, married James H. Kidd in 1895 and produced four children. Edwin, born in 1871, married Susan Amory in 1904 and sired a daughter, Betty, in 1906. Edwin was a businessman and the family lived in Albany, New York.

Bartlett's daughter Edith never married. After she died in 1959, she was interred next to her parents. Her grave is in the foreground on the right. Courtesy Donna Kasuba.

Susan passed away in 1910 and Edwin in 1918. The twins Robert and William were born in 1874. Robert moved west and eventually married Ruth Robinson in 1900; their daughter Agnes was born in 1901. Robert passed away on March 30, 1906, after a week-long struggle with appendicitis. His brother William married Ella de Long in 1903; he died on May 9, 1906. Edith, the last of Frank's children, was born in 1876. She never married and died in 1959.[19]

After Frank died, Mary Agnes never remarried. She moved out of the house that her husband had built some time after his death. In 1887, Colo-

Look to the right of the porch post in this image of the 1895 reunion of the 49th Massachusetts. Mrs. Bartlett can be seen fourth to the right. Courtesy Berkshire Historical Society, Pittsfield, MA.

nel Cutting built an eight-room "cottage" for Mary Agnes on Bartlett Avenue, in which she lived until her death. Mary Agnes remained very interested in her late husband's career. She was particularly fond of the 49th Massachusetts, and the veterans of that unit returned the love. The men affectionately called her "the mother of the 49th." Mary Agnes attended as many veterans' functions as she could, and presented a stand of colors to the local Sons of Union Veterans post, named General William F. Bartlett post in honor of the general. Mary Agnes was a member of the Berkshire Relief Corps and a charter member of the William W. Rockwell Woman's Relief Corps. She was an annual fixture at the Memorial Day observances for the unknown dead in Pittsfield Cemetery.[20]

Mary Agnes was a corporate member of the House of Mercy Hospital in Pittsfield, as well as the Berkshire County Home for Aged Women. She also belonged to various social organizations such as the Pittsfield Country Club and the Wednesday Morning Club. Like her husband, Mary Agnes became a member of St. Stephen's Episcopal Church in Pittsfield. In February 1909, she developed a very bad cold which soon developed into pneumo-

Opened on September 2, 1912, this school on Onota Street in Pittsfield was named for the general. A bronze tablet in the vestibule was inscribed as follows: "William Francis Bartlett. Patriot, soldier, statesman, loyal son of Massachusetts. Friend of boys and girls. To his fellows an example in private life and civic duty." After the school was closed, it was renovated as an apartment building. Courtesy Berkshire Athenaeum, Pittsfield, MA.

nia. This illness caused her death on February 17. Her funeral took place at the church three days later. A huge crowd turned out for the obsequies. All four surviving children attended. Mary Agnes was buried in Pittsfield Cemetery beside her husband.[21]

As the years went by after Frank's death, the nation's knowledge of his meteoric military career waned. His name appeared in books written about relevant campaigns that included Ball's Bluff, Yorktown, Port Hudson, and Petersburg. Frank's name appeared in scores of contemporary letters and diaries that have been published in past decades, including the 1991 publication of the letters of Henry L. Abbott. Regimental histories of the 20th (published in 1906 and 2005) and 57th (published in 1896 and 1990) Massachusetts, of course, include copious references to Bartlett. Most recently, a DVD entitled "Shot to Pieces" recreates Frank's Civil War service for modern viewers.[22]

William Francis Bartlett was a true American hero. His life previous to 1861 was not much to talk about. He was an indifferent student and apparently had no plans for his future career. But the army changed all that. Bartlett took to army life as a duck does to water. His letters clearly indicate that he loved being an officer in charge of other men. Frank could be a martinet at times, but he also understood his responsibility and did his best to ensure that his men were well-cared for and drilled. Soldiers might complain loudly about all their drilling, but in battle they realized the value of Frank's ceaseless drilling.

As a reviewer wrote, it is unfortunate that Bartlett never had the chance to command large bodies of troops. As a company commander, his sole engagement was Ball's Bluff, and he did as well as could be expected under the circumstances. Promoted to colonel, Frank organized the 49th Massachusetts and led it capably in its first engagement at Plains' Store. A few days later, he was badly wounded in a forlorn charge at Port Hudson. At the head of the 57th Massachusetts, Frank led his new command into the Wilderness, where he was lightly wounded and carried from the field. Promoted to brigadier general, Frank led his brigade into the Crater and was captured that frightful day. The sources for this battle generally blame Frank's superior, James H. Ledlie, for garbling General Burnside's order of attack. But as shown in the Crater chapter of this book, the contemporary sources are at odds as to what were the exact orders to Ledlie's division. In turn, the orders to Bartlett and his interpretation of them are still open to question.

Following the war, Frank turned to a business career but never managed to find an enjoyable position anywhere. First in Massachusetts with a paper mill, then in Massachusetts and Virginia with iron ore, Frank struggled to make enough money to ensure his fam-

After Mary Agnes Pomeroy Bartlett died in 1909, she was laid to rest near her husband in Pittsfield Cemetery. This view shows the double headstone made for husband and wife. Across the bottom is inscribed "Love lives on and hath a power to bless." There is conflicting evidence as to exactly where the general is buried. Did he remain under the memorial boulder or was he moved next to his beloved wife? Courtesy Donna Kasuba.

ily's comfort. His strenuous efforts to provide for his family wore down his
already frail health caused by wounds and imprisonment during the war.
Frank's sojourn in postwar Richmond led him to advocate a policy of reconciliation with the defeated South. His speeches pleading for this policy
attracted national media attention and Frank became something of a celebrity
for a couple of years.

When examining Bartlett's short but hectic life, it becomes clear that he
was a man of steel, in spite of his weak body. The army was Frank Bartlett
and vice versa. The Civil War gave this young man the opportunity of a life-
time and he made the most of it. When his leg was amputated in April 1862,
Frank could have gone home and rested on his laurels. But he didn't, and
continued his fledgling military career. Above all, he stood for the restora-
tion of the Union and everything it stood for. Americans today would do well
to emulate Frank's iron will.

Scott Paradise, in writing for the readers of the Andover Phillips Academy, perhaps summed up Frank's career the best of any of his biographers:

> But the element of disappointment and misfortune was always present
> even in his success. He never shared a triumph with the troops he had
> trained so thoroughly and so well. Unfortunate combinations of cir-
> cumstances, through no fault of his own, denied him the political
> honors he might have had, and even withheld the modest business
> prosperity that would have given peace of mind and a sense of security
> to his last years. But above all there is tragedy in the gradual failing of
> his glorious physical strength, until worn out by his war-time priva-
> tions, by worry, and by constant pain from his wounds, even his
> courageous spirit welcomed the repose of death.[23]

CHAPTER NOTES

Chapter 1

1. Levi Bartlett, *Sketches of the Bartlett Family in England and America* (Lawrence, MA: George S. Merrill & Crocker, Printers, 1876), 9–11.

2. *Ibid.,* 13–21.

3. *Ibid.,* 22–23; D. Hamilton Hurd, *History of Essex County, Massachusetts,* 2 volumes (Philadelphia: J. W. Lewis and Company, 1888), 2: 2010.

4. Charles L. Bartlett obituaries (unidentified newspaper clippings), in William F. Bartlett file, Harvard University.

5. *Ibid.;* Channing Howard to Mr. Griffin, November 4, 1940, copy of this letter provided to Martin Sable by G. David Hubbard. The Bartlett family owned this house until 1887, when Orlando Belcher purchased it, including an adjacent barn and seventeen acres. Belcher was an entrepreneur who began buying land and cottages in 1871 so that he could take advantage of Winthrop's growing popularity as a seaside resort. A year after buying the Bartlett house, he rebuilt the structure, doubling its size. Belcher eventually had more than thirty-five acres and many buildings, as well as a boat dock. After the business declined during World War I, Belcher sold out and retired. The old Bartlett house was eventually torn down and the property divided into building lots. This information was supplied by the Winthrop Public Library.

6. Bartlett, *Sketches of the Bartlett Family,* 32; C. L. Bartlett obituaries, Harvard University. Edwin had already become quite rich by his successful managing of the guano trade from South America to Europe, routed through New York, as well as the sale of Peruvian bark, which was used to make quinine. See Bartlett, *Sketches of the Bartlett Family,* 25–33, for more detailed information about Edwin's career.

7. Oral story told by Hubbard to Martin Sable.

8. A Garibaldi timeline can be found in "Life and Times of Giuseppe Garibaldi," found at www.reformation.org/garibaldi. html. See also Harry N. Gay, "Garibaldi's American Contacts and His Claims to American Citizenship," *American Historical Review* 38 (October 1932), reprinted in Anthony P. Campanella (editor), *Pages from the Garibaldian Epic* (Sarasota, FL: Institute of Garibaldian Studies, 1984), 8, 12; C. L. Bartlett obituaries, Harvard University.

9. William F. Bartlett student card #783, archives of Phillips Academy. Student records prior to 1902 were destroyed in a flood, and thus there are no other Bartlett records than his student card. Telephone conversation between Richard A. Sauers and Ruth Quattlebaum, September 10, 2007.

10. Ronald Story, *The Forging of an Aristocracy: Harvard & the Boston Upper Class, 1800–1870* (Middletown, CT: Wesleyan University Press, 1980), 117, 124.

11. Story, *Forging of an Aristocracy,* 120, 128.

12. Francis W. Palfrey, *Memoir of William Francis Bartlett* (Cambridge, MA: H. O. Houghton, Osgood and Company, 1878), 1; Harvard University Archives, UA III 15.74.6, Rank Scales, 1827–1858.

13. This paragraph is taken from notes compiled by author Richard F. Miller while researching Frank's academic record in the Harvard University Archives, and summarized in a letter to the author. These notes are taken from UA III.5.4, Faculty Records, Volume XV, 319, 385, 428, 481, 496; Volume XVI, 19, 92, 99; UAI.45.890.3, President Felton's Papers, Volume 5, Felton to Charles Bartlett, May 22, 1860. Miller stated to Richard A. Sauers in a telephone conversation on July 21, 2005, that Frank's Harvard record was probably average when compared to his classmates.

14. Palfrey, *Memoir*, 2; Richard F. Miller, *Harvard's Civil War: A History of the Twentieth Massachusetts Volunteer Infantry* (Hanover, NH: University Press of New England, 2005), 11.

15. Miller, *Harvard's Civil War*, 12–15.

16. *Ibid.*, 16.

17. *Ibid.*, 16–17; Palfrey, *Memoir*, 2–3.

18. Miller, *Harvard's Civil War*, 19.

19. *Ibid.*, 17–21; Palfrey, *Memoir*, 3. Abbott wrote to his father that his first weeks in uniform proved to be a pleasant time. "[T]he work is just hard enough to give you a rousing appetite," he wrote, and said that being in the army was a pleasant way to pass the summer; however, he dreaded being ordered back without doing anything. Henry Abbott to Josiah Abbott, May 1861, in Abbott Family Papers, Houghton Library, Harvard University; see the printed version of this letter in Robert G. Scott (editor), *Fallen Leaves: The Civil War Letters of Major Henry Livermore Abbott* (Kent, OH: Kent State University Press, 1991), 30–32.

Chapter 2

1. Palfrey, *Memoir*, 4; George A. Bruce, *The Twentieth Regiment of Massachusetts Volunteer Infantry 1861–1865* (Boston: Houghton, Mifflin and Company, 1906), 1. All such nominations were subject to the final approval of Governor Andrew.

2. Palfrey, *Memoir*, 4.

3. *Ibid.*, 1–2, 298.

4. *Ibid.*, 5; Anthony J. Milano, "The Copperhead Regiment: The 20th Massachusetts Regiment," *Civil War Regiments* 3 #1 (1993): 37; Bruce, 20th Massachusetts, 3.

5. Bruce, *20th Massachusetts*, 2–3; Miller, Harvard's Civil War, 31–33.

6. Bruce, *20th Massachusetts*, 4–5.

7. *Ibid.*, 7; Palfrey, *Memoir*, 5–6.

8. Bruce, *20th Massachusetts*, 7–9; William F. Fox, *Regimental Losses in the American Civil War* (Albany, NY: Albany Publishing Company, 1889), 5.

9. Bruce, *20th Massachusetts*, 9.

10. *Ibid.*, 9–12; James Moore, *History of the Cooper Shop Volunteer Refreshment Saloon* (Philadelphia: James B. Rodgers, 1866), 133.

11. Bruce, *20th Massachusetts*, 12–14; Miller, Harvard's Civil War, 46–47.

12. Palfrey, *Memoir*, 8; Macy to My Dear Lincoln, September 25, 1861, Macy Papers.

13. Palfrey, *Memoir*, 8–9; Macy to Lincoln, September 25, 1861.

14. Palfrey, *Memoir*, 9; Bruce, 20th Massachusetts, 14–15.

15. Palfrey, *Memoir*, 11; Bruce, *20th Massachusetts*, 16–17; Macy to Lincoln, September 25, 1861. Stone's command was organized as follows: First Brigade, Brig. Gen. F. W. Lander: 19th, 20th MA, 1st Co. MA Sharpshooters, 7th MI. Second Brigade, Brig. Gen. Willis A. Gorman: 1st MN, 34th, 82nd NY. Third Brigade, Col. Edward D. Baker: 69th, 71st, 72nd, 106th PA. Unassigned: 15th MA, 42nd NY. Cavalry: 3rd NY (4 companies), District of Columbia company. Artillery: Battery I, 1st US; Battery B, 1st RI; Co. K, 9th NY State Militia Battery; 82nd NY battery section

16. Bruce, *20th Massachusetts*, 18.

17. Palfrey, *Memoir*, 13–14; Macy to Lincoln, September 25, 1861. Captain Bartlett himself was wet to begin with even before the rain. About midnight a small boat moored along the Maryland shore of the Potomac broke loose and floated off. The captain stripped and swam after it, and brought it back to shore. "I did not take any cold. I am beyond that now," he wrote. For some more details of this picket work, see Mark D. Howe (editor), *Touched With Fire: Civil War Letters and Diary of Oliver Wendell Holmes, Jr., 1861–1864* (Cambridge: Harvard University Press, 1947), 8–12.

18. Palfrey, *Memoir*, 14; Macy to Lincoln, September 25, 1861.

19. Palfrey, *Memoir*, 14–15; Macy to Lincoln, September 25, 1861.
20. Macy to Lincoln, September 25, 1861.
21. Macy to Dear Amasa, October 9, 1861. Macy did not identify the island, and probably did not know its name. Perusal of a map indicates that Seldon Island, in the Potomac just south of Edwards Ferry, is approximately three miles in length, and may have been the island in question.
22. Ibid.

Chapter 3

1. Macy to Lincoln, October 22, 1861, Macy Papers.
2. James A. Morgan III, *A Little Short of Boats: The Fights at Ball's Bluff and Edwards Ferry, October 21–22, 1861* (Fort Mitchell, KY: Ironclad Publishing, 2004), 23–24.
3. *Ibid.*, 23–25.
4. *Ibid.*, 1, 25–28.
5. *Ibid.*, 26–30.
6. *Ibid.*, 30–32; Miller, *Harvard's Civil War*, 56–57.
7. Morgan, *A Little Short of Boats*, 32–33.
8. *The War of the Rebellion: A Compilation of the Official Records of the Union and Confederate Armies*, 70 volumes in 128 parts (Washington, D.C.: Government Printing Office, 1880–1901), volume 5, 299–300. Future references to the *Official Records* are abbreviated as *O.R.*, followed by the volume and part numbers.
9. Morgan, *A Little Short of Boats*, 35–37. Miller, *Harvard's Civil War*, 58, writes that Colonel Lee sent two companies instead of the required one because his companies were not at full strength; thus two companies fielded enough men for the single company as ordered by General Stone.
10. Henry Abbott to Josiah Abbott, October 22, 1861 (Scott, *Fallen Leaves*, 60).
11. Morgan, *A Little Short of Boats*, 39–40.
12. *Ibid.*, 40.
13. *Ibid.*, 41.
14. *Ibid.*, 41–43; Palfrey, *Memoir*, 21. Riddle was thus the first battle casualty of the 20th Massachusetts. His arm was amputated and although he was promoted to lieutenant and then captain, Riddle spent much of the next two years recuperating from his wound.

He was injured by a fleeing horse at the Battle of Seven Pines (May 31, 1862), was sent home, and medically discharged in September 1863.
15. Morgan, *A Little Short of Boats,* 43.
16. *Ibid.,* 44–46.
17. *Ibid.,* 46–58.
18. Palfrey, *Memoir*, 21–22; *Report of the Joint Committee on the Conduct of the War*, 3 volumes (Washington, D.C.: Government Printing Office, 1863), volume 3, 476 (future citations of this volume in this chapter are abbreviated as *C.C.W.*); O.R., volume 5, 318 (Bartlett's report).
19. *C.C.W.,* 477; Morgan, *A Little Short of Boats*, 58–60. Bartlett, in his report, wrote that Devens advanced his regiment again at 11:00 a.m. (O.R., volume 5, 318–9).
20. Morgan, *A Little Short of Boats*, 60–61. At this time, General McClellan had not informed Stone that McCall's division was under orders to march back to its camp, thus freeing Colonel Evans from worry that McCall would proceed toward Leesburg and force him to evacuate the area. When planning his movements, Stone was acting under the assumption that McCall was ready to aid his river crossings.
21. *Ibid.,* 61–67.
22. Palfrey, *Memoir*, 22. Lee made it clear in his congressional testimony (*C.C.W.*, 477) that he carried out his orders to the letter, remaining in line to cover any withdrawal by the 15th Massachusetts rather than move his troops out to join Colonel Devens.
23. Heidler, *Encyclopedia of the American Civil War*, 1: 161–62.
24. Morgan, *A Little Short of Boats*, 68–71.
25. *Ibid.,* 79–100.
26. *Ibid.,* 100–110; Miller, *Harvard's Civil War*, 65–66.
27. Morgan, *A Little Short of Boats*, 110.
28. *Ibid.,* 111–126, 132–34. Lee (*C.C.W.*, 479) said that he gave a reluctant order to fire by file, commencing on the right of the line. The colonel mentioned the rising ground to his front, and said that his men would advance a few steps toward the crest, fire their shots, then fall back to reload under cover of the high ground in their front.
29. Palfrey, *Memoir*, 23–24.
30. Henry Abbott to Josiah Abbott, October 22, 1861 (Scott, *Fallen Leaves*, 62); Bruce, *20th Massachusetts*, 48–49.

31. Palfrey, *Memoir*, 25; Morgan, *A Little Short of Boats*, 142.

32. Morgan, *A Little Short of Boats*, 134–45; Miller, *Harvard's Civil War*, 73.

33. Morgan, *A Little Short of Boats*, 147–49; *C.C.W.*, 480–1.

34. Morgan, *A Little Short of Boats*, 149–152; see Miller, *Harvard's Civil War*, 73–75, for this portion of the battle, in which he details Cogswell's attempt to break through toward Edwards Ferry.

35. *Ibid.*, 152–54; *C.C.W.*, 481. Bruce, *20th Massachusetts*, 51, mistakenly wrote that Bartlett's attack was designed to bring the two howitzers off the field.

36. Palfrey, *Memoir*, 25.

37. *Ibid.*, 25–26; *O.R.*, volume 5, 319 (Bartlett's report).

38. Henry Abbott to Josiah Abbott, October 22, 1861 (MS Am 800.26[15]), quoted by permission of the Houghton Library, Harvard University (Scott, *Fallen Leaves*, 62–63).

39. Morgan, *A Little Short of Boats*, 153–59.

40. *Ibid.*, 161–66, 168–71.

41. Palfrey, *Memoir*, 26–27.

42. *Ibid.*, 27; Macy to Lincoln, October 22, 28, 1861; Bruce, *20th Massachusetts*, 54–55; *O.R.*, volume 5, 319 (Bartlett's report); Miller, *Harvard's Civil War*, 76–78.

43. Palfrey, *Memoir*, 27–29; Henry Abbott to Josiah Abbott, October 22, 1861 (Scott, *Fallen Leaves*, 63); Bruce, *20th Massachusetts*, 56–57; *O.R.*, volume 5, 319–20 (Bartlett's report); Miller, *Harvard's Civil War*, 79–80.

44. Palfrey, *Memoir*, 29–32; *C.C.W.*, 481; Bruce, *20th Massachusetts*, 54; *O.R.*, volume 5, 308, 320; Morgan, *A Little Short of Boats*, 178. Morgan enumerates a total of 553 Union prisoners, which suggests that the remaining missing, a total of 161, were probably shot and drowned in the river. Bruce, *20th Massachusetts*, lists the casualties of Company I as three killed, ten wounded, and seven missing. Miller, *Harvard's Civil War*, 81–82, enumerates the regiment's loss as 204.

45. Henry Abbott to Josiah Abbott, October 22, 1861 (MS Am 800.26[16], quote by permission of the Houghton Library, Harvard University; Abbott to Josiah Abbott, December 31, 1861 (Scott, *Fallen Leaves*, 73–74, 94).

46. Palfrey, *Memoir*, 33–34.

Chapter 4

1. Palfrey, *Memoir*, 29–30. Frank also wrote the required official report of the regiment's actions; the report was dated October 23. See *O.R.*, volume 5, 318–20, for this report. Palfrey also wrote a brief report (October 24, in *O.R.*, volume 5, 317–8) in which he simply enumerated the regiment's strength and losses in the engagement.

2. Bruce, *20th Massachusetts*, 70–72.

3. Palfrey, *Memoir*, 35–36; Macy to Lincoln, November 6, 1861, Macy Papers.

4. Palfrey, *Memoir*, 36. Macy echoed Palfrey's comments in a December 4 letter to his friend Lincoln: "...he has a great military genius and puts us through the most intricate battalion movements like an old veteran."

5. Bruce, *20th Massachusetts*, 72–73; Macy to Lincoln, November 14, 25, 1861; Henry Abbott to Josiah Abbott, November 23, 1861 (Scott, *Fallen Leaves*, 79).

6. Palfrey may have glossed over this period of the regiment's history for good reason. As will be noted in the following paragraphs, there was dissension in the regiment over the return of fugitive slaves. Palfrey also got into a long feud with Governor Andrew over the appointment of officers to replace those who had been killed, wounded, or captured at Ball's Bluff. For details, see Miller, *Harvard's Civil War*, 96–104.

7. Anthony J. Milano, "The Copperhead Regiment: The 20th Massachusetts Infantry," *Civil War Regiments* 3 #1 (1993): 31–32; Miller, *Harvard's Civil War*, 96.

8. Milano, "Copperhead Regiment," 32; Anthony J. Milano, "Letters from the Harvard Regiments: The Story of the 2nd and 20th Massachusetts Volunteer Infantry Regiments from 1861 Through 1863 as Told by the Letters of Their Officers. Part One: The Twentieth Massachusetts Regiment–From the Outbreak of War Through the Seven Days," *Civil War* #13 (1989): 21; Bruce, 20th Massachusetts, 72. Macy's promotion to captain meant a transfer to the command of Company B in December. See Macy to Lincoln, December 20, 1861.

9. Many Union soldiers who were in the war to preserve the Union, after they came in contact with the living conditions of black slaves in the South, came to feel that the abolishment of slavery must become one of the

war's end results. Numerous Massachusetts soldiers who went with General Ambrose E. Burnside's expedition to North Carolina in early 1862 eventually supported the demise of slavery after coming into contact with slaves on the Carolina coastal area.

10. Macy to Lincoln, December 4, 1861; Henry Abbott to Josiah Abbott, December 20, 1861 (Scott, *Fallen Leaves*, 88–92).

11. Henry Abbott to Josiah Abbott, December 16, 1861 (Scott, *Fallen Leaves*, 86).

12. Henry Abbott to Josiah Abbott, December 31, 1861 (MS Am 800.26[16]), quoted by permission of the Houghton Library, Harvard University (Scott, *Fallen Leaves*, 94–96).

13. Henry Abbott to Caroline Abbott, February 5, 1862 (Scott, *Fallen Leaves*, 100).

14. Henry Abbott to Josiah Abbott, November 4, 1861 (Scott, *Fallen Leaves*, 70–1).

15. For a thorough investigation of the committee's activities, see Bruce Tap, *Over Lincoln's Shoulder: The Committee on the Conduct of the War* (Lawrence: University Press of Kansas, 1998). In short, Stone was the victim of rage by the Radicals. Governor Andrew turned over the November 1861 anonymous letter about the 20th, and friends of Colonel Baker used the committee to whitewash his ineffective handling of the battle. McClellan had no hesitation in arresting Stone, in short, selling his subordinate out to protect his own errors, according to critics of McClellan. A detailed review of the Ball's Bluff testimony is beyond the purview of this book.

16. *Ibid.*, 102–3; Frederick H. Dyer, *A Compendium of the War of the Rebellion* (Des Moines, IA, 1908; reprinted in three volumes, New York: Thomas Yoseloff, 1959); 1: 276, 287, 291–93.

17. Bruce, *20th Massachusetts*, 78–79.

18. William J. Miller (compiler), "The Grand Campaign: A Journal of Operations in the Peninsula Campaign, March 17-August 26, 1862," in William J. Miller (editor), *The Peninsula Campaign of 1862: Yorktown to the Seven Days, Volume One, 179–82* (Campbell, CA: Savas Woodbury Publishers, 1993).

19. Bruce, *20th Massachusetts*, 79–80; Scott, Fallen Leaves, 106–7; Milano, "Letters from the Harvard Regiments," 21; Milano, "The Copperhead Regiment," 35; Miller, *Harvard's Civil War*, 107–8.

20. Henry Abbott to Josiah Abbott, March 8 and 17, 1862 (Scott, Fallen Leaves, 105–6, 108); Bruce, *20th Massachusetts*, 80; Milano, "The Copperhead Regiment," 40.

21. Miller, "The Grand Campaign," 183–84.

22. Henry Ropes to John C. Ropes, April 6, 1862.

23. Henry Ropes to John C. Ropes, April 9, 1862; Captain Macy listed the 42nd New York as part of this reconnaissance. See Macy to Lincoln, April 10, 1862. For the official version of the reconnaissance, see Bruce, *20th Massachusetts*, 81–83.

24. Palfrey, *Memoir*, 37.

25. Henry Ropes to John C. Ropes, April 6, 1862. In this missive, Lieutenant Ropes observed that Lieutenant Abbott led Company I forward to deploy as skirmishers. He moved straight forward toward the crest of a small hill, which would have exposed them to enemy fire. Seeing this, General Dana shouted at Abbott to move to the left to avoid being fired upon; the regimental surgeon ran forward and delivered Dana's order and saved the company from potential loss. Abbott failed to provide details of this reconnaissance in his letter home of April 9, calling it merely "a bloodless skirmish" (Henry Abbott to Caroline Abbott, April 9, 1862, in Scott, *Fallen Leaves*, 108).

26. Palfrey, Memoir, 38.

27. Henry Abbott to Caroline Abbott, April 20, 1862 (Scott, *Fallen Leaves*, 110–111); Palfrey, *Memoir*, 39.

28. Henry Ropes to John C. Ropes, April 15, 1862; Henry Abbott to Caroline Abbott, April 20, 1862 (Scott, *Fallen Leaves*, 111); Bruce, *20th Massachusetts*, 83–84.

29. Henry Ropes to John C. Ropes, April 25, 1862; Henry Abbott to Caroline Abbott, April 26, 1862 (Scott, *Fallen Leaves*, 112).

30. Herbert C. Mason to Sturgis, April 26, 1862, Mason Letters, Historical Society of Pennsylvania.

31. Henry Abbott to Caroline Abbott, April 26, 1862 (MS Am 800.26[16]), quoted by permission of the Houghton Library, Harvard University, (Scott, *Fallen Leaves*, 112).

32. Mason to Sturgis, April 26, 1862.

33. Palfrey, *Memoir*, 40, 43. See also Palfrey to Lieutenant W. F. Milton, April 25, 1862, in Bartlett's Compiled Service Record, National Archives. One of the cards in this

file indicates that the captain was wounded at noon, though Palfrey specifically wrote 11:15 a.m. in his brief report to General Dana's assistant adjutant general (Lieutenant Milton).

34. Henry Ropes to John C. Ropes, April 25, 1862; Henry Abbott to Caroline Abbott, April 26, 1862 (Scott, *Fallen Leaves*, 112); Palfrey, Memoir, 44.

35. Palfrey, *Memoir*, 43–44.

Chapter 5

1. Palfrey, *Memoir*, 44–47.

2. Quoted in Miller, *Harvard's Civil War*, 451–2. At some point after Frank returned home, Harvard University awarded him a bachelor's degree.

3. Palfrey, *Memoir*, 48–50.

4. *Ibid.*, 51; William Schouler, *A History of Massachusetts in the War* (New York: E. P. Dutton, 1868), 650.

5. Henry T. Johns, *Life with the Forty-ninth Massachusetts Volunteers* (Pittsfield, MA: the author, 1864), 19, 32–35.

6. *Ibid.*, 33–36.

7. *Ibid.*, 48–49.

8. *Ibid.*, 58–59.

9. *Ibid.*, 51, 55–56. The Berkshire Bible Society provided a copy of the New Testament to every man in the regiment (Stuart Murray, *A Time of War: A Northern Chronicle of the Civil War* [Lee, MA: Berkshire House Publishers, 2001], 160).

10. Palfrey, *Memoir*, 51; *Biographical Review, Volume XXXI: Containing Life Sketches of Leading Citizens of Berkshire County, Massachusetts* (Boston: Biographical Review Publishing Company, 1899), 287–89; "Mrs. W. F. Bartlett Dies at Bartlett Avenue Home," *Berkshire County Eagle*, February 17, 1909; Howe, *Touched with Fire*, 12, 143.

11. Schouler, *Massachusetts in the War*, 650; Johns, *Life with the 49th*, 64–65; Scrapbook 2, 230, Berkshire Athenaeum.

12. Scrapbook 2, 230, Berkshire Athenaeum; Johns, *Life with the 49th*, 65–66.

13. Johns, *Life with the 49th*, 68; Corporal John C. Gamwell wrote in his diary that weapons were distributed on November 26; see Doris G. Wendell, *Civil War Diary of Cpl. John Milton Gamwell, Co. B, 49th. Mass. Vols.* (N.p., 1987), entry for November 26, 1862.

14. *Ibid.*, 72–73; Schouler, *Massachusetts*

in the War, 651; Scrapbook 2, 231, Berkshire Athenaeum; Wendell, *Gamwell Diary*, entries for November 28–29, 1862.

15. "The Forty-Ninth in New York," Scrapbook 2, 268, Berkshire Athenaeum; partially quoted in Palfrey, *Memoir*, 53–54. See also a letter from another onlooker published in the *Pittsfield Sun*, Scrapbook 2, 231, Berkshire Athenaeum. Johns quoted from it in *Life with the 49th*, 73–75.

The writer of this article was amazed at Bartlett's equestrian ability. Frank must have pulled the wool over this man's eyes, for as late as December 31, the colonel wrote that his horse was "wild, fractious, and stubborn." He assigned one of his men to work with the horse and break him in. Frank, though, admitted that riding was a "delightful sensation to me, to move about on a horse after hobbling around on crutches so long." Palfrey, *Memoir*, 54–55.

16. Johns, *Life with the 49th*, 72–73, 75; "The 49th Reach New York," Scrapbook 2, 231, Berkshire Athenaeum.

17. Palfrey, *Memoir*, 53–56; Schouler, *Massachusetts in the War*, 651; Wendell, *Gamwell Diary*, entry for December 4, 1862.

18. Palfrey, *Memoir*, 55; Johns, *Life with the 49th*, 90–91.

19. Johns, *Life with the 49th*, 88–91.

20. Wendell, *Gamwell Diary*, entries for entries for December 7–31, 1862, and January 1–23, 1863. Gamwell was on detached duty as part of the provost guard and recorded his experience on this duty in many of the entries for this period.

21. Schouler, *Massachusetts in the War*, 651; Johns, Life with the 49th, 107–8; Scrapbook 2, 235, Berkshire Athenaeum.

22. Johns, *Life with the 49th*, 110–117; Wendell, *Gamwell Diary*, entries for January 26–30, 1862.

23. *Ibid.*, 123; Joseph Tucker, "The Forty-ninth in the Field," Scrapbook 1, 37, Berkshire Athenaeum; Palfrey, Memoir, 56; Wendell, *Gamwell Diary*, entries for February 1, 7, 10, 1863.

Chapter 6

1. For Butler, see his *Autobiography and Personal Reminiscences of Major-General Benj. F. Butler: Butler's Book* (Boston: A. M. Thayer and Company, 1892), and the modern biog-

raphy by Hans L. Trefousse, *Ben Butler: The South Called Him Beast!* (New York: Twayne Publishers, 1957). General Orders 28 stipulated that any woman insulting a United States soldier would be "regarded and held liable to be treated as a woman of the town plying her avocation."

2. For Banks, see Fred H. Harrington, *Fighting Politician, Major General N. P. Banks* (Philadelphia: University of Pennsylvania Press, 1948).

3. Dyer, *Compendium*, 1: 552; Johns, *Life with the 49th*, 123–24; Palfrey, *Memoir*, 56; Wendell, *Gamwell Diary*, entry for February 10, 1863. Gamwell indicated this date for debarkation from the steamer, while John wrote February 9.

4. Johns, *Life with the 49th*, 124–25.

5. *Ibid.*, 125–28.

6. *Ibid.*, 128–31; Wendell, *Gamwell Diary*, entry for February 11, 1863.

7. *Ibid.*, 128, 130–32; Palfrey, *Memoir*, 57.

8. Johns, *Life with the 49th*, 132–33; Palfrey, *Memoir*, 57–58.

9. Johns, *Life with the 49th*, 133–34; Wendell, *Gamwell Diary*, entry for February 18, 1863.

10. David S. and Jeanne T. Heidler (editors), *Encyclopedia of the American Civil War*, 5 volumes (Santa Barbara, CA: ABC-CLIO, 2000), 1: 147; Dyer, *Compendium*, 1: 552. Augur's First Division also included the Second Brigade, Brigadier General Godfrey Weitzel (75th, 114th, 160th, 174th New York, 8th Vermont, 12th Connecticut, 1st Louisiana), Third Brigade, Colonel Nathan A. M. Dudley (30th, 50th Massachusetts, 91st, 161st New York, 2nd Louisiana), plus artillery (1st Maine Battery, 6th Massachusetts Battery, Battery A, 1st United States), cavalry (1st Louisiana, 2nd Rhode Island Battalion, Company B, Massachusetts Battalion), and four regiments of African American volunteers. It was the strongest division in the corps.

11. Johns, *Life with the 49th*, 135–36; Palfrey, *Memoir*, 58.

12. Palfrey, *Memoir*, 58, 66. Corporal Gamwell noted in his diary on February 28 that after brigade review that day, Colonel Bartlett "says we made a good impression."

13. Johns, *Life with the 49th*, 143.

14. Palfrey, *Memoir*, 67; Wendell, *Gamwell Diary*, entry for March 4, 1863.

15. *Ibid.*, 68–70; Wendell, *Gamwell Diary*, entry for March 7, 1863.

16. Heidler, *Encyclopedia of the American Civil War*, 3: 1546; O.R., volume 15, 251–52.

17. Johns, *Life with the 49th*, 165; Palfrey, *Memoir*, 73.

18. Palfrey, *Memoir*, 74–75. Wendell, *Gamwell Diary*, entry for March 14, 1862. Gamwell wrote that the regiment camped for the night on a Rebel plantation and the men helped themselves to whatever they could find.

19. *Ibid.*, 74–76; Johns, *Life with the 49th*, 170; O.R., volume 15, 251–53.

20. Palfrey, *Memoir*, 75–76; Wendell, *Gamwell Diary*, entry for March 15, 1863.

21. *Ibid.*, 76–77.

22. *Ibid.*, 77–78; Johns, *Life with the 49th*, 170–1.

23. Palfrey, *Memoir*, 78–79; O.R., volume 15, 254, 266–67.; Wendell, *Gamwell Diary*, entry for March 16, 1863.

24. Palfrey, *Memoir*, 60–61, 79–80; Wendell, *Gamwell Diary*, entries for March 17–20, 1863.

25. *Ibid.*, 80; Johns, *Life with the 49th*, 177–79.

26. Johns, *Life with the 49th*, 179, 182–84; Wendell, *Gamwell Diary*, entry for March 22. Gamwell commented on the cold weather in his diary entries of March 24, 25, 30, and 31; on diarrhea in the regiment on April 4 (Gamwell seemed to have diarrhea quite often, as noted in many diary entries); and on the hot weather on April 7, 8, 22, and 28. On May 5, according to Gamwell, Bartlett limited drill to two and a half hours per day, before noon, to keep the men out of the hottest part of the day.

27. The best research on Banks' campaign on the Bayou Teche and move to Alexandria is that of David C. Edmonds, Volume One of *The Guns of Port Hudson* (Lafayette, LA: Arcadia Press, 1983), includes details on this expedition. The relevant reports are found in *O.R.*, volume 15, 292–400.

28. Palfrey, *Memoir*, 63.

Chapter 7

1. Joseph Tucker, "The Forty-ninth in the Field," Scrapbook 1, 37, Berkshire Athenaeum.

2. Johns, *Life with the 49th*, 203, 205–7;

Wendell, *Gamwell Diary*, entry for May 20, 1863.

3. Palfrey, *Memoir*, 63–64.

4. *Ibid.*, 64; "General Bartlett's War Career," *Springfield Republican*, May 8, 1904; Tucker, "49th in the Field"; Johns, *Life with the 49th*, 207.

5. Palfrey, *Memoir*, 64–65.

6. Edmonds, *Guns of Port Hudson*, 2: 1–5.

7. *Ibid.*, 6–7; *O.R.*, volume 26, part 1, 121 (Dudley's report).

8. Johns, *Life with the 49th*, 207–8.

9. Edmonds, *Guns of Port Hudson*, 2–3.; Lawrence Lee Hewitt, *Port Hudson, Confederate Bastion on the Mississippi* (Baton Rouge: Louisiana State University Press, 1987), 127.

10. Edmonds, *Guns of Port Hudson*, 8–9.

11. Hewitt, *Port Hudson*, 128; *O.R.*, volume 26, part 1, 121 (Dudley's report).

12. Hewitt, *Port Hudson*, 128–29; *Supplement to the Official Records of the Union and Confederate Armies*, 100 volumes (Wilmington, NC: Broadfoot Publishing Company, 1995–2000), volume 4, 724 (Chapin's report). Further references to this volume are abbreviated as *O.R.S.*

13. Edmonds, *Guns of Port Hudson*, 9.

14. *Ibid.*, 9–10; Tucker, "49th in the Field"; Johns, *Life with the 49th*, 208; *O.R.S.*, volume 4, 724 (Chapin's report).

15. Johns, *Life with the 49th*, 209–10. The accounts of the 49th Massachusetts in this engagement are at odds with each other. Corporal Gamwell, in his diary entry for May 21, wrote that the 49th was ordered "through the ravine to cut off their retreat." He further wrote that Company B deployed as skirmishers as Rebel artillery shells "whistle through the trees over our heads." Over all, the Union reports reflect the confusion that reigned on the field during this brief engagement.

16. Edmonds, *Guns of Port Hudson*, 10–11; *O.R.S.*, volume 4, 725–6.

17. Edmonds, *Guns of Port Hudson*, 11–12; Hewitt, *Port Hudson*, 129–30.

18. *O.R.*, volume 26, part 1, 67; *O.R.S.*, volume 4, 767 (Miles' report); Edmonds, *Guns of Port Hudson*, 13.

19. Hewitt, *Port Hudson*, 130–32; Johns, *Life with the 49th*, 213–14; Wendell, *Gamwell Diary*, entry for May 22, 1863.

20. Johns, *Life with the 49th*, 215–16; *O.R.S.*, volume 29, 473; Wendell, *Gamwell Diary*, entry for May 24, 1863.

21. *Ibid.*, 217–18.

22. Hewitt, *Port Hudson*, 135–36; Edmonds, *Guns of Port Hudson*, 33–35.

23. Johns, *Life with the 49th*, 219–220; Edmonds, *Guns of Port Hudson*, 27.

24. Johns, *Life with the 49th*, 220–1.

25. *Ibid.*, 221–24.

26. Hewitt, *Port Hudson*, 140–55; Edmonds, *Guns of Port Hudson*, 36–78.

27. Hewitt, *Port Hudson*, 156–62.

28. Johns, *Life with the 49th*, 225–27; Edmonds, *Guns of Port Hudson*, 79–80.

29. Johns, *Life with the 49th*, 227; Edmonds, *Guns of Port Hudson*, 80–81.

30. Johns, *Life with the 49th*, 227–28.

31. *Ibid.*, 228; Edmonds, *Guns of Port Hudson*, 81–82.

32. *O.R.S.*, volume 4, 731 (report of Colonel Elijah D. Johnson, 21st Maine); Edmonds, *Guns of Port Hudson*, 82; Palfrey, *Memoir*, 82.

33. Roswell G. Harris, "Assault on Port Hudson," *National Tribune*, February 14, 1907; O.R.S., volume 4, 731 (Johnson's report); Johns, *Life with the 49th*, 228–29.

34. Solomon Nelson, "Storming Port Hudson," *The Bivouac Banner*, fall 2007, online magazine at www.bivouacbooks.com.

35. Johns, *Life with the 49th*, 229; Harris, *National Tribune*; Edmonds, *Guns of Port Hudson*, 84–86.

36. *O.R.S.*, volume 4, 768 (report of Colonel Miles); Edmonds, *Guns of Port Hudson*, 83–84.

37. Johns, *Life with the 49th*, 229–30. See also Nelson, "Storming Port Hudson," for a similar experience at the abatis after the attack clearly failed.

38. *Ibid.*, 230–32.

39. *Ibid.*, 231; Edmonds, *Guns of Port Hudson*, 85.

40. Johns, *Life with the 49th*, 233–34; Hewitt, *Port Hudson*, 164; Palfrey, *Memoir*, 82; Edmonds, *Guns of Port Hudson*, 86; Welsh, *Medical Histories of Union Generals*, 21; Scrapbook 2, 237, Berkshire Athenaeum, clipping from a newspaper quoting the *New York Times* description of the attack.

41. Frederick Winsor, "The Surgeon at the Field Hospital," *Atlantic Monthly* 46 (1880): 184–5.

42. *Ibid.*, 185–6.

43. *Ibid.*, 186–7.

44. Edmonds, *Guns of Port Hudson*, 103–4, 107–115; O.R.S., volume 29, 491–2.

45. Palfrey, *Memoir*, 83–84; "The Siege of Port Hudson," *Harper's Weekly*, June 27, 1863, 411.

46. *O.R.*, volume 26, part 1, 47 (Banks' report); *O.R.S.*, volume 29, 473–4; Johns, *Life with the 49th*, 251–3.

47. Harris, *National Tribune*. Palfrey, *Memoir*, 82, noted that Frank wrote in his journal about the journey in the ambulance: "The ride reminded me of mine from Yorktown to Shipping Point a year before."

48. Palfrey, *Memoir*, 84–85.

49. *Ibid.*, 88–89.

50. Winsor, *Atlantic Monthly*, 188.

51. Palfrey, *Memoir*, 84–85.

52. *Ibid.*, 86, 90; Scrapbook 2, 238, Berkshire Athenaeum.

53. Schouler, *Massachusetts in the War*, 653.

54. Scrapbook 2, 239–41, Berkshire Athenaeum.

55. Ibid.; Schouler, *Massachusetts in the War*, 653; Murray, *A Time of War*, 231–32.

Chapter 8

1. Scrapbook 2, 265, Berkshire Athenaeum.

2. Palfrey, *Memoir*, 90; Warren Wilkinson, *Mother, May You Never See the Sights I Have Seen: The Fifty-seventh Massachusetts Veteran Volunteers in the Army of the Potomac, 1864–1865* (New York: Harper & Row, 1990), 2. Wilkinson notes that Bartlett was commissioned colonel of the 57th to date from August 17 (page 2), but on page 406 writes that Frank was not mustered out of service as colonel of the 49th until September 1. Frank was indeed mustered out of service as colonel of the 49th on September 1, but was not mustered into service as colonel of the 57th Massachusetts until April 9, 1864. See Frederick C. Ainsworth to George P. Lawrence, January 31, 1903, in Bartlett's Compiled Service File, Record Group 94, Records of the Office of the Adjutant General, National Archives.

3. Wilkinson, *57th Massachusetts*, 2, 406–7, 409, 428, 440, 464, 482, 505–6, 532, 545–5, 582, 600–1. Upon hearing Hollister's decision to resign, Frank penned the following in his journal: "He is going to resign,

I am sorry to say. His wife has persuaded him. It is the weakest thing I ever saw in him. I lose faith in man's firmness and woman's fortitude." See Palfrey, *Memoir*, 96.

4. Wilkinson, *57th Massachusetts*, 8–9.

5. *Ibid.*, 5–7, 10–12.

6. Palfrey, *Memoir*, 90–1.

7. *Ibid.*, 91–2.

8. Wilkinson, *57th Massachusetts*, 18, 410, 634–5. Dr. White had previously served with the 47th New York.

9. *Ibid.*, 20–22, 27, 29–30, 635–37.

10. Wilkinson, *57th Massachusetts*, 31; "Presentation to Col. Bartlett," Scrapbook 2, 265, Berkshire Athenaeum. See also Palfrey, *Memoir*, 94–96, for Palfrey's version of Frank's presentation speech.

11. Wilkinson, *57th Massachusetts*, 31–32; "Speeches of Gov. Andrew and Col. Bartlett," Scrapbook 2, Berkshire Athenaeum; Palfrey, *Memoir*, 96–98; John Anderson, *The Fifty-seventh Regiment of Massachusetts Volunteers in the War of the Rebellion, Army of the Potomac* (Boston: E. B. Stillings & Company, Printers, 1896), 11–14.

12. Wilkinson, *57th Massachusetts*, 32–33.

13. *Ibid.*, 34–41. The official history of the Cooper Shop omits the arrival and feeding of the 57th. The author noted that the list of regiments fed was deficient for April 1864. See Moore, *History of the Cooper Shop Volunteer Refreshment Saloon*, 181.

14. For background on Burnside and the Ninth Corps, see William Marvel, *Burnside* (Chapel Hill: University of North Carolina Press, 1991), and Augustus A. Woodbury, *Major General Ambrose E. Burnside and the Ninth Army Corps* (Providence, RI: Sidney S. Rider and Brother, 1867).

15. Warner, *Generals in Blue*, 477–78; *O.R.*, volume 36, part 1, 113.

16. Wilkinson, *57th Massachusetts*, 43–44.

17. *Ibid.*, 44–46.

18. *Ibid.*, 47–48.

19. *Ibid.*, 48–49.

20. *Ibid.*, 51–57.

21. Palfrey, *Memoir*, 99.

22. *Ibid.*, 99; Wilkinson, *57th Massachusetts*, 59–61.

23. Wilkinson, *57th Massachusetts*, 61–64; Christopher L. Kolakowski, " 'A Rough Place and a Hard Fight': Thomas Stevenson's Divi-

sion on the Brock and Plank Roads, May 6, 1864," *Civil War Regiments* 6 #4, available on the publisher's website: www.savaspublishing.com/Wilderness,html.

24. Wilkinson, *57th Massachusetts*, 65–66; Kolakowski, "Stevenson's Division." For details of Burnside's movement with Potter's and Willcox's divisions, see Gordon C. Rhea, *The Battle of the Wilderness, May 5–6, 1864* (Baton Rouge: Louisiana State University Press, 1994), 324–32. Rhea notes the difficulties Burnside faced, as well as his dilatory movement to the front in the first place, which led to increased Rebel opposition and Grant's decision to send Burnside against Hill's flank rather than filling a gap in the line.

25. Wilkinson, *57th Massachusetts*, 67–69; Kolakowski, "Stevenson's Division."

26. Wilkinson, *57th Massachusetts*, 69–72; *O.R.*, volume 36, part 1, 441 (Captain Joseph W. Spaulding's report, 19th Maine).

27. Wilkinson, *57th Massachusetts*, 72–73.

28. *Ibid.*, 73–74; Palfrey, *Memoir*, 99–100.

29. Wilkinson, *57th Massachusetts*, 74–80.

30. Rhea, *Wilderness*, 351–62.

31. *Ibid.*, 362–64.

32. *Ibid.*, 365–66; Wilkinson, *57th Massachusetts*, 77–78, 80–81; Palfrey, *Memoir*, 99–102.

33. Wilkinson, *57th Massachusetts*, 82–83, 625. *The Official Records* (volume 36, part 1, 131), lists the regimental casualties at 57 killed, 158 wounded, and 30 missing, for a total of 245. Wilkinson stated that his figures are more accurate, reflecting his extensive research in compiled service records at the National Archives.

34. Palfrey, *Memoir*, 99–101.

35. *Ibid.*, 101–2.

36. Andrew to Burnside, April 30, 1864; Andrew to Stanton, May 6, 1864; Andrew to Wilson, May 20, 1864; and Andrew to Stanton, May 30, 1864, all in Bartlett's Compiled Service Record, RG 94.

37. Palfrey, *Memoir*, 102–3.

38. *Ibid.*, 103–4.

39. *Ibid.*, 104–5.

40. *Ibid.*, 106–9.

Chapter 9

1. *O.R.*, volume 40, part 3, 370–72, 388. When Frank's regiment had marched off from Annapolis in May, the Ninth Corps was an independent command. Burnside ranked Meade in seniority, so Grant placed Burnside's corps as an attached command which received orders direct from the lieutenant general. But this chain of command proved cumbersome, and when it was suggested that the Ninth Corps be assigned to the Army of the Potomac, Burnside magnanimously agreed to serve under Meade's command. Thus, when Bartlett arrived at City Point, he was unaware that he should first report to army headquarters for assignment.

2. Faust, *Historical Times Encyclopedia*, 192–3; Dyer, *Compendium*, 313.

3. Wilkinson, *57th Massachusetts*, 136–43.

4. *Ibid.*, 173–79.

5. *O.R.*, volume 40, part 1, 195, 246.

6. Wilkinson, *57th Massachusetts*, 224, 625–6.

7. Palfrey, *Memoir*, 110.

8. Jerome B. Yates to Marie Yates Swanson, July 19, 1864, in Robert G. Evans (editor and compiler), *The 16th Mississippi Infantry: Civil War Letters and Reminiscences* (Jackson: University Press of Mississippi, 2002), 276.

9. Richard A. Sauers (editor), *The Civil War Journal of Colonel William J. Bolton, 51st Pennsylvania, April 20, 1861–August 2, 1865* (Conshohocken, PA: Combined Publishing, 2000), 220–23; William H. Powell, "The Battle of the Petersburg Crater," in Robert U. Johnson and Clarence C. Buel (editors), *Battles and Leaders of the Civil War*, 4 volumes (New York: The Century Company, 1884–1888; reprint edition, New York: Thomas Yoseloff, 1956), 4: 559.

10. Palfrey, *Memoir*, 112–13.

11. *Ibid.*, 113–14.

12. *O.R.*, volume 40, part 3, 528–29.

13. Palfrey, *Memoir*, 116.

14. *O.R.*, volume 40, part 3, 525–6.

15. For recent scholarship about Hancock's foray, see Bryce A. Suderow, "Glory Denied: The First Battle of Deep Bottom, July 27th–29th, 1864," *North & South* 3 #7 (September 2000): 17–32.

16. *War Diary and Letters of Stephen Minot Weld, 1861–1865* (Cambridge, MA: Privately printed by the Riverside Press, 1912; 2nd edition, Boston: Massachusetts Historical Society, 1979), 344; Palfrey, *Memoir*, 116–17.

17. Palfrey, *Memoir*, 118.

Chapter 10

1. *O.R.,* volume 40, part 2, 220.

2. *Ibid.,* 396–7; Michael A. Cavanaugh and William Marvel, *The Petersburg Campaign: The Battle of the Crater, "The Horrid Pit"* (Lynchburg, VA: H. E. Howard, Inc., 1989), 4–5.

3. *Report of the Committee on the Conduct of the War on the Attack on Petersburg, on the 30th Day of July, 1864* (Washington, D.C.: Government Printing Office, 1865), 112–13. Future references to this volume are abbreviated as *C.C.W.*

4. Cavanaugh and Marvel, *Crater,* 5. Pleasants' version of the entire episode is at odds with other accounts. Although the story here generally follows the Pleasants version, Colonel Pleasants became bitter after the failure of the July 30 assault. Dr. Earl J. Hess, who is working on a new book about this event, will show that General Meade did not act as Pleasants claimed he did. Meade was a trained engineer and knew full well that a tunnel could be dug; he doubted the success of an attack after the mine was exploded.

5. *Ibid.,* 5–6.

6. *C.C.W.,* 113.

7. Cavanaugh and Marvel, *Crater,* 8.

8. *Ibid.,* 6–7, 9.

9. *Ibid.,* 10; Gary W. Gallagher (editor), *Fighting for the Confederacy: The Personal Recollections of General Edward Porter Alexander* (Chapel Hill: University of North Carolina Press, 1989), 444–45.

10. Gallagher, *Fighting for the Confederacy,* 445–46.

11. Cavanaugh and Marvel, *Crater,* 11; Gallagher, *Fighting for the Confederacy,* 450–1. See also *O.R.,* volume 40, part 3, 819–20, for reports of the Confederate digging operation. When the mine was exploded on July 30, a Confederate digging crew was at work in the righthand tunnel, but were unaffected by the explosion, which created the crater to their left and thus allowed them to escape being buried alive. No one was at work in the left tunnel, which was destroyed by the blast.

12. Cavanaugh and Marvel, *Crater,* 11–12; *C.C.W.,* 113–14.

13. *O.R.,* volume 40, part 1, 130–32.

14. *Ibid.,* volume 40, part 3, 438.

15. *Ibid.,* volume 40, part 1, 557; part 3, 479; *C.C.W.,* 114–15.

16. *Ibid.,* volume 40, part 3, 476–77.

17. Cavanaugh and Marvel, *Crater,* 17–18. Burnside issued orders to Ferrero on July 17 to collect his troops and begin training. When he testified before the Committee on the Conduct of the War in December 1864, Burnside wrongfully thought that the start of the training "must have been some three weeks before the attack was made," see *C.C.W.,* 15.

18. *C.C.W.,* 17–18. During the afternoon on July 28, Grant left his City Point headquarters and went north of the James to visit the battle front there to observe the progress of General Hancock's foray toward Richmond's defenses. The general returned to headquarters by nine o'clock that evening, as indicated by a telegram he sent to Washington. See *O.R.,* volume 40, part 3, 551.

19. See *O.R.,* volume 40, part 3, 553–54, for Meade's and Grant's messages to each other.

20. *Ibid.,* 608.

21. *C.C.W.,* 18, 79. At this time, General Ledlie was not a part of the conversation at corps headquarters. There is some disagreement in the sources whether or not Ledlie was originally called to this conference or not called until after Meade's departure.

22. *Ibid.,* 18.

23. *Ibid.,* 18, 79, 85.

24. *Ibid.,* 85.

25. *O.R.,* volume 40, part 3, 596–7.

26. *Ibid.,* 611–12.

27. *C.C.W.,* 18–19.

28. *O.R.,* volume 40, part 1, 535.

29. Wilkinson, *57th Massachusetts,* 238.

30. Stephen M. Weld, "The Petersburg Mine," *in Papers of the Military Historical Society of Massachusetts,* 5: 207. See also Weld's *War Diary and Letters,* 351, where the colonel said Bartlett told the regimental officers that the objective was Cemetery Hill.

31. Wilkinson, *57th Massachusetts,* 240.

32. *Ibid.,* 240–1.

33. *Ibid,* 241–42; column from an unidentified newspaper regarding Chaplain Dashiell in Scrapbook Collection, Berkshire Athenaeum.

34. Cavanaugh and Marvel, *Crater,* 37.

35. *Ibid.,* 37–39.

36. George W. Ward, *History of the Second Pennsylvania Veteran Heavy Artillery (112th Regiment Pennsylvania Volunteers) From 1861*

to 1866, Including the Provisional Second Pen-n'a. Heavy Artillery (Philadelphia: George W. Ward, Printer, 1904), 205.

37. William G. Gavin, *Campaigning with the Roundheads: The History of the Hundredth Pennsylvania Veteran Volunteer Infantry Regiment in the American Civil War 1861–1865* (Dayton, OH: Morningside House, Inc., 1989), 515.

38. Cavanaugh and Marvel, *Crater*, 41–42. For the reaction of soldiers watching the falling debris, see William H. Powell, "The Battle of the Petersburg Crater," in Robert U. Johnson and Clarence C. Buel (editors), *Battles and Leaders of the Civil War*, 4 volumes (New York: The Century Company, 1884–1889), 4: 551. Powell was one of General Ledlie's aides.

39. Charles H. Houghton, "In the Crater," *Battles and Leaders*, 4: 561–2.

40. Robert G. Scott (editor), *Forgotten Valor: The Memoirs, Journals, and Civil War Letters of Orlando B. Willcox* (Kent, OH: Kent State University Press, 1999), 555–6.

41. Powell, "Petersburg Crater," 551; Weld, "Petersburg Mine," 208.

42. Powell, "Petersburg Crater," 551.

43. Weld, "Petersburg Mine," 209.

44. Cavanaugh and Marvel, Crater, 42–43.

45. *O.R.*, volume 40, part 1, 541; Ward, *2nd Pennsylvania*, 206.

46. Wilkinson, *57th Massachusetts*, 248; Gavin, *100th Pennsylvania*, 517.

47. Wilkinson, *57th Massachusetts*, 249, taken from Anderson's history, 208.

48. Dashiell account, Scrapbook Collection, Berkshire Athenaeum.

49. See Allen D. Albert, *History of the Forty-fifth Regiment Pennsylvania Veteran Volunteer Infantry 1861–1865* (Williamsport, PA: Grit Publishing Company, 1912), 154, for a description of the Confederate entrenchments.

50. Cavanaugh and Marvel, *Crater*, 42–46.

51. *Ibid.*, 46, 51–52.

52. *Ibid.*, 42–43.

53. *O.R.*, volume 40, part 1, 103–4, 118–19.

54. Cavanaugh and Marvel, *Crater*, 56–58, 85–90.

55. *Ibid.*, 89–91.

56. *Ibid.*, 53–58, 87–88, 91, 93. Meade had earlier ordered Warren to probe the Rebel right flank after signal officers plainly could see Mahone's troops moving north, but by the time Warren sent orders to subordinates, Meade had sent out his 9:30 order to cease all attacks.

57. *Ibid.*, 90–92.

58. Dashiell account, Scrapbook Collection, Berkshire Athenaeum.

59. Weld, "Petersburg Mine," 210–11; Weld, *War Diary and Letters*, 356–57.

60. Powell, "Petersburg Crater," 553–54; Palfrey, *Memoir*, 119. Powell, in his "Petersburg Crater" article, pages 558–59, included a footnote in which he stated that Bartlett's wooden leg was hit by a shot that caused the general to totter and fall. Those around him thought he had been wounded until Bartlett told them it was his wooden leg that was hit. Major Houghton of the 14th New York Heavy Artillery, wrote that Bartlett "had received a shot, disabling his artificial leg, and he could not be carried to the rear" (Houghton, "In the Crater," 562).

61. Wilkinson, *57th Massachusetts*, 257–58.

62. *O.R.*, volume 40, part 1, 555. It is unknown why Bartlett chose Gregg, an officer in a regiment in Potter's division, as his field officer of the day. According to Captain Rees G. Richards of the 45th, Bartlett had witnessed the savage fighting that took place when the Rebels charged into the mass of Yankees just north of the Crater. During this fighting, Captain Gregg successfully defended himself against a Confederate officer who grabbed his throat and demanded that Gregg surrender. Richards recorded that Bartlett, impressed by Gregg's heroics, even offered Gregg his own sword that had been presented to him by the 57th Massachusetts, telling Gregg, "you know how to use it." But Gregg returned the sword at some unspecified time. See Albert, *45th Pennsylvania*, 157, for this story.

63. Freeman S. Bowley, "The Battle of the Mine," *Overland Monthly* 4 (1870): 325–26.

64. *O.R.*, volume 40, part 3, 663.

65. Cavanaugh and Marvel, *Crater*, 97–98; George Clark, "Alabamians in the Crater Battle," *Confederate Veteran* 3 (1895): 68; John C. Featherston, "Graphic Account of Battle of Crater," *Southern Historical Society Papers* 33 (1905): 360–1.

66. Cavanaugh and Marvel, *Crater*, 98; Clark, "Alabamians in the Crater," 68–69; Powell, "Petersburg Crater," 558.

67. *O.R.,* volume 40, part 1, 556, 568, 579; Featherston, "Graphic Account," 364.

68. Featherston, "Graphic Account," 364.

69. Palfrey, *Memoir*, 119; O.R., volume 40, part 1, 555–56.

70. Gavin, *100th Pennsylvania*, 519; Clark, "Alabamians," 69; Bowley, "Battle of the Mine," 326–27; Cavanaugh and Marvel, *Crater*, 100–2.

71. Palfrey, *Memoir*, 119; Featherston, "Graphic Account," 365; Clark, "Alabamians," 69. Featherston also recounted that Bartlett's captors detailed two captured black soldiers to help him out of the pit, but the general refused their help, then was given white assistance. If true, it seems that Frank was echoing the prevalent view of nineteenth century white America in regard to blacks in general.

72. Cavanaugh and Marvel, *Crater*, 128–29.

73. For the military court of inquiry, see *O.R.,* volume 40, part 1, 42–163. For a summary of the court findings, see Cavanaugh and Marvel, *Crater*, 108–111.

74. Cavanaugh and Marvel, *Crater*, 111.

Chapter 11

1. Palfrey, *Memoir*, 120.

2. *Ibid.*

3. *Ibid.* Colonel Weld, also captured and marched through Petersburg, wrote that the prisoners were placed on an island in the Appomattox River overnight.

4. *Ibid.;* James I. Robertson, Jr., "Houses of Horror: Danville's Civil War Prisons," *Virginia Magazine of History and Biography* 69 (1961): 329–31; George H. Putnam, A Prisoner of War in Virginia, 1865–1865 (New York, 1912; reprint edition, Arivaca, AZ: Proofmark, 2000), 26.

5. Palfrey, *Memoir*, 119–20. Weld wrote that the train was delayed because of a prior accident on the line (Weld, *War Diary and Letters*, 359).

6. Palfrey, *Memoir*, 120.

7. Robertson, "Houses of Horror," 332–33; Weld, War *Diary and Letters*, 359.

8. Robertson, "Houses of Horror," 339; Palfrey, *Memoir*, 120–23.

9. Palfrey, *Memoir*, 121–22; Dashiell account, Scrapbook Collection, Berkshire Athenaeum.

10. *Ibid.*, 123–24.

11. *Ibid.*, 124.

12. *Ibid.*, 124–25.

13. *Ibid.*, 125–26. In a letter home written on August 20, Bartlett indicated that his ailment was dysentery, brought on by exposure after overexertion and exhaustion on July 30. *Ibid.*, 128.

14. *Ibid.*, 126–27. Bartlett's use of peach stones to make rings was a favorite pastime of bored prisoners, many of whom used bits of bone to craft their wares. For an example, see Abner R. Small, "Personal Observations and Experiences in Rebel Prisons, 1864–1865," 311, in Military Order of the Loyal Legion of the United States, Maine Commandery, *War Papers, Volume One* (Portland, ME: Thurston Print, 1898). Small, an officer in the 16th Maine, was captured in August 1864 and eventually wound up at Danville.

15. Palfrey, *Memoir*, 128–30.

16. *Ibid.*, 131.

17. *Ibid.*, 131; Heidler, *Encyclopedia of the American Civil War*, 4: 2061; Ezra J. Warner, *Generals in Gray* (Baton Rouge: Louisiana State University Press, 1959), 324; *O.R.,* Series 2, Volume 7, 599, 605.

18. Heidler, *Encyclopedia of the American Civil War*, 3: 1179–80. For more details on Libby, see Sandra V. Parker, *Richmond's Civil War Prisons* (Lynchburg, VA: H. E. Howard, Inc., 1990).

19. Palfrey, *Memoir*, 131–32.

20. *Ibid.*, 132–33.

21. *Ibid.*, 133–34, 140.

22. *Ibid.*, 134–35.

23. *Ibid.*, 136–37.

24. *Ibid.*, 139–42.

25. *Ibid.*, 142. Ross is identified in Parker, *Richmond's Civil War Prisons*, 11.

26. Palfrey, *Memoir*, 142–43.

27. *Ibid.*, 142–43. Although Bartlett could not know it, the diarrhea he had contracted while in Libby Prison would haunt him for the rest of his life. See Welsh, *Medical Histories of Union Generals*, 22.

28. *Ibid.*, 144–45.

Chapter 12

1. Palfrey, *Memoir*, 144–45.

2. *Ibid.*, 146–49; Bartlett to General Edward T. Townsend, May 23, 1865, Bartlett service file.

3. Palfrey, *Memoir*, 149–50; Dyer, *Compendium*, 1: 313.

4. Dyer, *Compendium*, 1: 313–315.

5. Palfrey, *Memoir*, 150–1.

6. *Ibid.*, 152, 155–56; Assistant Adjutant General R. Chandler to Bartlett, July 14, 1865, Bartlett service record.

7. Palfrey, *Memoir*, 155–56. By the time Frank left the corps, Major General Christopher C. Augur, commander of the Department of Washington, had issued an order suspending all duty except the necessary guard and fatigue duties. He further dictated that "all indulgence promotive of enjoyment and not inconsistent with the requirements of military discipline and good order" was granted to the troops. See Sauers, *Bolton Journal*, 267 (Colonel Bolton's journal entry for July 4, 1865).

8. Palfrey, *Memoir*, 157–58.

9. *Ibid.*, 152–54, with original in Bartlett service record.

10. Stanton to Bartlett, August 12, 1865; Stanton to Assistant Adjutant General Edward T. Townsend, September 18, 1865; Bartlett to Townsend, September 22, 1865; Bartlett to Stanton, September 24, 1865, all in Bartlett service record.

11. Palfrey, *Memoir*, 159–60. A wedding notice appeared in the *Berkshire Eagle*, October 19, 1865, but the brief paragraph is very general. The Pittsfield *Sun* of October 19 listed the marriage in its "Marriages" column, then inserted a paragraph in the "Local Intelligence" section that detailed their departure for Europe. No other wedding details have been located.

12. Palfrey, *Memoir*, 159–66.

13. *Ibid.*, 166–70.

14. *Ibid.*, 171–77.

15. *Ibid.*, 177–79.

16. *Ibid.*, 179–81.

17. *Ibid.*, 182, 184. For background on Garibaldi, see http://www.reformation.org/garibaldi.html.

18. Palfrey, *Memoir*, 182–87.

19. *Ibid.*, 187–95. Bartlett's leave of absence was extended for two months on March 13, 1866. See Bartlett to Townsend, June 14, 1866, Bartlett service record. The leave extension also meant that his mustering

out of service was delayed. See E. D. Townsend memorandum of April 17, 1866, Bartlett service record.

20. Bartlett to Townsend, June 14, 1866; F. C. Ainsworth to George P. Lawrence, January 31, 1903, both in Bartlett service record.

Chapter 13

1. Palfrey, *Memoir*, 196–202.

2. *Ibid.*, 196–204.

3. *Ibid.*, 205–9.

4. *Ibid.*, 205–214. On the final page of his *Memoir*, Palfrey clarified Frank Bartlett's inheritance from Uncle Edwin at the insistence of his widow, who wished readers to know that Bartlett "borrowed largely" from both Edwin's estate and his aunt, and that these loans were never repaid (*Memoir*, 310).

5. *Ibid.*, 214–5.

6. *Ibid.*, 215–6.

7. *Ibid.*, 217–8.

8. *Ibid.*, 219. Frank's health must have improved somewhat, for on December 20, 1869, he delivered a lecture on iron to the Scientific Section of the Young Men's Association in Pittsfield. For a brief report, see "Gen. Bartlett's Lecture," *Berkshire County Eagle*, December 23, 1869.

9. *Ibid.*, 219–222.

10. *Ibid.*, 222–23.

11. *Ibid.*, 223–25.

12. *Ibid.*, 225–26, 236–39.

13. *Ibid.*, 226–7.

14. Eric Foner, *Reconstruction: America's Unfinished Revolution, 1863–1877* (New York: Harper & Row, 1988), 499–502.

15. Mary R. Dearing, *Veterans in Politics: The Story of the G.A.R.* (Baton Rouge: Louisiana State University Press, 1952), 199–200.

16. Palfrey, *Memoir*, 227–32; Bartlett to William Schouler, April 14, 21, 1872, in Schouler Papers, Massachusetts Historical Society.

17. Foner, *Reconstruction*, 502–3.

18. Palfrey, *Memoir*, 231; Bartlett to Schouler, May 20, July 31, 1872, Schouler Papers.

19. Bartlett to Schouler, July 20, 1872, Schouler Papers; Foner, *Reconstruction*, 502–10.

20. Palfrey, *Memoir*, 231–2. That June,

Frank received an honorary M.A. from Harvard.

21. *Ibid.*, 232.
22. *Ibid.*, 232–34.
23. *Ibid.*, 234–35, 240–42.
24. *Ibid.*, 242–43; Foner, *Reconstruction*, 512.
25. Palfrey, *Memoir*, 248–49, 262–3.
26. *Ibid.*, 249–50.
27. *Ibid.*, 250–52.
28. *Ibid.*, 252–3.
29. *Ibid.*, 252–56.
30. *Ibid.*, 257–8.
31. Richmond *Daily Dispatch*, April 29, 1875.
32. *Ibid.*
33. Palfrey, *Memoir*, 259.
34. *Ibid.*, 259–60.
35. *Ibid.*, 260–1.
36. *Ibid.*, 262–4.
37. *Ibid.*, 274–81.
38. *Ibid.*, 264–74, 277–8, 282–3.
39. *Ibid.*, 283–85; Janet Schwartzberg, "Tredegar Iron Works: An Introduction," in *The Richmond National Parks Quarterly Newsletter*, Spring 2000.
40. Palfrey, *Memoir*, 285–289. Frank went to Europe alone, without his family, as inferred from his letters home.
41. *Ibid.*, 289–91.
42. *Ibid.*, 291–93.
43. *Ibid.*, 293–95.
44. *Ibid.*, 295–96; Welsh, *Medical Histories of Union Generals*, 22; "Funeral of General Bartlett," *Springfield Republican*, December 21, 1876; Scrapbook 2, 270, Berkshire Athenaeum.
45. *Springfield Republican*, December 21, 1876; Henry M. Rogers, *Annals of the Commandery of the State of Massachusetts From Its Institution, March 4, 1868, to May 1, 1918, and the Proceedings at the Fiftieth Anniversary, March 6, 1918* (Boston: Atlantic Printing Company, 1918), 13. Frank Bartlett had been elected to MOLLUS on October 6, 1868. *See Register of the Commandery of the State of Massachusetts, November 1, 1912* (Cambridge: The University Press, 1912), 35.

Chapter 14

1. Scrapbook 2, 269, Berkshire Athenaeum. *The New York Times*, on December 22, 1876, printed a lengthy obituary that was copied from the *Springfield Republican* of December 18, 1876.

2. Military Order of the Loyal Legion of the United States, Commandery of Massachusetts, *Tribute to the Memory of Companion Brevet Major General William F. Bartlett, U. S. Volunteers* (N.p., 1877).

3. Stanton Garner, *The Civil War World of Herman Melville* (Lawrence: University Press of Kansas, 1993), 9, 32, 194–195, 266–69.

4. *Ibid.*, 32–36. For the complete poem, see Herman Melville, *Battle-Pieces and Aspects of the War* (New York: Harper & Brothers, Publishers, 1866; reprint edition, New York: DaCapo, 1995), 120–1.

5. "Tribute to Gen. Wm. Francis Bartlett," *Boston Advertiser*, December 1876.

6. Harte's poem about Bartlett can be found in Charles M. Kozlay (compiler), *Stories and Poems and Other Uncollected Writings of Bret Harte* (Boston: Houghton, Mifflin, 1921), 267–68.

7. A. G. Sedgwick, "William Francis Bartlett," *The Nation* #677 (June 20, 1878): 406–7.

8. James L. High, "My Hero," in *Military Essays and Recollections: Papers Read Before the Commandery of the State of Illinois, Military Order of the Loyal Legion of the United States*, (Chicago: Dial Press, 1899), volume 3, 155–71; Mrs. H. Neill Watson, "Sketch of the Life of Gen. William F. Bartlett," *Collections of the Berkshire Historical and Scientific Society 3* (1899): 363–76. High was a member of the 46th Wisconsin during the Civil War. There is another Bartlett article by Scott H. Paradise, "Some Eminent And-over Alumni, 21: William Francis Bartlett, 1840–1876," *The Phillips Bulletin* (October 1931): 11–22. This article was taken largely from Palfrey's *Memoir* and added nothing new to any writing on Bartlett.

9. "A Monument in the West," *Pittsfield Sun*, May 14, 1891; Susan Greendyke Lachevre to Martin Sable, March 7, 2002.

10. The entire text of Holmes' speech can be located on the Internet at www.people.virginia.edu/~mmd5f/memorial.htm.

11. The information for this paragraph is taken from several clippings and reports found in Bartlett's Harvard University file (HUG 300).

12. "Legislative Eulogies of Gen. Bartlett When the $20,000 Statue was Voted," *Pittsfield Sun*, April 4, 1901; *Maj.-Gen. W. F. Bartlett, A Pittsfield Soldier*, 8, 10, Berkshire Athenaeum; *A Record of the Dedication of the Statue of Major General William Francis Bartlett. A Tribute of the Commonwealth of Massachusetts, May 27, 1904* (Boston: Wright and Potter Printing Company, State Printers, 1905), 18–19.

13. *Maj.-Gen. W. F. Bartlett, A Pittsfield Soldier*, 1, 14 (Scrapbook of clippings in the Berkshire Athenaeum); *Record of the Dedication*, 18.

14. *Ibid.*, 1, 14–15.

15. *Ibid.*, 3–8, 15–23.

16. Unidentified newspaper clipping in Bartlett's Harvard File, B2012; the two Confederate tributes are included in *Record of the Dedication of the Statue*, 75–82. For more details on the ceremony, see "Unveiled the Bartlett Statue. Little Grandson of the Distinguished Soldier Did It Very Successfully," *Boston Globe*, May 28, 1904; "Veil Drawn from Bartlett Statue," *Boston Herald*, May 27, 1904; "State Honors a Noble Son," *Boston Globe*, May 27, 1904; "Maj. Gen. Bartlett's Statue Unveiled," *Boston Globe*, May 28, 1904.

17. "The Gen. Bartlett Statue," *Pittsfield Sun*, November 10, 1904; Statue Dedication, Pittsfield Sun, December 8, 1904.

18. "A Pittsfield Hero Gets a New Home,"*Berkshire Eagle*, March 15, 1963; Murray, *A Time of War*, 304.

19. "Children of William Francis Bartlett," Bartlett files, Harvard University; *1862–Class Report–1912, Class of 'Sixty-Two, Harvard University, Fiftieth Anniversary* (Cambridge, 1912), 7–8; Robert Pomeroy Bartlett obituary, *Pittsfield Sun*, April 2, 1903.

20. "Historical Data: Items from the Pittsfield Sun Newspaper, Series 80," by Bruce N. Honig, dates of July 20, 1881, August 11, 1887, September 1, 1887, from copy in Berkshire Athenaeum; "Mrs. W. F. Bartlett Dies at Bartlett Avenue Home," *Berkshire Eagle*, February 17, 1909; clipping from unknown newspaper with Mary Agnes' obituary, Bartlett file, Harvard University.

21. Ibid.; "Mrs. William F. Bartlett. Widow of General was Buried Yesterday at Pittsfield," unidentified newspaper clipping, Bartlett file, Harvard University.

22. *Shot to Pieces*, produced by Inecom Entertainment, 2002. This 80-minute DVD has received mixed reviews. See Amazon.com for this product and several reviews.

23. Paradise, "Bartlett," 22.

BIBLIOGRAPHY

Unpublished Primary Sources

Abbott, Henry L. Civil War Letters. In Abbott Family Papers. Houghton Library, Harvard University.

Bartlett, William F. Compiled Service and Pension Files. In National Archives, Record Group 94, Records of the Office of the Adjutant General.

_____. Scholastic Files. Harvard University.

Macy, George N. Papers. In William Wyles Collection. University of California at Santa Barbara.

Mason, Herbert C. Letters. Historical Society of Pennsylvania.

Ropes, Henry. Letters. In Twentieth Regiment Collection. Boston Public Library.

Schouler, William. Papers. Massachusetts Historical Society.

Published Primary Sources

Bowley, Freeman S. "The Battle of the Mine." *Overland Monthly* 4 (1870): 319–27.

Clark, George. "Alabamians in the Crater Battle." *Confederate Veteran* 3 (1895): 68–69.

Evans, Robert G. (editor and compiler). *The 16th Mississippi Infantry: Civil War Letters and Reminiscences.* Jackson: University Press of Mississippi, 2002.

Featherston, John C. "Graphic Account of Battle of Crater." Richmond *Times-Dispatch*, October 22, 1905; reprinted in *Southern Historical Society Papers* 33 (1905): 358–74; edited and reprinted as "The Battle of the 'Crater' as I Saw It," *Confederate Veteran* 14 (1906): 23–26.

Gallagher, Gary W. (editor). *Fighting for the Confederacy: The Personal Recollections of General Edward Porter Alexander.* Chapel Hill: University of North Carolina Press, 1989.

Harris, Roswell G. "Assault on Port Hudson." *National Tribune*, February 14, 1907.

Honig, Bruce N. "Historical Data: Items from the *Pittsfield Sun* Newspaper, Series 80." Copy in Berkshire Athenaeum.

Hosmer, James K. *A Corporal's Notes of Military Service in the Nineteenth Army Corps.* Boston: Walker, Wise & Company, 1864.

Houghton, Charles H. "In the Crater." In Robert U. Johnson and Clarence C. Buel (editors), *Battles and Leaders of the Civil War.* 4 volumes. New York: The Century Company, 1884–1888; reprint edition, New York: Thomas Yoseloff, 1956, volume 4: 561–62.

Howe, Mark D. (editor). *Touched With Fire: Civil War Letters and Diary of Oliver Wendell Holmes, Jr., 1861–1864.* Cambridge: Harvard University Press, 1947.

Johns, Henry T. *Life with the Forty-ninth Massachusetts Volunteers.* Pittsfield, MA: the author, 1864.

Maj.-Gen. W. F. Bartlett, A Pittsfield Soldier. Scrapbook of clippings in the Berkshire Athenaeum.

Nelson, Solomon. "Storming Port Hudson." *Bivouac Banner,* Fall 2007. Online magazine at www.bivouacbooks.com.

Palfrey, Francis W. (editor). *Memoir of William Francis Bartlett.* Cambridge, MA: Houghton, Osgood and Company, 1878.

Powell, William H. "The Battle of the Petersburg Crater." In Robert U. Johnson and Clarence C. Buel (editors), *Battles and Leaders of the Civil War.* 4 volumes. New York: The Century Company, 1884–1888; reprint edition, New York: Thomas Yoseloff, 1956, volume 4: 545–60.

Putnam, George H. *A Prisoner of War in Virginia, 1865–1865.* New York, 1912; reprint edition, Arivaca, AZ: Proofmark, 2000.

Sauers, Richard A. (editor). *The Civil War Journal of Colonel William J. Bolton, 51st Pennsylvania, April 20, 1861–August 2, 1865.* Conshohocken, PA: Combined Publishing, 2000.

Scott, Robert G. (editor). *Fallen Leaves: The Civil War Letters of Major Henry Livermore Abbott.* Kent, OH: Kent State University Press, 1991.

_____. *Forgotten Valor: The Memoirs, Journals, and Civil War Letters of Orlando B. Willcox.* Kent, OH: Kent State University Press, 1999.

Scrapbook Collection. Berkshire Athenaeum.

"The Siege of Port Hudson." *Harper's Weekly,* June 27, 1863, p. 411.

Small, Abner R. "Personal Observations and Experiences in Rebel Prisons, 1864–1865." Military Order of the Loyal Legion of the United States. Maine Commandery. *War Papers, Volume One,* pages 295–317. Portland, ME: Thurston Print, 1898.

Supplement to the Official Records of the Union and Confederate Armies. 100 volumes. Wilmington, NC: Broadfoot Publishing Company, 1995–2000.

United States Congress. Joint Committee on the Conduct of the War. *Report of the Joint Congressional Committee on the Conduct of the War.* 3 volumes. Washington, D.C.: Government Printing Office, 1863.

_____. *Report of the Committee on the Conduct of the War on the Attack on Petersburg, on the 30th Day of July, 1864.* Washington, D.C.: Government Printing Office, 1865.

United States War Department. *The War of the Rebellion: A Compilation of the Official Records of the Union and Confederate Armies.* 70 volumes in 128 parts. Washington, D.C.: Government Printing Office, 1880–1901.

Weld, Stephen M. "The Petersburg Mine." *Papers of the Military Historical Society of Massachusetts.* Volume 5 (1906), 207–219.

_____. *War Diary and Letters of Stephen Minot Weld, 1861–1865.* Boston: Massachusetts Historical Society, 1979.

Wendell, Doris G. *Civil War Diary of Cpl. John Milton Gamwell, Co. B, 49th. Mass. Vols.* N.p., 1987.

Winsor, Frederick. "The Surgeon at the Field Hospital." *Atlantic Monthly* 46 (1880): 183–88.

Unit Histories

Albert, Allen D. *History of the Forty-fifth Regiment Pennsylvania Veteran Volunteer Infantry 1861–1865.* Williamsport: Grit Publishing Company, 1912.

Anderson, John. *The Fifty-seventh Regiment of Massachusetts Volunteers in the War of the Rebellion, Army of the Potomac.* Boston: E. B. Stillings & Company, Printers, 1896.

Bruce, George A. *The Twentieth Regiment of Massachusetts Volunteer Infantry 1861–1865.* Boston: Houghton, Mifflin and Company, 1906.

Gavin, William G. *Campaigning with the Roundheads: The History of the Hundredth Pennsylvania Veteran Volunteer Infantry Regiment in the American Civil War 1861–1865.* Dayton, OH: Morningside House, Inc., 1989.

Miller, Richard F. *Harvard's Civil War: A History of the Twentieth Massachusetts Volunteer Infantry.* Hanover, NH: University Press of New England, 2005.

Ward, George W. *History of the Second Pennsylvania Veteran Heavy Artillery, (112th Regiment Pennsylvania Volunteers) From 1861 to 1866, Including the Provisional Second Penn'a. Heavy Artillery.* Philadelphia: George W. Ward, Printer, 1904.

Wilkinson, Warren. *Mother, May You Never See the Sights I Have Seen: The Fifty-seventh Massachusetts Veteran Volunteers in the Army of the Potomac, 1864–1865.* New York: Harper & Row, 1990.

Secondary Studies

Bartlett, Levi. *Sketches of the Bartlett Family in England and America.* Lawrence, MA: George S. Merrill & Crocker, Printers, 1876.

Biographical Review, Volume XXXI: Containing Life Sketches of Leading Citizens of Berkshire County, Massachusetts. Boston: Biographical Review Publishing Company, 1899.

Campanella, Anthony P. (editor). *Pages from the Garibaldian Epic.* Sarasota, FL: Institute of Garibaldian Studies, 1984.

Cavanaugh, Michael A., and William Marvel. The Petersburg Campaign: *The Battle of the Crater, 'The Horrid Pit."* Lynchburg, VA: H. E. Howard, Inc., 1989.

1862-Class Report-1912, Class of 'Sixty-Two, Harvard University, Fiftieth Anniversary. Cambridge, 1912.

Dearing, Mary R. *Veterans in Politics: The Story of the G.A.R.* Baton Rouge: Louisiana State University Press, 1952.

Dyer, Frederick H. *A Compendium of the War of the Rebellion.* Des Moines, IA, 1908; reprinted in 3 volumes, New York: Thomas Yoseloff, 1959.

Edmonds, David C. *The Guns of Port Hudson.* 2 volumes. Lafayette, LA: The Arcadia Press, 1983–1984.

Faust, Patricia L. (editor). *Historical Times Illustrated Encyclopedia of the Civil War.* New York: Harper & Row, 1986.

Foner, Eric. *Reconstruction: America's Unfinished Revolution, 1863–1877.* New York: Harper & Row, 1988.

Garner, Stanton. *The Civil War World of Herman Melville.* Lawrence: University Press of Kansas, 1993.

"Gen. Bartlett's War Career." *Springfield Republican,* May 8, 1904.

Heidler, David S., and Jeanne T. Heidler (editors). *Encyclopedia of the American Civil War.* 5 volumes. Santa Barbara, CA: ABC-CLIO, 2000.

Hewitt, Lawrence L. *Port Hudson, Confederate Bastion on the Mississippi.* Baton Rouge: Louisiana State University Press, 1987.

High, James L. "My Hero." *Military Essays and Recollections: Papers Read Before the Commandery of the State of Illinois, Military Order of the Loyal Legion of the United States,* volume 3: 155–71.

Holien, Kim B. "The Battle at Ball's Bluff, October 21, 1861." *Blue & Gray Magazine* 7 (February 1990): 8–18, 46–59.

Hoyt, David W. *The Old Families of Salisbury and Amesbury, Massachusetts, With Some Related Families of Newbury, Haverhill, Ipswich, and Hampton, and of York County, Maine.* Reprint edition, Baltimore: Genealogical Publishing Company, 1982.

Hurd, D. Hamilton. *History of Essex County, Massachusetts*. 2 volumes. Philadelphia: J. W. Lewis and Company, 1888.

Kolakowski, Christopher L. " 'A Rough Place and a Hard Fight': Thomas Stevenson's Division on the Brock and Plank Roads, May 6, 1864." *Civil War Regiments* 6 #4, available on publisher's website: www.savaspublishing.com/Wilderness.html.

Melville, Herman. *Battle-Pieces and Aspects of the War*. New York: Harper & Brothers, 1866; reprint edition, New York: DaCapo, 1995.

Milano, Anthony J. "The Copperhead Regiment: The 20th Massachusetts Infantry." *Civil War Regiments* 3 #1 (1993): 31–63.

_____. "Letters from the Harvard Regiments: The Story of the 2nd and 20th Massachusetts Volunteer Infantry Regiments from 1861 Through 1863 as Told by the Letters of Their Officers. Part One: The Twentieth Massachusetts Regiment-From the Outbreak of War Through the Seven Days." *Civil War* #13 (1989): 15–27.

Military Order of the Loyal Legion of the United States. Commandery of Massachusetts. *Tribute to the Memory of Companion Brevet Major General William F. Bartlett, U. S. Volunteers*. N.p., 1877.

Miller, William J. (compiler). "The Grand Campaign: A Journal of Operations on the Peninsula, March 17-August 26, 1862." In Miller, William J. (editor), *The Peninsula Campaign of 1862: Yorktown to the Seven Days, Volume One*, pages 177–205. Campbell, CA: Savas Woodbury Publishers, 1993.

Morgan, James A., III. *A Little Short of Boats: The Fights at Ball's Bluff and Edwards Ferry, October 21–22, 1861*. Fort Mitchell, KY: Ironclad Publishing, 2004.

Murray, Stuart. *A Time of War: A Northern Chronicle of the Civil War*. Lee, MA: Berkshire House Publishers, 2001.

Paradise, Scott H. "Some Eminent Andover Alumni, 21: William Francis Bartlett, 1840–1876." *The Phillips Bulletin* (October 1931): 11–22.

A Record of the Dedication of the Statue of Major General William Francis Bartlett. A Tribute of the Commonwealth of Massachusetts, May 27, 1904. Boston: Wright and Potter Printing Company, State Printers, 1905.

Register of the Commandery of the State of Massachusetts, November 1, 1912. Cambridge: The University Press, 1912.

Rhea, Gordon C. *The Battle of the Wilderness*, May 5–6, 1864. Baton Rouge: Louisiana State University Press, 1994.

Robertson, James I. Jr. "Houses of Horror: Danville's Civil War Prisons." *Virginia Magazine of History and Biography* 69 (1961): 329–45.

Rogers, Henry M. *Annals of the Commandery of the State of Massachusetts From Its Institution, March 4, 1868, to May 1, 1918, and the Proceedings at the Fiftieth Anniversary, March 6, 1918*. Boston: Atlantic Printing Company, 1918.

Schouler, William. *A History of Massachusetts in the War*. New York: E. P. Dutton, 1868.

Schwartzberg, Janet. "Tredegar Iron Works: An Introduction." *Richmond National Parks Quarterly Newsletter* (Spring 2000): 1–2.

Sedgwick, A. G. "William Francis Bartlett." *The Nation* #677 (June 20, 1878): 406–7.

Story, Ronald. *The Forging of an Aristocracy: Harvard & the Boston Upper Class, 1800–1870*. Middletown, CT: Wesleyan University Press, 1980.

Warner, Ezra J. *Generals in Gray*. Baton Rouge: Louisiana State University Press, 1959.

Watson, Mrs. H. Neill. "Sketch of the Life of Gen. William F. Bartlett." *Collections of the Berkshire Historical and Scientific Society* 3 (1899): 363–76.

Welsh, Jack D. *Medical Histories of Union Generals*. Kent, OH: Kent State University Press, 1996.

INDEX

Numbers in **_bold italics_** indicate pages with illustrations